SEASONING SUBSTITUTIONS

SWAPS AND STAND-INS FOR SWEET OR SAVORY CONDIMENTS AND FLAVORINGS

Jean B. MacLeod

MacLeod How-To Books
Seasoning Substitutions:
Swaps and Stand-ins for Sweet or Savory Condiments and Flavorings

ISBN-13: 9780997446470

For Bob
The salt of the earth

INTRODUCTION

We cooks love to experiment in the kitchen. We like to try new recipes, hone our culinary chops, and test new procedures. We like to stay abreast of the latest food trends and keep up with the latest advances. What we don't want, however, is waste. For instance, you bought an obscure spice for a recipe you thought might be a winner but turned out a loser: There the spice sits, silently sulking, gathering dust, and taking up space. It's a constant reminder of a wasteful expenditure because you know it will not be called into service again.

The way to get around this common occurrence is the time-tested art of substitution, also known as using what you have on hand. Until a recipe has proved its worth and deserves a dedicated ingredient, you can test it with a reasonable facsimile. It won't be the real thing of course. But it will give you a pretty good indication of its potential. Plus, you won't face an assembly of disgruntled aging ingredients. And, more important, you won't have to appease your waste-free sensibilities. I'm a great believer in substitutions when it comes to experimental dishes. Nothing ventured, nothing gained. And no pricey reminders of the losers.

Other circumstances call for substituting. The all-too-familiar scenario when you are out of a necessary ingredient the recipe calls for, or the item is difficult to obtain, or you'd like a more healthful version. Not to worry! The book covers those situations and replaces them with practical alternatives, either readymade or one you can make yourself.

If you are on board with this philosophy, love being a creative maverick, and are committed to avoiding needless waste, you will find *Seasoning Substitutions* an invaluable tool. Filled with hundreds of substitutions for common and not-so-common flavorings, this book can save you time, money, and exasperation.

Cooking is about feeding our souls as well as nurturing our bodies, a creative outlet that takes place in kitchens worldwide. How else would we have the plethora of recipes we now enjoy? It shouldn't require a nosedive into the food budget to engage in culinary exploration. To experiment with a new recipe, or try a new procedure. All it takes is a little ingenuity and a deft hand at substituting.

A

ACHIOTE/ACHUETE *See ANNATTO OIL; ANNATTO SEEDS*

ACHIOTE PASTE (Latin American seasoning and coloring agent) – 1 tablespoon
- 2 teaspoons ground annatto seeds or powdered annatto/*bijol* (for coloring; lacks seasoning)
- 1 teaspoon Goya Sazón, turmeric, or paprika (for coloring)

AGRODOLCE (Italian sweet-sour flavoring agent) – 1 cup
Make Your Own Bring 1/2 cup red wine vinegar and 1/2 cup sugar to a boil, stirring to dissolve the sugar. Cool and store in a tightly sealed jar in the refrigerator; it will keep indefinitely.

AGRUMATO-LEMON OIL (Italian citrus oil) *See LEMON OLIVE OIL*

AJI AMARILLO CHILI POWDER/AJI MOLIDO (Peruvian) – 1 teaspoon
- 1 teaspoon aji amarillo paste/*pasta de amarillo*
- 1 teaspoon hot paprika mixed with 1/2 teaspoon ground turmeric
- 3/4 teaspoon ground cayenne pepper or crushed red pepper flakes

AJI AMARILLO PASTE/PASTA DE AMARILLO (Peruvian) – 1 tablespoon
- 1 tablespoon sambal oelek (for a small amount)

AJI VERDE (Peruvian condiment) – 1 cup
- 1 cup Mexican tomatillos salsa/*salsa verde* plus 2 tablespoons grated Cotija cheese/*queso añejo* blended until smooth

AJWAIN/AJOWAN/CAROM SEEDS (Indian and Pakistani seasoning) – 1 teaspoon
- 3/4 teaspoon lovage seeds plus 1/4 teaspoon fresh thyme leaves

⊫ 1 packed teaspoon dried thyme leaves, finely crumbled

ALATOPIPERIGANO (Greek seasoning salt) – 1 tablespoon
⊫ 2 teaspoons dried Greek oregano plus 1 teaspoon sea salt and a few grains of black pepper (stir before using to redistribute)

ALCAPARRADO (Caribbean and Latin American condiment) – 2 tablespoons
⊫ 1 tablespoon each drained and chopped pimiento-stuffed olives and brined capers
⊫ 1 teaspoon each diced green olives, red pimiento, capers, and a touch of garlic

ALEPPO/HALABY CHILI POWDER (Turkish/Middle Eastern) – 1 teaspoon
⊫ 1 teaspoon Urfa or ancho chili powder
⊫ 1/2 teaspoon crushed red pepper flakes

ALEPPO/HALABY PEPPER FLAKES (Turkish/Middle Eastern) – 1 teaspoon
⊫ 1 teaspoon Marash pepper flakes/*Maras biber* (smokier)
⊫ 1 teaspoon Urfa pepper flakes/*Urfa biber* (darker colored; smokier tasting)
⊫ 3/4 teaspoon Aleppo, Urfa, ancho, or gochugaru CHILI powder
⊫ 3/4 teaspoon Hungarian sweet/mild paprika plus 1/4 teaspoon ground cayenne pepper
⊫ 1/2 teaspoon crushed red pepper flakes

ALLSPICE, JAMAICAN/PIMENTO BERRIES, DRIED – 1 teaspoon ground
⊫ 1 teaspoon ground Mexican or Central American allspice (larger berries; less aromatic)
⊫ Scant 1/2 teaspoon each ground cloves and cinnamon plus scant 1/4 teaspoon ground nutmeg
⊫ 1/2 teaspoon ground cinnamon plus 1/8 teaspoon ground cloves

ALMOND BUTTER – 1 cup
⇨ 1 cup coconut butter or cashew butter
Make Your Own Grind 2 cups roasted almonds with 1/2 teaspoon sea salt (optional) in a food processor until reduced to a paste, about 10 minutes, scraping down the sides of the bowl as needed. Transfer to a sterilized jar and store in the refrigerator; it will last for up to 4 weeks.

ALMOND EXTRACT – 1/2 teaspoon
⇨ 1 drop bitter almond oil
⇨ 1/2 teaspoon amaretto extract
⇨ 1 tablespoon almond-flavored liqueur

ALMOND LIQUEUR/ALMOND-FLAVORED SPIRIT (such as amaretto, crème d'amande, or ratafia) – 1 tablespoon for cooking
⇨ 1/4 teaspoon almond extract plus 1 tablespoon vodka or water

ALMOND PASTE – 1 cup
Make Your Own Pulse 1 cup finely ground blanched almonds, 3/4 cup granulated sugar, 2 tablespoons water, and 1/2 teaspoon pure almond extract in a food processor until a paste forms, and then knead until smooth. It will keep, well-wrapped, for up to 1 month in the refrigerator, or up to 1 year in the freezer.

ALMOND SYRUP/ORZATA (Greek sweetener) – 1 tablespoon
⇨ 1 tablespoon orgeat syrup

AMARILLO PEPPER See AJI AMARILLO CHILI POWDER

AMCHUR/AMCHOOR/GROUND MANGO POWDER (Indian souring agent) – 1 teaspoon
⇨ 1/2 teaspoon tamarind powder
⇨ 1/3 teaspoon powdered citric acid (found in the canning section of the supermarket)
⇨ 1 teaspoon ground sumac or powdered lemon peel
⇨ 1 to 2 teaspoons very finely grated lemon zest (spread it out to dry slightly before using; for sprinkling as a garnish)

ANARDANA *See POMEGRANATE SEEDS, DRIED SOUR*

ANCHO (dried red poblano chili) – 1
- 1 dried black Urfa chili
- 1 dried choricero pepper
- 1 dried California, guajillo, mulato, pasilla, or New Mexico chili, plus a pinch of sweet smoked paprika
- 1 tablespoon ancho chili powder (or pasilla or New Mexico Hatch chili powder plus a small pinch of mild/sweet smoked paprika)
- 1 tablespoon ancho paste

ANCHO CHILI PASTE *See CHILI PASTE, MILD*

ANCHO CHILI POWDER – 1 tablespoon *See also CHILI POWDER, MILD*
- 1 medium ancho chili, dry toasted, stemmed, and ground
- 1 tablespoon New Mexico, pasilla, or mild chili molida powder
- 1 tablespoon ancho pepper paste
- 1 1/2 to 2 tablespoons hot Hungarian paprika

ANCHOVY FILLETS, OIL PACKED – 2 fillets (1 1/2 teaspoons finely chopped)
- 2 to 3 salt-packed anchovy fillets, rinsed, or 1 salt-packed anchovy, rinsed and filleted (firmer texture; soak in water until flexible, 5 to 10 minutes, or 30 minutes to remove salt)
- 1 to 1 1/2 teaspoons anchovy paste or extract (contains vinegar and sugar)
- 1 or 2 fresh, frozen, or canned smelts
- 1/2 teaspoon Asian fish sauce, such as *nam pla* or *nuoc nam*; Filipino anchovy/shrimp sauce/*bagoong isda*; or vegetarian fish sauce/*nuoc mam an chay*
- 1 teaspoon Japanese *ayu* fish sauce (less salty)
- 1 generous tablespoon drained chopped capers

ANCHOVY PASTE – 1 teaspoon
- 1 salt-packed anchovy, rinsed, boned, minced, and mashed to a paste with a little olive oil

- 1 oil-packed anchovy fillet, rinsed, minced and mashed to a paste (or put through a garlic press)
- 1 firmly packed tablespoon finely chopped water-packed tuna
- 1 teaspoon dark miso, such as *inaka* or *hatcho*
- 1 teaspoon Worcestershire sauce plus 1/2 teaspoon powdered kelp or crushed dried dulse flakes
- 1/2 teaspoon sugar-free Asian fish sauce or Italian anchovy syrup/ *colatura di alici*

ANCHOVY SAUCE/MAM NEM (Vietnamese cooking condiment) – 1 tablespoon
- 2 teaspoons anchovy paste plus 1 teaspoon water

ANCHOVY SYRUP/COLATURA DI ALICI (Italian condiment) – 1 tablespoon
- 1 tablespoon Asian fish sauce (such as *nam pla* or *nuoc nam*)

ANISE EXTRACT – 1 teaspoon
- 1 1/2 tablespoons anise seeds, ground in a mortar or a spice/coffee grinder
- 2 teaspoons ground anise seeds
- 1/8 teaspoon anise oil

ANISE HYSSOP/LICORICE MINT/AGASTACHE FOENICULUM, FRESH – 1 tablespoon chopped
- 1 tablespoon chopped fresh Korean mint/*Agastache rugosa* or young Mexican giant hyssop
- 1 1/2 teaspoons each chopped fresh thyme and mint

ANISE LIQUEUR/ANISE-FLAVORED SPIRIT (such as Absente, arak, Herbsaint, ouzo, pastis, Pernod, Ricard, sambuca, xtabentún, or other unsweetened anise-flavored spirit) – 1 tablespoon for cooking
- 1 tablespoon vodka plus 1 teaspoon ground anise seeds
- 1/2 teaspoon anise extract plus 2 teaspoons water

ANISE SEEDS – 1 teaspoon
- 2 whole star anise pods, crushed or coarsely ground, or 1 1/2 teaspoons broken pieces
- 1/4 teaspoon anise extract
- 1 1/4 teaspoons fennel or caraway seeds

ANNATTO OIL/ACEITE/DAU MAU DIEU/MANTECA DE ACHIOTE (Asian and Latin American coloring agent) – 1/4 cup
- 1/4 cup olive oil plus 1 teaspoon sweet paprika

Make Your Own Slowly heat 1 to 2 tablespoons annatto seeds and 1/4 cup vegetable oil until the oil turns orangey-red and the seeds begin to crackle, 5 to 7 minutes; strain and cool. Store in an airtight container in the refrigerator; it will keep for up to 1 year. (For annatto chili oil, include 1 small crushed dried red chili when heating the seeds and oil.)

ANNATTO SEEDS/ACHIOTE (Latin American and Caribbean spice and coloring agent) – 1 teaspoon
- 3/4 teaspoon achiote paste/*condimento de achiote* (contains oregano and other ingredients), or Yucatan achiote paste/*recado rojo/Achiote recado* (contains garlic and vinegar)
- 1 teaspoon pesticide-free dried marigold petals, preferably pot marigold/*Calendula officinalis*, steeped in 1 or 2 tablespoons warm water for 5 minutes (use the liquid for color and discard the petals)
- 1/4 teaspoon sweet California or Hungarian paprika and 1/2 teaspoon ground turmeric, preferably Madras
- 1/2 teaspoon crumbled azafrán (Mexican saffron) or 1/8 teaspoon pure saffron

APPELSTROOP (Dutch apple syrup) – 1 cup
- 4 cups fresh apple juice, simmered until reduced to 1 cup, 45 to 60 minutes
- 1 cup *keukenstroop*, molasses, or strong honey

APPLE BRANDY/APPLEJACK (such as Calvados or Laird's) – 2 tablespoons
- 1 tablespoon each apple juice concentrate and brandy
- 2 tablespoons hard cider

APPLE PIE SPICE – 1 tablespoon
- 2 teaspoons ground cinnamon, 1/2 teaspoon ground nutmeg, and 1/2 teaspoon ground ginger (or a pinch of allspice)

ARAME, DRIED (Japanese mild shredded seaweed) – 1 ounce
- 1 ounce wakame (soak for 15 to 20 minutes; cut out the center rib, then slice the rest into thin ribbons)
- 1 ounce kiri kombu/long narrow kombu strands (soak for 10 minutes)
- 1 ounce alaria (saltier; soak for 30 minutes)
- 1 ounce hijiki (stronger tasting; soak for 10 minutes)

ARGAN OIL (Moroccan golden-colored unrefined oil) – 1 cup
- 1/2 cup each extra-virgin olive oil and peanut oil
- 1 cup peanut oil, hazelnut oil, or walnut oil

ARROPE (Spanish grape syrup) *See GRAPE MOLASSES/MUST SYRUP*

ASAFETIDA/ASAFOETIDA/HING/PERUNKAYA (pungent Indian seasoning) – 1 teaspoon ground lump asafetida
- 1 teaspoon yellow asafetida powder (milder; contains turmeric)
- 1/2 teaspoon each onion and garlic powder

ASAM GELUGOR/ASAM KEPING *See KOKUM*

ASHTAR (Lebanese clotted cream) *See CREAM, CLOTTED*

ASIAN DIPPING SAUCE – 1/4 cup
Make Your Own Stir together 2 tablespoons each soy sauce and unseasoned rice vinegar, 1 teaspoon finely minced green onion, and a little grated fresh ginger.

ASIAN FISH PASTE, FERMENTED/PRESERVED FISH/MAM CA SAC (Southeast Asian salty flavoring agent) – 1 teaspoon

- 1 teaspoon fermented shrimp paste: Filipino *bagoong,* Thai *kapi,* Indonesian *trassi/terasi* (more pungent), or Burmese *ngapi*
- 1 1/2 teaspoons French or Italian anchovy paste
- 1 whole salt-packed anchovy, deboned and mashed
- 2 oil-packed anchovies, rinsed and mashed
- 1 tablespoon Japanese red *inaka* miso or brown *hatcho* mi

ASIAN FISH SAUCE/NAM PLA/NUOC NAM/PATIS/SHOTTSURU/TUK TREY (Southeast Asian salty seasoning) – 1 tablespoon

- 1 tablespoon Vietnamese vegetarian fish sauce/*nuoc mam an chay*
- 1 tablespoon Japanese *ayu* sweet fish sauce (more delicate) or *ishiri* fermented squid sauce (stronger flavor)
- 1 tablespoon Italian anchovy sauce/syrup/*colatura di alici,* or Vietnamese anchovy sauce/*mam nem*
- 2 to 3 teaspoons Thai unfiltered fish sauce/*pla ra* or *pla ra* powder (stronger flavor)
- 2 teaspoons anchovy paste mixed with 1/2 teaspoon soy sauce or Maggi Seasoning
- 1 1/2 teaspoons each Golden Mountain Seasoning sauce and soy sauce
- 1 tablespoon soy sauce and 1 finely minced anchovy fillet
- 2 tablespoons white or Thai soy sauce
- 1/4 teaspoon salt (or to taste)

ASIAN FISH SAUCE, VEGETARIAN – 1/4 cup

- 1/4 cup coconut aminos plus 1 teaspoon sea salt

Make Your Own Break 1 small dried shiitake mushroom into pieces and combine with 1/2 cup water plus 1 1/2 teaspoons each sea salt and soy sauce. Simmer until reduced by half. Strain, cool, and store in the refrigerator. It will keep for up to 3 weeks.

ATE (Mexican concentrated fruit paste) See GUAVA PASTE; QUINCE PASTE

AVOCADO LEAF/HOJA DE AGUACATE, FRESH OR DRIED (Latin American seasoning and food wrapper) – 1 leaf (for seasoning)
- 1 scant teaspoon ground avocado leaf
- 1 fresh or dried hoja santa/yerba santa leaf
- 1 dried California bay leaf
- 1 small piece fresh fennel frond
- 1 teaspoon fennel seeds

B

BABA GHANOUSH (Middle Eastern spread or dip) – about 1 1/4 cups
Make Your Own Peel 1 medium cooked eggplant (about 1 pound, preferably grilled) then process with1 or 2 medium garlic cloves, 1 or 2 tablespoons each lemon juice and olive oil, and 2 tablespoons tahini in a blender or food processor until smooth. Season with salt.

BACON BITS – 1/4 cup
- 1/4 cup crumbled smoked tempeh
- 1/4 cup dry-roasted tamari sunflower seeds
- Kiri kombu/sea vegetable, fried in 350°F oil until crisp, 1 to 2 minutes, and then crumbled (measure after crumbling)

BAHARAT/LEBANESE SEVEN-SPICE MIX (Middle Eastern spice blend) – 1 tablespoon
- 1/2 teaspoon each ground cloves, ground cumin (preferably roasted), paprika, ground black pepper, and ground cinnamon (or allspice)
- 1 teaspoon each ground coriander and cumin plus 1/2 teaspoon each ground cinnamon and paprika
- 1 tablespoon garam masala or *ras el hanout* spice blend

BAKER'S CARAMEL/CARAMEL COLOR (powdered non-sweet coloring agent) – 1 teaspoon
- 1 teaspoon gravy browner, such as Gravy Master or Kitchen Bouquet
- 1 tablespoon extra-strong coffee

Make Your Own Melt 1/4 cup granulated sugar over low heat, stirring constantly, until very dark brown, about 3 minutes; cool completely, about 10 minutes, before slowly stirring in 1/4 cup hot water. Use 1 to 2 teaspoons in place of baker's caramel. Store in a tightly covered container at room temperature; it will keep for up to 3 months.

BALSAMIC GLAZE/CRÈMA DE BALSAMICO – 1/4 cup

Make Your Own Simmer 1 cup balsamic vinegar gently until syrupy and reduced to 1/4 cup, about 15 minutes. This will keep in the refrigerator for up to 1 month.

BALSAMIC GLAZE, SWEET – 1/4 cup

Make Your Own Gently simmer 1/2 cup balsamic vinegar and 1 1/2 teaspoons granulated sugar until reduced to 1/4 cup, 7 to 10 minutes. Store, refrigerated, for up to 1 month.

BALSAMIC VINEGAR – 1 tablespoon

- 1 tablespoon Chianti or red wine vinegar, preferably aged, plus 1/8 teaspoon sugar or honey
- 1 tablespoon Chinese aged black-rice vinegar, preferably Chinkiang
- 1 tablespoon white balsamic vinegar (milder; less sweet and syrupy)
- 1 tablespoon apple balsamic vinegar (less sweet)
- 4 teaspoons cranberry juice

BALSAMIC VINEGAR, AGED/ACETO BALSAMICO TRADIZIONALE (Italian grape-based) – 1 tablespoon

- 1 tablespoon reduced non-artisanal balsamic vinegar (Simmer 1 cup non-artisanal balsamic until syrupy and reduced by one-half or more, then measure.)
- 1 tablespoon Italian apple balsamic vinegar
- 1 tablespoon Greek grape Corinthian vinegar (more fruity flavored)

BALSAMIC VINEGAR, WHITE (Italian mild, unaged grape-based) – 1 tablespoon

- 1 tablespoon Moscatel vinegar
- 1 tablespoon white wine vinegar or unseasoned rice vinegar plus 1/8 to 1/4 teaspoon sugar

BANANA SAUCE/TAMIS ANGHANG (Filipino condiment) – 1 tablespoon
- 1 tablespoon ketchup

BANYULS (French fortified wine) – 2 tablespoons
- 1 tablespoon each syrah and ruby port
- 2 tablespoons tawny port, Madeira, or dry vermouth

BANYULS VINEGAR/VINAIGRE de BANYULS (French aged wine vinegar) – 1 tablespoon
- 1 tablespoon aged sherry or balsamic vinegar
- 1 tablespoon red wine vinegar

BAOBAB LEAF POWDER (West African flavoring and thickening agent) – 1 tablespoon
- 1 tablespoon filé/sassafras leaf powder (added at the end of cooking)
- 2 cups sliced fresh okra, or 1 (10-ounce) package sliced frozen okra, or whole frozen okra cut into 1/4-inch rounds (cooked with the stew)

BARBECUE SAUCE – 1 cup
- 1 cup tomato sauce plus 1 tablespoon (or more) smoky seasoning blend, barbecue spice blend, rib and chicken rub, steak seasoning, or Cajun seasoning
- 1 cup ketchup plus 2 teaspoons Worcestershire sauce
- 1 cup Chinese hoisin, chee hou, or char siu barbecue sauce

Make Your Own Stir together1 cup ketchup, 1/4 teaspoon (or more) liquid smoke or hickory smoke powder (optional), 1 or 2 tablespoons molasses or brown sugar, and a pinch of garlic powder. For hot barbecue sauce add 1 teaspoon hot pepper sauce; for smoky hot sauce add 2 to 3 teaspoons liquid from canned chipotles in adobo; for thinner sauce add 1 to 2 tablespoons cider or rice vinegar or red wine (regular or nonalcoholic).

BARBECUE SEASONING/DRY RUB – 1/3 cup
Make Your Own Stir together 1 tablespoon each paprika, brown sugar, kosher salt, and ground black pepper. If desired, add 1/2 teaspoon

onion or garlic powder or 1 tablespoon of one of the following: dried crumbled sage, dried oregano, ground cumin, dried thyme leaves, mustard powder, mild chili powder, or Cajun seasoning.

BARBERRIES, DRIED/ZERESHK (Persian souring agent) – 1 cup
- 1 cup coarsely chopped dried cranberries or sour/tart cherries
- 1 cup dried currants (red or Zante) soaked in a little lemon juice

BARLEY MALT SYRUP, PLAIN/MOOL YUTI (non-diastatic liquid grain sweetener) – 1 tablespoon
- 1 tablespoon non-diastatic barley malt powder
- 2 teaspoons diastatic barley malt powder
- 1 tablespoon wheat malt syrup
- 1 tablespoon Chinese brown rice syrup/*yinnie*
- 1 tablespoon honey
- 1 tablespoon dark brown sugar
- 2 teaspoons mild unsulphured molasses

BAROLO WINE VINEGAR, AGED – 1 tablespoon
- 1 tablespoon red wine vinegar or raspberry vinegar

BASIL, AFRICAN BLUE – 1 tablespoon chopped fresh leaves
- 1 tablespoon chopped fresh Thai basil or anise hyssop (less camphor taste)

BASIL, HOLY/BAI KRAPAU/KAPHRAO/TULSI – 1 tablespoon chopped fresh leaves
- 1 1/2 teaspoons chopped fresh mint and small-leafed Mediterranean basil (if using in a cooked dish, add at the last minute)
- 1 tablespoon chopped fresh Peruvian/spice basil, Thai basil, or anise/licorice basil
- 1 teaspoon jarred holy basil paste or holy basil seasoning

BASIL, SWEET/MEDITERRANEAN/GENOVESE – 1 tablespoon chopped fresh leaves

- ⯈ 1 scant tablespoon Greek basil (smaller leaves and softer stems; stronger flavor)
- ⯈ 1 teaspoon sweet dried Mediterranean basil leaves, crumbled
- ⯈ 3/4 teaspoon sweet dried California, French, Italian, Peruvian/spice, or opal basil
- ⯈ 1 to 2 tablespoons chopped lettuce leaf basil (milder flavor)
- ⯈ 1 teaspoon dried Italian seasoning or dried crushed thyme leaves
- ⯈ 2 to 3 teaspoons finely chopped fresh mint leaves
- ⯈ Scant 1/2 teaspoon basil pesto (for marinara sauce)

BASIL, SWEET/MEDITERRANEAN/GENOVESE – 1 cup chopped fresh leaves, for pesto

- ⯈ 1 cup coarsely chopped arugula, flat-leaf parsley leaves, cilantro stems and leaves, radish tops, stemmed baby spinach, shiso leaves, or any peppery green

BASIL, THAI/ASIAN BASIL/ANISE BASIL/HUNG QUE – 1 tablespoon chopped fresh leaves

- ⯈ 1 tablespoon chopped fresh Holy basil or anise basil/licorice basil
- ⯈ 1 1/2 teaspoons chopped small fresh regular/sweet basil leaves and small fresh mint leaves

BASIL SALT

Make Your Own Layer fresh basil leaves in kosher salt in a small container (make sure the salt completely covers the leaves); seal and leave several days for the salt to develop flavor.

Or

Pulse 1 or 2 cups fresh basil leaves and 1/2 cup kosher salt in a food processor until combined; spread on a baking sheet and dry at 160°F, 30 to 40 minutes, stirring halfway through. Cool, then pulse again to a fine powder. (For a coarser product, dry the leaves first, pulverize to a powder, then stir into the salt.)

BAY LEAF POWDER – 1 teaspoon
- 8 to 10 dried Turkish bay leaves, stem and spines removed, pulverized in a spice/coffee grinder (add a little raw rice, if necessary, to help the grinding process)

BAY LEAF, CALIFORNIA, DRIED – 1
- 2 dried Turkish bay leaves
- 1 very small fresh bay leaf (or part of a larger one)
- 1/4 teaspoon crushed dried bay leaf
- Scant 1/8 teaspoon bay leaf powder/ground dried bay leaf
- 2 fresh bayberry leaves/*Myrica pensylvanica* (milder flavor)

BAY LEAF, INDIAN See CASSIA LEAF/CINNAMON LEAF/TEJ PATTA

BAY LEAF, TURKISH, DRIED – 1
- 1/2 dried California bay leaf (best for quick-cooking dishes)
- 1/8 teaspoon Turkish bay leaf powder
- 1 or 2 fresh bayberry leaves/*Myrica pensylvanica*

BEAN PASTE, FERMENTED See MISO; CHINESE YELLOW BEAN SAUCE; KOREAN SOYBEAN PASTE

BEAN SAUCE See BLACK BEAN GARLIC SAUCE; SICHUAN BEAN SAUCE; VIETNAMESE YELLOW BEAN SAUCE

BEANS, FERMENTED, SALTED BLACK See FERMENTED BLACK BEANS

BEAU MONDE SEASONING – 1 teaspoon
- 1/2 teaspoon each onion powder and celery salt
- 1 teaspoon seasoning salt

BEE BALM/BERGAMOT (mint-family herb) – 1 tablespoon chopped fresh leaves
- 1 tablespoon chopped fresh oregano

BEECH MUSHROOM/BROWN BEECH/PIOPPINI/SHIMEJI – *7 ounces*
- 7 ounces golden enoki, oyster, or small cremini mushrooms

BEER – *1 cup for cooking*
- 1 cup porter, stout, or other slightly bitter dark ale (for braised meat dishes)
- 1 cup light beer (3% alcohol), low-alcohol beer (less than 2% alcohol), near beer (0.5% alcohol), or nonalcoholic beer (lowest in calories)
- 1 cup gluten-free beer, such as Bard's, Green's, New Grist, or Redbridge; or vegan lager beer
- 1 cup hard cider (gluten-free)
- 1 cup wine (regular or nonalcoholic)
- 1 cup beef or chicken stock
- Small amount beer extract powder (for rubs and blends)

BENGALI FIVE-SPICE MIX/PANCH PHORON (Bengali seasoning) – *1/3 cup*
Make Your Own Combine 1 tablespoon each black cumin seeds, fenugreek seeds, black or brown mustard seeds, nigella seeds, and fennel seeds; store in an airtight container in a cool, dry place.

BENITADE SPROUTS/RED WATER PEPPER (Japanese garnish) – *1 cup*
- 1 cup alfalfa sprouts (for the taste)
- 1 cup finely shredded red cabbage (for the color)

BERBERE (Ethiopian spice blend) – *1 tablespoon*
- 1 tablespoon harissa powder or peri peri seasoning (for powder blend)
- 1 tablespoon harissa (for paste blend)
- 2 teaspoons hot or bittersweet/semi-hot paprika plus 1 teaspoon Chinese chili garlic sauce (for paste blend)

BERMUDA HOT PEPPER SHERRY *See SHERRY PEPPER SAUCE*

BESSARA (Moroccan dip) – 1 cup
- 1 cup hummus, preferably with sweet red peppers

BIBER SALÇASI/ACI BIBER See RED PEPPER PASTE, HOT

BIRCH SYRUP – 1 cup
- 1 cup maple syrup
- 1 1/3 cups brown sugar plus 1/4 cup water heated until the sugar melts

BITTER ORANGE See ORANGE, SOUR/BITTER/SEVILLE

BITTERS (aromatic flavoring agent, such as Angostura or Peychaud's) – 1/4 teaspoon
- 1/2 teaspoon Worcestershire sauce (regular or vegetarian)

BLACHAN/BLACAN/BALACHAN See SHRIMP PASTE, FERMENTED

BLACK BEAN GARLIC SAUCE/DOUCHI (Chinese salty cooking condiment) – 1 tablespoon
- 1 tablespoon Chinese fermented black beans, rinsed, mashed, then combined with 1 teaspoon soy sauce and a touch of garlic paste
- 1 tablespoon Japanese dark miso, such as *hatcho*, or Korean soybean paste/*doenjang*

BLACK BEANS, FERMENTED SALTED See FERMENTED BLACK BEANS

BLACK CURRANT JUICE – 1 cup
- 1 cup 100% pure pomegranate juice

BLACK CURRANT VINEGAR – 1 tablespoon
- 1 tablespoon red wine vinegar plus a few drops of black currant liqueur, such as crème de cassis
- 1 tablespoon raspberry vinegar

BLACKENING SEASONING (New Orleans spice rub) – 3 tablespoons
- 2 teaspoons salt plus 1 teaspoon each garlic powder, ground black pepper, hot paprika, onion powder, dried thyme leaves, dried oregano, and ground cayenne pepper to taste

BLACK FOOD COLORING – few drops
- Few drops squid or cuttlefish ink

BLACK GARLIC See FERMENTED BLACK GARLIC

BLACK MINT See HUACATAY

BLACK SUGAR See JAPANESE BLACK SUGAR

BOLDO/BOLDINA LEAF/HOJA DE BOLDO, DRIED (South American seasoning) – 1 leaf
- 1 small fresh or dried California bay leaf

BOTTARGA DI MUGGINE (salt-cured, dried gray mullet roe) – 1 ounce
- 1/2 ounce powdered dried mullet bottarga (milder)
- 1 ounce tuna bottarga/*bottarga di tonno* (stronger flavor and moister texture; harder to grate so thinly shave with a knife)
- 1 ounce Japanese salt-cured, dried mullet roe/*karasumi* (softer texture)
- 1 ounce Spanish salt-cured, dried tuna loin/*majama* (moister; less expensive)
- 1 ounce Chinese dried scallop/*conpoy* (expensive flavoring agent)

BOUILLON – 1 cup
- 1 beef bouillon cube, 1 teaspoon beef bouillon granules, or 1 envelope instant broth, dissolved in 1 cup boiling water
- 1 seasoning packet from a 3-ounce-package beef-flavored ramen noodles dissolved in 1 cup boiling water
- 4 teaspoons dark miso (or 5 teaspoons light) added to 1 cup very hot (not boiling) water a little at a time and stirred until smooth

☞ 1 porcini-flavored bouillon cube or 1 teaspoon wild mushroom bouillon granules dissolved in 1 cup boiling water
☞ 1 cup water plus a little soy sauce for flavor

BOUILLON CUBE, BEEF – 1
☞ 4 teaspoons Japanese dark miso, such as *hatcho*; Korean soybean paste/*doenjang*; or tamari

BOUKOVO PEPPER FLAKES (Greek) – 1 teaspoon
☞ 1/2 to 3/4 teaspoon hot Spanish paprika or chipotle chili powder

BOUQUET GARNI (fresh seasoning herbs tied in a bundle) – 1
☞ 1 teaspoon dried parsley, 1/2 teaspoon dried thyme, and 1 whole or crumbled bay leaf, wrapped in a 6-inch square of cheesecloth or placed in a reusable muslin tea bag or metal tea infuser
☞ 1 bay leaf (in a pinch)

BRANDY EXTRACT – 1 teaspoon
☞ 2 tablespoons brandy or rum; reduce the liquid in the recipe by 2 tablespoons

BRINE SOLUTION, SALTWATER (flavoring agent for pork and poultry) – 1 quart
☞ 1/4 cup kosher salt (or 2 tablespoons table salt) dissolved in 1 quart cold water (for plain brine)
☞ 1/2 cup kosher salt (or 1/4 cup table salt) and 1/4 cup granulated sugar dissolved in 1 quart cold water (for sweetened brine)
☞ 1 to 4 tablespoons kosher salt (for poultry dry brine; rub salt evenly over the bird, including cavity and under breast skin; refrigerate, lightly covered, at least 24 hours before roasting)

BROWNING/BURNT SUGAR See BAKER'S CARAMEL/CARAMEL COLORING

BROWN RICE SYRUP/YINNIE (Chinese naturally processed sweetener) – 1 cup *See also JAPANESE BLACK SUGAR SYRUP*
- 3/4 cup mild-flavored liquid honey or maple syrup plus 2 tablespoons water
- 1 cup agave syrup/nectar or coconut nectar

BROWN RICE VINEGAR *See JAPANESE BROWN RICE VINEGAR/GEN-MAIZU*

BROWN SAUCE, BOTTLED (British condiment) – 1 tablespoon
- 1 tablespoon HP sauce, A-1 sauce, steak sauce, or gluten-free brown sauce, such as Granovita
- 1 1/2 teaspoons each Worcestershire sauce and ketchup

BROWN SUGAR SYRUP/KURO MITSU (Japanese sweetener) – 1 cup
- 1 1/3 cups (firmly packed) brown sugar, a pinch of salt, and 1/2 cup boiling water, simmered until syrupy

BUTTER, BRITTANY (cooking butter containing sea salt crystals) – 2 ounces (1/4 cup)
- 2 ounces softened unsalted European butter plus 2 teaspoons coarse sea salt, thoroughly combined

BUTTER, CLARIFIED – 4 ounces (1/2 cup) for cooking
- 1/2 cup pure ghee/*usli ghee*, vegetable-oil ghee/*vanaspati ghee*, light sesame oil, macadamia nut oil, or refined coconut oil
- 1/2 cup nonhydrogenated solid vegetable shortening (or rendered leaf lard) plus a few drops toasted sesame oil (or hazelnut oil) for the taste
- 5 ounces unsalted butter (lower smoke point; be careful not to overheat)

Make Your Own Slowly heat 5 ounces unsalted butter in a small saucepan until melted (or microwave for 2 minutes on High in a loosely covered large microwave-safe bowl); let sit until the milk solids settle, about 30 minutes, then gently pour the butter into a container, and leave the milky residue behind.

BUTTER, CULTURED – 4 ounces (1/2 cup)

☞ Homemade butter made with 1 cup heavy cream (not ultra-pasteurized) and 1/2 cup crème fraîche instead of all heavy cream

BUTTER, EUROPEAN-STYLE/HIGH FAT (82 to 84% butterfat) – 4 ounces (1/2 cup)

☞ 1/2 cup plus 2 teaspoons North American–style butter; reduce the liquid in the recipe by 1 tablespoon

BUTTER, PRUNE See PRUNE PURÉE/BUTTER

BUTTER, REDUCED-FAT SOFT SPREAD – 1 pound

Make Your Own Beat 8 ounces (1 cup/2 sticks) room-temperature butter until creamy, then slowly beat in 1 cup chilled evaporated milk. Transfer to an airtight container and keep refrigerated.

BUTTER, SALTED – 8 ounces (1 cup/2 sticks)

☞ 8 ounces unsalted butter plus increase salt in the recipe by 1/2 teaspoon

BUTTER, SOFT SPREAD – 1 cup

Make Your Own Beat 4 ounces (1/2 cup/1 stick) unsalted butter until creamy, then slowly beat in 1/2 cup grapeseed or canola oil; pour into an airtight container and keep refrigerated. Alternatively, pulse the oil and butter in a blender, then pour into a container; it will harden when chilled. (Light or mild-tasting olive oil can be used, but extra-virgin olive oil can turn bitter when whipped; for a salted spread, use salted butter plus 1/4 teaspoon fine sea salt.)

BUTTER, WHIPPED – 1 cup

☞ 2/3 cup firm butter, beaten until light and fluffy

BUTTER-FLAVORED GRANULES – 1 tablespoon (for seasoning)

☞ 4 tablespoons (2 ounces/1/4 cup/1/2 stick) salted or unsalted butter

BUTTERMILK, EUROPEAN-STYLE – 1 cup
☞ 3/4 cup cultured buttermilk whisked with 1/4 cup plain full-fat yogurt until smooth

BZAR (Middle Eastern seasoning mix) – 1 teaspoon
☞ 1 teaspoon garam masala spice blend

C

CABERNET SAUVIGNON VINEGAR – 1 tablespoon
- 1 tablespoon Zinfandel vinegar or other mellow red wine vinegar
- 1 tablespoon sherry vinegar
- 1 to 2 tablespoons red wine (regular or nonalcoholic)

CACHAÇA/AGUARDENTE/PINGA (Brazilian clear sugarcane alcohol) – 2 tablespoons
- 2 tablespoons white (light) rum

CAJUN SEASONING – 1 tablespoon
- 1/2 teaspoon each ground black pepper, white pepper, ground cayenne pepper, garlic powder, onion powder, and paprika. Or, in place of white pepper, use dried thyme or increase paprika to 1 teaspoon.
- 1 tablespoon Creole seasoning

CAKE GLAZE – 1 cup *See also FRUIT GLAZE*
- 1 cup store-bought frosting plus a little liquid (water, milk, cream) heated in a small pan over low heat, stirring constantly, until liquid enough to pour

CALABRESE RED PEPPER POWDER, SWEET/PEPE ROSSA (Italian seasoning) – 1 tablespoon
- 1 tablespoon mild/sweet Spanish paprika

CALABRIAN BOMB (Italian spicy condiment paste) – 1 tablespoon
- 1 tablespoon Calabrese sweet pepper paste
- 1 tablespoon spicy red chili paste, such as harissa or sambal oelek

C

C

C   24

CALABRIAN CHILI PASTE/SILAFUNGHI HOT CHILI SAUCE – 1 generous tablespoon
- ☞ 1 tablespoon minced jarred roasted red pepper, 1/2 teaspoon each olive oil and lemon juice, plus 1/4 teaspoon each crushed red pepper flakes and smoked Spanish paprika

CALABRIAN CHILI/PEPERONCINO (Italian hot chili) – 1
- ☞ 1 oil-packed Calabrian chili
- ☞ 1 fresh red cayenne or Thai chili

CALABRIAN RED PEPPER POWDER, HOT (Italian seasoning powder) – 1 tablespoon
- ☞ 1 tablespoon ground cayenne pepper

CALAMINT See NEPITELLA

CAMBODIAN FISH SAUCE/TUK TREY See ASIAN FISH SAUCE

CANDLENUT/KEMIRI/BUAH KERAS (Southeast Asian thickening agent) – 1/2 ounce (4 to 5 nuts)
- ☞ 1/2 ounce unsalted, unroasted macadamia nuts (5 or 6), or 1/2 ounce medium unsalted cashews (9 or 10)

CANELA See CINNAMON, GROUND (Ceylon, Sri Lanka, Mexican, canela)

CANE SUGAR, RAW/UNREFINED See SUGAR, DEMERARA; SUGAR, TURBINADO CANE

CANE SYRUP/INVERT SYRUP (Caribbean and Creole strong-flavored sweetener) – 1 cup
- ☞ 1 cup plain barley malt syrup or dark corn syrup
- ☞ 1/2 cup each molasses and light-colored corn syrup
- ☞ 1 cup sorghum syrup, unsulphured molasses, or treacle

CANE VINEGAR, DARK/SUKANG ILOKO (Caribbean and Southeast

Asian dark sugarcane vinegar) – tablespoon
- 1 tablespoon sherry vinegar, cider vinegar, or brown rice vinegar

CANE VINEGAR, WHITE/SUKANG MAASIM *(Filipino mild, all-purpose sugarcane vinegar)* **– 1 tablespoon**
- 1 tablespoon unseasoned rice vinegar or rice wine vinegar
- 1 scant tablespoon distilled white vinegar

CANISTEL/EGG FRUIT *See LÚCUMA PULP*

CANOLA OIL/RAPESEED OIL *(neutral-flavored oil)* **– 1 cup**
- 1 cup grapeseed, safflower or sunflower oil

CAPERS/CAPER BUDS, BRINED – 1 tablespoon
- 9 to 12 large salt-packed capers, soaked in cold water 20 or more minutes then drained; if very salty, soak in 3 or 4 changes of water or for 2 hours in warm water (less firm)
- 1/4 cup brined caperberries, stemmed and rinsed (larger, starchier, milder flavor; best for garnish)
- 2 tablespoons tubed caper paste
- 1 to 2 tablespoons chopped green olives or dill pickles
- 2 tablespoons pickled green nasturtium buds, pickled green coriander seed, or pickled young marsh mallow buds (*Althaea officinalis*)

CAPPUCCINO PASTE *(flavoring agent)* **– 1 tablespoon**
- 1 tablespoon espresso or coffee paste
- 3 1/2 tablespoons instant espresso powder mixed with enough heavy cream to form a thick paste

CARAMEL COLORING *See BAKER'S CARAMEL/CARAMEL COLORING*

CARAMEL PASTE/DULCE DE LECHE/CAJETA/AREQUIPE/MANJAR – 1 cup
Make Your Own Heat the contents of 1 (14-ounce) can sweetened condensed milk, uncovered, in a double boiler over low heat until

golden, 2 to 3 hours, replacing water as needed (it will thicken on cooling).

Or

Simmer 1 cup firmly packed dark brown sugar, 1/3 cup butter, and 1/4 cup heavy cream (or evaporated milk) until slightly thickened; remove from heat and add 1 teaspoon vanilla extract.

CARAMEL SYRUP/NUOC MAU (Vietnamese sweetener) – 1 teaspoon
⇝ 1 1/2 teaspoons granulated sugar

CARAWAY SEEDS – 1 tablespoon
⇝ 1 tablespoon anise, fennel, or dill seeds

CARDAMOM, GROUND – 1 teaspoon
⇝ Seeds from 6 to 8 green or white cardamom pods, finely ground with a mortar and pestle
⇝ 1 or 2 drops Elaichi essence (Indian cardamom seed essence)
⇝ 3 drops cardamom extract
⇝ 3/4 teaspoon ground cinnamon plus 1/4 teaspoon finely grated lemon zest
⇝ 1/2 teaspoon each ground cloves and nutmeg (or cinnamon)

CARDAMOM PODS, BLACK/BROWN – 1 tablespoon
⇝ 1 tablespoon Chinese cardamom/*Amomum globosum* (less expensive; more pungent)
⇝ 2 or 3 whole cloves

CARDAMOM PODS, GREEN OR WHITE – 1 tablespoon
⇝ 1 teaspoon ground cardamom
⇝ 1 tablespoon Ethiopian koreima/*Aframomum korarima* (less expensive; more camphor overtones)

CARNE SÊCA/CHARQUE/CHARKI/CARNE DE SOL (South American dried salted beef) – 4 ounces
⇝ 4 ounces Cuban tasajo, Cajun tasso, or Mexican cecina

☞ 4 ounces spicy salted beef jerky

CAROB SYRUP/MOLASSES/HARNUP PEKMEZI (Middle Eastern sweetener) *See DATE MOLASSES*

CAROM SEEDS *See AJWAIN*

CARRAGEENAN/IRISH MOSS (thickening agent) – 1 tablespoon
 ☞ 1 tablespoon gelatin
 ☞ 1 teaspoon powdered agar/kanten

CASHEW BUTTER – 1 cup
 ☞ 1 cup smooth, natural peanut butter (less sweet)
Make Your Own Process 2 cups whole roasted, unsalted cashews and 1/4 teaspoon sea salt in a food processor until reduced to a paste, 6 to 10 minutes, scraping down the sides of the bowl and adding a little oil if needed. Store in a sterilized jar in the refrigerator; it will last for up to 4 weeks.

CASHEW CREAM – 1 to 1 1/4 cups
Make Your Own Soak 1 cup whole raw unsalted cashews in 2 cups water for 4 to 8 hours; drain and rinse, then blend with 1/2 cup water until completely smooth; strain if necessary. For a faster procedure, soak 1 cup cashew pieces in 1/2 cup boiling water 30 minutes. For a thicker, richer cream use 1/3 cup water and 1/4 cup refined coconut oil. For a thinner, pourable cream use 1 1/2 cups water. Store, refrigerated, for up to 4 days, or freeze for up to 6 months.
Or
Soak 1/3 cup whole raw unsalted cashews in 2/3 cup water for 4 to 8 hours; drain and rinse, then blend with 2/3 cup unsweetened soy milk until completely smooth; strain if necessary. Store, refrigerated, for up to 4 days or freeze for up to 6 months.

CASHEW VINEGAR/GOAN VINEGAR – 1 tablespoon
 ☞ 1 tablespoon cider vinegar

CASSAREEP (Caribbean thick black cassava sweetener) – 1 cup
- 1 cup blackstrap molasses or *yacón* syrup

CASSIA *See CINNAMON, GROUND*

CASSIA BARK *See CINNAMON STICK, INDONESIAN*

CASSIA LEAF/CINNAMON LEAF/TEJ PATTA (Indian flavoring agent) – 1 dried leaf
- 1 whole clove or small pinch ground cloves
- 1 small dried Turkish bay leaf and a few grains cassia cinnamon

CATALAN RED CHILI, DRIED (Spanish mild chili) – 1
- 1 dried red California, New Mexico, or guajillo chili
- 2 dried ñora chilis
- 1 tablespoon crushed red pepper flakes

CAYENNE PEPPER, GROUND/GROUND RED PEPPER – 1/2 teaspoon
- 1/2 teaspoon Aleppo, de árbol, or Thai chili powder
- 1/2 teaspoon hot paprika
- 3/4 teaspoon crushed red pepper flakes
- 3 to 4 drops hot pepper sauce, such as Tabasco or Crystal

CELERY FLAKES
- Celery leaves, dried in a preheated 200°F oven until brittle, then coarsely crushed

CELERY SALT – 1 tablespoon
Make Your Own Grind 1 1/2 teaspoons whole celery seeds in a coffee/spice grinder (or use 1 teaspoon ground celery seed) and mix with 2 teaspoons salt; cover and let sit for a few days to develop flavor.

CELERY SEEDS – 1 teaspoon
- 1/2 teaspoon ground celery seed
- 3/4 teaspoon celery salt, and reduce the salt in the recipe by 1/2 teaspoon

➤ 1 tablepoon finely minced celery leaves
➤ 1 teaspoon dill seeds

CELERY SOUP, CANNED CREAM OF (for recipes) – 1 (10.5-ounce) can
➤ 1 cup thick homemade white sauce plus 2 to 3 tablespoons finely chopped sautéed celery and 1/2 teaspoon celery salt; stir until combined

CHAI SEASONING/YOGI TEA (Thai and Indian spice mix for tea) – 2 teaspoons
➤ 1 teaspoon ground cardamom plus 1/4 teaspoon each ground allspice, ground cinnamon, ground ginger, and ground nutmeg
➤ 1-inch cinnamon stick, 2 green cardamom pods, and 3 whole cloves

CHAMOMILE FLOWERS, DRIED – 1 tablespoon
➤ 2 chamomile tea bags (contents removed)
➤ 2 tablespoons finely chopped fresh chamomile leaves

CHANCACA (Latin American unrefined sugar) See PILONCILLO/PANELA/PANOCHA

CHARDONNAY VINEGAR – 1 tablespoon
➤ 1 tablespoon champagne vinegar or white wine vinegar

CHAROLI NUTS/CHIRONGI/CALUMPANG (Indian sweetmeat garnish) – 1 ounce
➤ 1 ounce slivered blanched almonds
➤ 1 ounce chopped unsalted pistachios or hazelnuts

CHAR SIU SAUCE See CHINESE BARBECUE SAUCE

CHEE HOU SAUCE/CHU HOU PASTE (Chinese braising sauce) – 1/4 cup
➤ 1/4 cup hoisin sauce diluted with a little rice vinegar

CHEESE, MELTING (soft or semifirm cheese; used for pizza, lasagna, sauces, and fondues) – 1 ounce

⊩ 1 ounce American, mild Cheddar, Colby, Edam, Emmental, fontina, Gruyère, Gouda, Havarti, Jarlsberg, Manchego, Monterey Jack, mozzarella, or provolone

CHEESE CURDS (firm, chewy unprocessed cheddar lumps) – 1 cup

⊩ 1 cup kasseri cheese cubes
⊩ 1 cup fresh salted mozzarella, cut into small pieces

CHEESE POWDER – 1 cup

⊩ 1 cup nutritional yeast powder

Make Your Own Spread 1 1/2 cups grated cheddar cheese on parchment paper-lined trays and dry in a dehydrator at high setting until the oil is released, 8 to 12 hours. Drain on paper towels until cool, then pulse in a blender or food processor until powdery. Store in a tightly sealed container; it will keep for up to 1 year in the refrigerator.

CHEESE SAUCE – 1 cup

⊩ 2/3 cup condensed cheese soup, 1/3 cup milk, plus a few drops hot pepper sauce, whisked together and heated

Make your own: Whisk together 1/2 cup condensed cream of mushroom soup and 1/2 cup milk; bring to a boil, then remove from the heat and stir in 2/3 cup shredded cheese until the cheese is melted.

CHERRIES, MARASCHINO, JARRED – 1 cup cherries plus 1 cup liquid

Make Your Own Combine 1 cup fresh pitted cherries, 1 cup vodka, 1/2 cup granulated sugar, and 1/2 teaspoon pure almond extract in a sterilized jar and place in a cool, dark place for 5 to 6 days, shaking the jar daily. Store, refrigerated, for up to 4 months.

CHERRY EXTRACT – 1 teaspoon

⊩ 2 to 3 tablespoons cherry juice or liquid from jarred maraschino cherries (sweeter; reduce the liquid in the recipe by 2 to 3 tablespoons)

CHERRY LIQUEUR/CHERRY-FLAVORED SPIRIT (such as Cherry Heering, Cherry Marnier, Cherry Rocher, Cusenier Heering, or Kirschenliqueur) – 2 tablespoons
- 2 tablespoons crème de cerise or crème de griotte
- 2 tablespoons cherry schnapps or kirsch (less sweet)
- 1/2 to 1 teaspoon cherry extract plus 2 tablespoons vodka or water

CHERVIL/CICELY/SWEET CICELY, FRESH – 8 sprigs (1 tablespoon finely chopped leaves)
- 1 teaspoon dried crumbled chervil leaf
- 2 teaspoons chopped fresh flat-leaf parsley plus 1 teaspoon chopped fresh tarragon
- 1/2 teaspoon dried parsley plus 1/4 teaspoon dried tarragon
- 1 tablespoon finely chopped fennel fronds

CHESAPEAKE BAY SEASONING – 1 teaspoon
- 1 teaspoon shrimp boil seasoning

CHIA SEEDS/SALBA SEEDS – 2 tablespoons
- 1 1/2 tablespoons chia powder or 2 tablespoons ground flaxseed/flaxmeal (sprouted or regular)
- 2 tablespoons sesame seeds (lacks omega-3s and gelatinous property)

CHICKEN DEMI-GLACE *See POULTRY GLAZE/GLACE DE VOLAILLE*

CHICKEN SOUP, CANNED CREAM OF (for recipes) – 1 (10.5-ounce) can
- 1 cup thick homemade white sauce plus 1 teaspoon chicken bouillon granules or crumbled bouillon cube
- 1 (8-ounce) package cream cheese, 1/2 cup water, and 1/2 teaspoon chicken soup base, thoroughly combined

CHILI BEAN SAUCE/TOBANJIANG/DOUBANJIANG (Chinese condiment) – 2 generous tablespoons
- 2 tablespoons black bean sauce (or black bean and garlic sauce) plus a little chili oil, hot pepper sauce, or chopped hot chili

⊨ 1 tablespoon chili bean paste mixed with 1 crushed garlic clove and 2 teaspoons each soy sauce and rice vinegar

CHILI GARLIC SAUCE/LA JIAO JIANG (Chinese condiment) – 1 tablespoon

⊨ 1 tablespoon Chinese chili sauce or sambal oelek, plus minced fresh garlic

⊨ 1 teaspoon crushed red pepper flakes plus few grains granulated garlic

⊨ 2 teaspoons Chinese chili oil

Make Your Own Process in a food processor 5 (3-inch) fresh, chopped, seeded red chilis, 3 garlic cloves, and 2 tablespoons seasoned rice vinegar. Store, refrigerated, for up to 1 week.

CHILI JELLY See JALAPEÑO JELLY

CHILI OIL/DAU OT/LA JIAO YOU (Chinese condiment) – 1 teaspoon

⊨ 1 teaspoon Asian sesame oil (or peanut oil) plus 1/8 teaspoon ground cayenne pepper or hot chili powder

⊨ 1/8 teaspoon (or more) crushed red pepper flakes or hot sauce, such as Tabasco or Crystal

⊨ 1 teaspoon Thai or Malaysian chili oil (more pungent)

Make Your Own Slowly heat 1/2 cup peanut or sesame oil and 1/4 cup crushed red pepper flakes until the oil becomes a shade darker, about 5 minutes (or microwave in a 2-cup glass measuring jug for 1 minute). Let sit, covered, for 24 hours, then strain through a fine-mesh sieve; discard the pepper flakes and store the oil for up to 6 months in the refrigerator. Makes about 1/2 cup.

CHILI OIL, ITALIAN/OLIO PEPERONCINO/OLIO SANTA (bean soup condiment) – 1/4 cup

Make Your Own Combine 1/4 cup olive oil and 1 to 2 tablespoons crushed red pepper flakes (or ground medium-hot dried chili) and gently heat until infused, 3 to 4 minutes, stirring occasionally. Use within 2 or 3 days.

CHILI PASTE WITH GARLIC – 1/4 cup (about)

Make Your Own Stem, peel, seed, and chop 1 fresh mild chili (New Mexico, Anaheim, or poblano, then soften in hot water to cover for about 20 minutes before draining and pureeing with 2 or 3 garlic cloves. (Wear plastic gloves when handling chilis and avoid touching your face.)

CHILI PASTE, HOT – 1/4 cup (about) See also SAMBAL OELEK

Make Your Own Toast 1/2 cup dried hot chilis (bird's eye, pequín, or tepín) in a preheated 300°F oven until plump, about 5 minutes. Bring to a boil with 1/2 cup water, 1 tablespoon rice vinegar, and 1/2 teaspoon salt; cool, stem, then process to a paste. (Wear plastic gloves when handling the chilis and avoid touching your face.)

CHILI PASTE, MILD (cooking condiment) – 1/4 cup

Make Your Own Stem, seed, and chop fresh or dried mild chilis, such as ancho, New Mexico, mulato, or pasilla; simmer in water to cover until very soft, about 15 minutes. Drain, cool, then process to a paste with some of the soaking water. Alternatively, soak the seeded chilis in boiling water until softened, about 20 minutes, and then scrape the pulp off the skin with a knife. (Wear plastic gloves when handling the chilis and avoid touching your face.)

CHILI POWDER, HOT – 1/4 cup (about)

Make Your Own Toast 1 ounce (2/3 to 1 cup) hot dried red chilis (cayenne, de árbol, japonés pequín, or tepín/chiltepin) in a dry skillet over medium-high heat, stirring constantly, until crispy and fragrant, 3 to 5 minutes. Cool, then grind until powdery in a food processor or spice/coffee grinder. (Let the dust settle before removing the lid and avoid inhaling the fumes.) Store in an airtight container in a cool, dry place; it will keep for up to 3 months.

CHILI POWDER, MEXICAN/CHILI CON CARNE SEASONING – 1/4 cup

☞ 3 tablespoons mild chili powder, such as ancho or New Mexico, seasoned with 1 teaspoon ground cumin, 1 teaspoon dried oregano (preferably Mexican), 1/2 teaspoon garlic powder, and 1/2 teaspoon onion powder (Add ground cayenne pepper to taste for medium-hot chili, and cayenne and crushed red pepper flakes for extra-hot chili.)

CHILI POWDER, MILD – 1/2 cup (about)
Make Your Own Toast 6 mild dried chilis (ancho, New Mexico, mulato, or pasilla) in a dry skillet over medium heat until fragrant, 2 to 3 minutes per side (or in a preheated 350°F oven until fragrant and puffed, 5 to 6 minutes). Cool, remove stems and seeds, then grind until powdery. Store in an airtight container in a cool, dry place; it will keep for up to 3 months. (Wear plastic gloves when handling chilis, and avoid inhaling the fumes.)

CHILI SAUCE (tomato-based condiment) – 1 cup
⊢ 1 cup ketchup plus red hot-pepper sauce, such as Tabasco, to taste
Make Your Own Stir together 3/4 cup tomato sauce, 2 tablespoons firmly packed brown sugar (or 1/4 cup granulated sugar), 2 to 3 tablespoons cider or malt vinegar, and 1/4 teaspoon ground allspice (optional) until the sugar dissolves.

CHILI SAUCE, ASIAN – 1 teaspoon
⊢ 1 teaspoon Chinese chili sauce/*la jiao jiang*, Indonesian *sambal oelek*, Japanese chili yuzu paste/*yuzu koshu*, Thai *Sriracha*, or Vietnamese *tuong ot toi*
⊢ 1 teaspoon hot pepper sauce, such as Tabasco or Crystal

CHILI SOY SAUCE – 1 cup
⊢ 3/4 cup light soy sauce, and 3 tablespoons Chinese chili sauce
⊢ 3/4 cup light soy sauce, 1/4 cup deveined and seeded minced fresh chilis, plus sugar to taste (Wear plastic gloves when handling chilis and avoid touching your face.)

CHILI THREADS, DRIED RED See KOREAN RED PEPPER THREADS

CHILI VINEGAR, INDIAN – 1 cup
Make Your Own Chop 5 or 6 hot dried red chilis and place in a sterilized jar with 1 cup cider vinegar. Cover and let sit in a cool, dark place

for 7 to 10 days, shaking the bottle occasionally. Strain and discard the chilis. Store in an airtight container in a cool, dry place; it will keep for up to 6 months.

CHILTEPIN CHILI POWDER – 1 teaspoon
- 1 teaspoon Thai or piri-piri powder or ground cayenne pepper

CHIMAYO RED CHILI POWDER – 1 tablespoon
- 1 tablespoon New Mexico or ancho chili powder (less flowery aroma)

CHIMICHURRI SAUCE (Argentinean condiment) – 3/4 cup
- 1/4 to 1/2 teaspoon ground cayenne pepper or hot pepper sauce, such as Tabasco or Crystal, stirred into 3/4 cup parsley pesto

Make Your Own Process 1 packed cup flat-leaf parsley, 1/3 cup olive oil, 2 to 3 tablespoons red wine vinegar, 2 or 3 garlic cloves, and 1/4 teaspoon each kosher salt, dried oregano (optional), and cayenne to a paste in a food processor or blender. Let sit for 1 hour to develop the flavor before using.

CHINESE BARBECUE SAUCE/CHAR SIU CHIANG – 1 cup
- 1 cup oyster sauce
- 1 cup Chinese vegetarian barbecue sauce, such as AGV brand

CHINESE BROWN BEAN PASTE See CHINESE YELLOW BEAN SAUCE

CHINESE CHILI BEAN PASTE See SICHUAN CHILI BEAN PASTE

CHINESE CHILI FLAKES/LA JIAO MIAN – 1 tablespoon
- 1 tablespoon Korean coarse chili flakes/*gochugaru*
- 1 1/2 teaspoons Italian crushed red pepper flakes

CHINESE CHILI, DRIED/GAN LA JIAO – 1/4 cup
- 1/4 cup cayenne, de árbol, or Thai chilis

CHINESE CHIVES/CHINESE LEEK See GARLIC CHIVES

CHINESE COOKING WINE/LIAO JIU *See CHINESE YELLOW RICE COOKING WINE*

CHINESE CURRY POWDER – 1 teaspoon
- ⊨ 1 teaspoon mild Madras curry powder
- ⊨ 1/4 teaspoon each ground turmeric, cardamom, ginger, and cumin

CHINESE DATES *See JUJUBES*

CHINESE DIPPING SAUCE – 1 cup
- ⊨ 1/2 cup each soy sauce and brown rice vinegar plus 1 teaspoon grated fresh ginger (or chili oil)

Make Your Own Stir together 1/2 cup soy sauce, 1/4 cup water, 2 tablespoons seasoned rice vinegar, and 2 teaspoons sugar until the sugar dissolves. Add 2 tablespoons thinly sliced scallions or green onions, if desired.

CHINESE DRIED SCALLOP/CONPOY (flavoring agent) – 1 ounce
- ⊨ 1 ounce dried shrimp
- ⊨ 1 ounce tuna bottarga/*bottarga di tonno*

CHINESE DUCK SAUCE *See PLUM SAUCE*

CHINESE FIVE-SPICE POWDER – 1 teaspoon
- ⊨ 1/8 teaspoon each ground cinnamon, ground cloves, ground ginger, ground Sichuan pepper (or freshly ground black or white pepper), and ground star anise (or crushed anise or fennel seed)
- ⊨ 1 whole ground star anise (or 1/2 teaspoon star anise powder) plus a dash of ground white pepper or ginger
- ⊨ 1/2 teaspoon anise or fennel seeds, crushed, plus a dash of ground white pepper or ginger

CHINESE GARLIC STEMS/SUAN TAI – 4 ounces
- ⊨ 4 ounces garlic chives, or garlic scapes (curly garlic shoots)
- ⊨ 4 ounces green onions plus a little chopped garlic

☞ 4 ounces unsprayed wild garlic greens/shoots/onion grass/*Allium vineale*

CHINESE GINGER *See FINGERROOT*

CHINESE HAM (Yunnan or Jinhua) –4 ounces
☞ 4 ounces smoky Serrano ham, or dry-cured and smoked country-style ham, such as Smithfield

CHINESE PICKLED GARLIC – 1 cup
Make Your Own Separate and peel the cloves from 5 heads (about 8 ounces) of garlic. Heat with 1/2 cup unseasoned rice vinegar, 1 tablespoon sugar, and 1/2 teaspoon salt until boiling; let cool. Refrigerate in a covered jar for at least 1 month before using.

CHINESE PRESERVED CABBAGE/SALTED MUSTARD CABBAGE/ TIANJIN/TUNG TSAI – 1 tablespoon
☞ 1 tablespoon salt-packed capers, rinsed in cold water and patted dry
☞ 1 tablespoon sauerkraut or napa cabbage kimchi (milder)

CHINESE RED DATES *See JUJUBES*

CHINESE RED RICE POWDER/HONG QU FEN (coloring agent) – 1 tablespoon
☞ 1 tablespoon red rice (labeled red yeast rice) ground to a fine powder in a spice/coffee grinder

CHINESE RED RICE VINEGAR/DA HONG ZHE CU (vinegar dipping/condiment sauce) – 1 tablespoon
☞ 1 tablespoon Japanese rice vinegar (milder)
☞ 1 tablespoon red wine vinegar sweetened with a little sugar
☞ 1 tablespoon Chinese black rice vinegar or cider vinegar

CHINESE RICE WINE/HUANG JIN/CHIEW *See SHAOXING*

CHINESE SAUSAGE/LAP CHEONG (thin cured sweet seasoned sausage)
– 1 pound
- ⊫ 1 pound Spanish dry-cured chorizo
- ⊫ 1 pound Portuguese dry-cured chouriço or linguiça
- ⊫ 1 pound Italian pepperoni or dry salami

CHINESE SOY SAUCE See SOY SAUCE, CHINESE DARK; SOY SAUCE, CHINESE DOUBLE DARK; SOY SAUCE, CHINESE LIGHT

CHINESE SWEET-AND-SOUR SAUCE – 1/2 cup
- ⊫ 1/2 cup Italian sweet and sour sauce/*agrodolce*

Make Your Own Simmer 1/4 cup each plum jam and apricot (or peach) jam with 3 to 4 tablespoons cider vinegar until slightly thickened, about 10 minutes, or microwave on High for 4 minutes; let cool. (The sauce will thicken further as it cools.)

CHINESE SWEET BEAN PASTE/SAUCE See SICHUAN SWEET BEAN PASTE

CHINESE WHITE RICE VINEGAR/CLEAR RICE VINEGAR/BAI MI CU –
1/2 cup
- ⊫ 1/3 cup distilled white vinegar or cider vinegar plus 3 tablespoons water

CHINESE YELLOW BEAN SAUCE/SWEET BEAN SAUCE/HUANG JIANG –
1 tablespoon
- ⊫ 1 tablespoon canned, salted yellow beans, rinsed briefly in a fine sieve, then mashed with a fork
- ⊫ 1 tablespoon Vietnamese yellow bean sauce/*tuong ot* or Thai yellow bean sauce/*tao jiew*
- ⊫ 1 tablespoon Japanese all-purpose light miso, such as *shinshu*

CHINESE YELLOW RICE COOKING WINE/MICHIU/MI JIU – 1 tablespoon
- ⊫ 1 tablespoon pure yellow rice wine/*huang jiu,* such as Shaoxing/Shaohing, plus a few grains of salt
- ⊫ 1 tablespoon glutinous yellow rice wine/*gnow mei dew*

⊱ 1 tablespoon sake, dry vermouth, Latin American *vino seco*, or medium dry sherry, such as amontillado

CHIPOTLE CHILI POWDER – *1 teaspoon*

⊱ 2 teaspoons pureed chipotle chili from canned chipotle chilis in adobo
⊱ 1 teaspoon Urfa chili powder or 1 1/4 teaspoons Urfa pepper flakes
⊱ 1 1/2 teaspoons Aleppo chili powder, or 1 tablespoon ancho chili powder plus a touch of hickory smoke powder (or a drop of liquid smoke)
⊱ 1 teaspoon crushed red pepper flakes or ground cayenne pepper, plus a touch of hickory smoke powder (or a drop of liquid smoke)
⊱ 1/2 teaspoon Spanish hot paprika
⊱ Chipotle-flavored mini bouillon cube (add a small section to soups, chili, or stews; reduce the salt in the recipe accordingly)

CHIPOTLE HOT PEPPER SAUCE – *1 tablespoon*

⊱ Hot pepper sauce, such as Tabasco or Frank's RedHot, plus a few drops liquid smoke
⊱ Liquid from canned or jarred chipotles in adobo, thinned if necessary

CHIPOTLE MORA/MORITA/CHIPOTLE COLORADO (*smoked-dried jalapeño*) – *1*

⊱ 1 small dried chipotle meco chili
⊱ 1 large dried, smoked serrano
⊱ 1 small dried *pasilla de Oaxaca*
⊱ 1 de árbol or cascabel chili (spicy but not smoked)
⊱ 1 large canned chipotle in adobo, rinsed and dried (not for a concentrated seasoning paste)
⊱ 1/2 teaspoon chipotle chili powder, Morita chili powder, smoked red aji chili powder, Chilean *merkén*, or Spanish hot paprika
⊱ 1/4 teaspoon chipotle hot pepper sauce, such as Tabasco or Texas Pete

CHIPOTLE PASTE/PUREE – 1 tablespoon
- 2 or 3 drained chipotles in adobo, pureed until smooth
- 1 tablespoon ketchup plus 1 teaspoon hot chili sauce, such as Sriracha, and a pinch of smoked paprika

CHIVE OIL – 1/2 cup
Make Your Own Blanch 1 bunch chives in boiling water for 30 seconds, then dip in ice water; squeeze dry and process in a food processor or blender with 1/2 cup oil and a pinch of salt until combined, about 2 minutes. Store in the refrigerator.

CHIVES, FRESH, FROZEN, OR FREEZE DRIED – 4 ounces
- 4 ounces green parts of scallions or green onions, smashed and cut lengthwise into ribbons
- 4 ounces garlic chives or Chinese garlic stems (more garlicky tasting)
- 4 ounces garlic leaves, slivered (cut leaves sparingly when the plants are no more than 8 inches tall)
- 4 ounces Egyptian walking onion leaves, slivered
- 4 ounces unsprayed wild garlic foliage/shoots/*Allium vineale*

CHOCOLATE FUDGE TOPPING – 3/4 to 1 cup
Make Your Own Combine 1/2 cup each unsweetened cocoa powder, sugar, and boiling water, plus a pinch of salt; stir over low heat until smooth, about 2 minutes. The sauce hardens upon standing. (For a thinner sauce, use 1/3 cup cocoa powder.)
Or
Heat 1/2 cup heavy cream or evaporated milk and 2 tablespoons corn syrup just until boiling, then pour over 2/3 cup chocolate chips and stir until smooth.

CHOCOLATE LIQUEUR/CHOCOLATE-FLAVORED SPIRIT (such as Godiva, Haagen Dazs, Lejay-Lagoute, or Mozart) – 1 tablespoon for cooking
- 1 tablespoon crème de cacao or chocolate syrup (reduce the sugar in the recipe by 1 1/2 teaspoons)

CHOCOLATE MINT SAUCE – 1 cup
- 1/4 cup heavy cream (or soy or coconut creamer) stirred into 8 ounces chopped and melted chocolate peppermint creams (serve warm)

CHOCOLATE SYRUP – 3/4 cup (about)
- Simmer 1/2 cup water, 1/4 cup granulated sugar, 1/3 cup unsweetened cocoa powder and a pinch of sea salt for 3 or 4 minutes. Remove from the heat and add 1/2 teaspoon vanilla; store in a lidded jar in the refrigerator. (For a sweeter syrup, increase the sugar to up to 1 cup.)

CHORICERO PEPPER, DRIED (Spanish mild red pepper) – 1
- 1 dried ñora/murican pepper
- 1 dried ancho chili
- 1 1/2 teaspoons Choricero powder or smoked mild/sweet Spanish paprika/*Pimentón de la Vera Dulce*

CIDER MOLASSES – 1 cup
- 2 quarts unfiltered apple cider, gently boiled over medium heat until reduced to 1 cup, 40 to 50 minutes, stirring occasionally; store, refrigerated, for up to 1 month

CIDER VINEGAR/APPLE CIDER VINEGAR – 1 tablespoon
- 1 tablespoon white wine vinegar or unseasoned rice vinegar
- 1 tablespoon distilled colorless malt vinegar or distilled white vinegar (for pickling and preserving)
- 1 tablespoon vinegar powder (for barbecue spice rubs)

CIDER, BOILED (thick, pourable syrup) – 1 cup (12 ounces)
- 3 cups apple cider, boiled, uncovered, over moderate heat until reduced to 1 cup
- 1 cup thawed frozen apple juice concentrate

CIDER, HARD/CIDRE/SAGARDOA – *1 cup*

- 7/8 cup sweet apple cider plus 2 tablespoons bourbon
- 1 cup dry apple wine or dry white wine

CIDER, MEDIUM-HARD – *1 cup*

- 7/8 cup dry hard cider plus 2 tablespoons apple juice
- 2/3 cup organic apple juice plus 1/3 cup apple cider vinegar
- 1 cup lambic beer or ale (not light ale)

CIDER, SWEET APPLE – *1 cup*

- 1 tablespoon boiled cider mixed with 3/4 cup water
- 1 cup cold-pressed apple juice (less tangy)
- 1 or 2 teaspoons cider vinegar added to 1 cup apple juice
- 1 cup pear cider/perry

CILANTRO/FRESH CORIANDER LEAVES – *1 tablespoon chopped leaves*

- 1 teaspoon dried broken leaf cilantro
- 1 tablespoon chopped fresh sawleaf herb/*culantro*
- 1 tablespoon chopped Italian flat-leaf parsley leaves, 1/8 teaspoon sage, and 1/8 teaspoon finely grated lime or lemon zest
- 1 tablespoon chopped Italian flat-leaf parsley sprigs (for color)
- Small piece cilantro-flavored mini bouillon cube (for soups or stews; reduce the salt in the recipe accordingly)
- 1 to 2 tablespoons cilantro cooking base/*recaito* (for soups or stews; reduce the salt and seasoning accordingly)

CINNAMON, GROUND (Ceylon, Sri Lanka, Mexican, canela) – *1 teaspoon*

- 1-inch Ceylon/Sri Lanka cinnamon stick, crumbled or grated with a Microplane grater
- 2/3 teaspoon Indonesia/Korintje or China cassia cinnamon
- 1/4 to 1/2 teaspoon Vietnamese/Saigon cassia cinnamon

CINNAMON, GROUND (Indonesian, Korintje, Padang, cassia) – *1 teaspoon*

- 1 1/2 teaspoons pure Ceylon/Sri Lanka cinnamon/canela

☞ 1/4 teaspoon cinnamon extract
☞ 1/2 teaspoon ground allspice plus scant 1/8 teaspoon ground nutmeg
☞ 1/4 teaspoon ground cardamom plus 1/8 teaspoon ground nutmeg
☞ 1 teaspoon apple or pumpkin pie spice

CINNAMON, GROUND (Vietnamese/Saigon cassia) -1 teaspoon
☞ 1 1/4 teaspoons Indonesia/Korintje or China/Tung Hing cassia cinnamon
☞ 2 teaspoons pure Ceylon/Sri Lanka cinnamon/canela

CINNAMON OIL – 2 drops
☞ 1/2 teaspoon cinnamon extract
☞ 1 1/2 to 2 teaspoons ground cassia cinnamon

CINNAMON STICK, INDONESIAN KORINTJE – 1 (3- or 4-inch) stick
☞ 1 (5-inch) soft Ceylon cinnamon stick/canela
☞ 2 teaspoons ground cinnamon (to replace a smashed/crushed cinnamon stick used in cooking)
☞ 1/4 teaspoon ground cinnamon (to replace a whole cinnamon stick
   removed after cooking)
☞ 1 tablespoon cinnamon chunks (to flavor coffee, mulled wine, or
   cider)

CINNAMON SUGAR – 1 cup
☞ 2 tablespoons ground cinnamon thoroughly mixed with 1/2 cup
   granulated sugar
☞ 2 or 3 cinnamon sticks buried in a jar containing 1 cup sugar and
   then left for a few weeks

CINNAMON SYRUP – 1 cup
☞ 4 or 5 whole cinnamon sticks added to 1 cup heated heavy syrup
   (See SYRUP, SIMPLE) and simmered 1 or 2 minutes; strain and cool
   before using (for more intense flavor, let mixture sit a few hours
   before straining)

CITRIC ACID/CITRIC SALT (tart flavoring and anti-discoloration agent for fruits and vegetables) – 1 tablespoon powdered

➣ 1 heaping tablespoon citric acid crystals (lemon salt/sour salt), finely crushed and then measured to equal 1 tablespoon (found in the canning section of supermarkets)
➣ 1 tablespoon tartaric acid (found at wine supply stores)
➣ 1 teaspoon ascorbic acid powder (found in drugstores)
➣ Six (500-mg) ascorbic acid vitamin C tablets, crushed to a powder or dissolved in water

CITRON SALT/CITRUS SALT – 1 cup

Make Your Own Thoroughly combine 1 cup coarse sea salt or flake salt and 3 tablespoons freshly grated citron zest (or lemon zest), spread on a baking sheet, then dry in a preheated 200°F oven, about 1 hour; cool completely. Store in an airtight container. Alternatively, let sit at room temperature until completely dry, 8 to 12 hours.

CITRUS OIL, PURE (lemon, lime, orange, or tangerine) – 1/2 teaspoon

➣ 1 1/2 teaspoons pure citrus extract
➣ 3 or 4 teaspoons finely grated citrus zest from a scrubbed fruit, preferably organic (Place the whole fruit in the freezer until partly hardened, about 30 minutes, before grating.)

CITRUS SUGAR – 1 cup

Make Your Own Process 1 cup granulated sugar and 2 to 4 tablespoons finely grated zest (lemon, lime, or tangerine) in a blender or food processor until combined, 30 to 40 seconds, or in a spice/coffee grinder in batches. Alternatively, bury thin strips of zest in the sugar and store airtight at room temperature for at least 1 week before opening.

CITRUS SYRUP – 1 cup

Make Your Own Remove 8 to 10 strips of lemon, yuzu, or lime peel (scrub the fruit first) with a vegetable peeler and scrape away any white pith. Simmer with 1 cup heavy syrup (*See SYRUP, SIMPLE*) 1 to 2 minutes; strain and cool before using.

CITRUS ZEST, DRIED *See LEMON PEEL, DRIED; ORANGE PEEL, DRIED GRANULATED; TANGERINE/MANDARIN PEEL, DRIED*

CLAMATO JUICE – 1 cup for cooking
- 2/3 cup tomato juice and 1/3 third cup bottled clam juice

CLAM JUICE – 1 cup for cooking
- 20 to 30 shrimp shells and heads, sautéed in 1 or 2 teaspoons vegetable oil until bright orange (optional), then simmered with 2 cups water for 30 minutes, and strained
- 1 cup bottled/jarred clam juice (or 1/2 cup juice from canned clams and 1/2 cup water)
- 1 cup canned seafood stock
- 1/2 teaspoon bonito-flavored seasoning/soup stock, such as *hon-dashi* or *dashi-no-moto*, dissolved in 1 cup hot water
- 1/2 to 3/4 teaspoon concentrated clam or seafood base dissolved in 1 cup hot water
- 3/4 to 1 teaspoon clam flavored soup stock granules, such as Dashi-da, dissolved in 1 cup hot water.

CLOTTED CREAM *See CREAM, CLOTTED/DEVONSHIRE CREAM*

CLOUD EAR/BLACK TREE FUNGUS (Asian dried mushroom) – 1/2 ounce (1/4 to 1/3 cup)
- 1/2 ounce dried wood ear fungus (larger, thicker, tougher; increase the cooking time)
- 1/2 ounce dried silver ear/white fungus (white to pale gold)
- 1/2 ounce small dried shiitake mushrooms (triple the soaking time)

CLOVES, GROUND – 1 teaspoon
- 1 1/4 teaspoons whole cloves ground in a spice/coffee grinder
- 1/3 teaspoon each ground allspice, cinnamon, and nutmeg
- 1 teaspoon ground allspice

COCKTAIL SAUCE (sauce for shrimp cocktail) – 1 cup
Make Your Own Stir 2/3 cup ketchup or ketchup-based chili sauce, such as Heinz; 1/4 to 1/3 cup strained bottled horseradish (or 1 tablespoon

wasabi paste); and a few dashes of hot pepper sauce until combined. Alternatively, in place of the horseradish, increase the hot pepper sauce and add a dash of lemon juice plus a few drops of Worcestershire sauce.

COCOA BUTTER – 1 ounce
- 4 teaspoons unsalted butter, palm oil, grapeseed oil, or other neutral-tasting oil

COCONUT BUTTER/CREAMED COCONUT – 1 cup for cooking
- 1 cup vegetable shortening or unsalted butter (lacks coconut flavor)
  Make Your Own Process 4 cups dried unsweetened flaked or desiccated coconut in a food processor or high-speed blender until reduced to a paste, 15 to 20 minutes, scraping down the sides of the bowl as needed. Store in a lidded jar at room temperature up to 2 months.

COCONUT CREAM, UNSWEETENED – 1/2 cup
- 1/2 cup thick liquid that rises to the top of canned or homemade coconut milk after chilling it several hours
- 1/2 cup light cream or whipping cream plus 1/4 teaspoon coconut extract

COCONUT MILK BEVERAGE, BOXED – 1 cup
- 1/4 cup canned coconut milk mixed with 3/4 cup water
- 1 cup hemp milk

COCONUT MILK, FRESH – 1 cup
- 3 tablespoons canned cream of coconut plus enough water to make 1 cup

COCONUT NECTAR/PALM SYRUP/EVAPORATED COCONUT SAP/KITHUL TREACLE (thick, dark sweetener) – 1 cup
- 1 cup dark agave syrup/nectar, birch syrup, brown rice syrup, maple syrup, or yacón syrup
- 3/4 cup liquid honey plus 2 tablespoons water

COCONUT OIL, REFINED – *1 cup*
- 1 cup firm rendered leaf lard
- 1 cup solid shortening
- 1 cup liquid and pourable coconut oil, or neutral-flavored vegetable oil, such as canola

COCONUT PALM SUGAR, GRANULATED See PALM SUGAR, LIGHT

COCONUT SUGAR, POWDERED – *1 cup*
- 1/2 cup each confectioners' sugar and coconut milk powder, sifted together until thoroughly combined

COCONUT SYRUP, LIGHT – *1 cup* See also COCONUT NECTAR
- 1 tablespoon coconut extract added to 1 cup simple syrup (*See SYRUP, SIMPLE*)

COCONUT VINEGAR/SUKANG TUBA (Filipino low-acidity vinegar) – *1/3 cup*
- 1/3 cup organic coconut vinegar (sold in health food stores)
- 1/3 cup white sugarcane vinegar/*sukang maasim*
- 3 tablespoons cider vinegar plus 2 tablespoons water
- 1/4 cup rice vinegar plus 1 tablespoon water

COFFEE-BASED CREAM LIQUEUR (such as Bailey's) – *2 tablespoons for cooking*
- 1 tablespoon strong coffee, 1 1/2 teaspoons each heavy cream and whiskey, and 1 scant teaspoon sugar, preferably vanilla
- 2 tablespoons *crème de noyaux* (almond-flavored), or Tiramisu liqueur (chocolate-, coffee-, and almond-flavored)
- Few drops Irish cream flavoring; increase the liquid in the recipe by 2 tablespoons

COFFEE CONCENTRATE – *1 scant cup*
Make Your Own Combine 4 ounces (1 1/4 cups) regular-grind coffee with 2 cups cold water, cover, and let sit for 12 hours before straining; store in a small bottle in the refrigerator.

COFFEE ESSENCE – 1/3 cup
Make Your Own Bring 1/4 cup finely ground French roast or espresso roast and 1/2 cup water just to a boil, stir a few times, then cover and let steep for 3 to 4 minutes. Strain through a paper coffee filter or paper towel, then cool. Store, refrigerated, for up to 1 month.

COFFEE EXTRACT – 1 tablespoon
- 1 1/2 teaspoons instant espresso powder, such as Medaglia d'Oro, or 1 3/4 espresso granules dissolved in 1 tablespoon warm water; cool before using
- 2 teaspoons instant coffee granules dissolved in 1 tablespoon boiling water; cool before using
- 1 tablespoon coffee-flavored syrup; reduce the sugar in the recipe by 1 or more teaspoons

COFFEE LIQUEUR/COFFEE-FLAVORED SPIRIT (such as Kahlúa, Crème de Café, Tia Maria, or Pasha) – 1 tablespoon for cooking
- 1 tablespoon chocolate-, hazelnut-, or almond-flavored liqueur
- 1/2 teaspoon freeze-dried instant coffee dissolved in 1 tablespoon vodka or hot water
- 1/4 teaspoon chocolate extract and 1/4 to 1/2 teaspoon instant coffee dissolved in 1 tablespoon vodka or hot water
- 1 tablespoon mocha-flavored espresso drink

COFFEE PASTE – 1 tablespoon
- 1 tablespoon instant coffee dissolved in 1 tablespoon hot water

COFFEE, STRONG BREWED OR DOUBLE STRENGTH – 1 cup for flavoring
- The first cup from a pot of drip coffee
- 1 tablespoon instant espresso powder dissolved in 1 cup hot water
- 4 teaspoons freeze-dried instant coffee granules dissolved in 1 cup hot water

COGNAC (French brandy) – 2 tablespoons
- 2 tablespoons Armagnac

COLESLAW DRESSING – 1/4 cup
Make Your Own Whisk together 2 tablespoons mayonnaise, 1 table-spoon each sour cream (or plain yogurt) and white wine vinegar (or cider vinegar), and 1 teaspoon granulated sugar.

CONSOMMÉ – 1 cup
☞ 1 cup canned or boxed beef broth plus 1 1/2 teaspoons unflavored gelatin powder (dissolve the gelatin in the broth before heating)

CONSOMMÉ, DOUBLE – 1 cup
☞ 2 cups consommé, gently boiled in a large pan until reduced to 1 cup, 5 to 10 minutes

CORIANDER LEAVES See CILANTRO/FRESH CORIANDER LEAVES

CORIANDER ROOT/RAK PAK CHI/PAK CHEE MET (Thai) – 3 to 4 medium (1 tablespoon chopped)
☞ 3 tablespoons chopped cilantro stems

CORIANDER SEED, DRIED (European and Indian) – 1 tablespoon (1/8 ounce)
☞ 1 to 1 1/2 teaspoons ground coriander
☞ 2 tablespoons fresh green coriander seeds
☞ 1 tablespoon caraway or fennel seeds
☞ 1 1/2 teaspoons black cardamom seeds or cumin seeds

CORNICHONS (tiny French pickles) – 1/4 cup
☞ 1/4 cup Mexican fresh sour gherkins, brined gherkins, or other sour brined pickles, cut small
☞ 1/4 cup drained pickle relish (for chopped or minced cornichons)

CORN SMUT See HUITLACOCHE

COSTEÑO CHILI, DRIED – 1
☞ 1 chili de árbol or cayenne chili

CRAB BOIL SEASONING – 1 (3-ounce) packet
- 2 1/2 tablespoons Old Bay seasoning (regular or low-sodium) or Zatarain's seasoning
- 1 to 2 tablespoons pickling spice

CRANBERRIES, DRIED UNSWEETENED – 1 cup
- 1 cup sweetened dried cranberries; reduce the sugar in the recipe by 2 tablespoons
- 1 cup raisins or sultanas/golden raisins
- 1 cup dried blueberries, bilberries, or cherries
- 1 cup dried barberries/*Berberis vulgaris*, Oregon grape berries/*Mahonia aquifolium,* juneberries or serviceberries/*Amelanchiers* (for cooking)

CRANBERRY LIQUEUR/CRANBERRY-FLAVORED SPIRIT (such as DeKuyper, Boggs, or Flag Hill) – 1 tablespoon for cooking
- 1 tablespoon cranberry syrup (sweeter)
- 1/2 teaspoons cranberry extract plus 1 tablespoon water
- 1 tablespoon raspberry liqueur

CRANBERRY VINEGAR – 1 tablespoon
- 1 tablespoon raspberry vinegar or other red fruity vinegar

CRAYFISH/CRAWFISH, DRIED -1 ounce
- 1 ounce fermented fish powder/*pla ra powder*
- 1 ounce smoked dried shrimp
- 1 tablespoon Thai fish sauce/*nam pla*

CREAM CHEESE (38% butterfat) – 1 cup (8 ounces)
- 1 cup Neufchâtel cheese (23% butterfat; more moisture)
- 1 cup reduced-fat cream cheese (16.5 to 20% butterfat; more sodium)
- 1 cup fat-free cream cheese (nearly twice as much sodium; separates when heated)
- 1 cup fresh goat cheese/chèvre or thick fromage blanc (softer texture)

- 1 cup soy cream cheese or tofu cream cheese
- 3 cups plain yogurt and a pinch of salt stirred together, then drained for 12 to 24 hours in a sieve lined with dampened cheesecloth (or 2 basket-style paper coffee filters) and set over a bowl in the refrigerator (cover the sieve with a plate or plastic wrap)
- 1 1/2 cups lowfat cottage cheese, 2 tablespoons butter, and 1 tablespoon milk blended until smooth, then drained for 8 to 12 hours in a sieve lined with dampened cheesecloth and set over a bowl in the refrigerator (cover the sieve with a plate, cloth, or plastic wrap)
- 2 sticks (8 ounces) vegan margarine, such as Earth Balance, plus liquid cream cheese flavoring (for cakes, cookies, fillings, or frostings)

CREAM CHEESE, CREOLE – 8 ounces
- 1 teaspoon lemon juice stirred into 8 ounces softened cream cheese
- 8 ounces fromage blanc

CREAM CHEESE, WHIPPED (27.9% butterfat) – 1/2 cup
- 1 (3-ounce) package room-temperature cream cheese, beaten until light and fluffy (unlike whipped cream cheese, will not separate in cooking)

CREAM, CLOTTED/DEVONSHIRE CREAM (English cream containing 55 to 75% butterfat) – 1 cup
- 1/2 heavy cream slowly beaten into 3 ounces (1/3 cup) softened cream cheese until smooth
- 1 cup mascarpone

Make Your Own Pour 4 cups heavy cream (not ultra-pasteurized) into a wide ovenproof bowl or pot and set in a preheated 175°F oven for 8 hours. Cool; cover and refrigerate for 8 to 12 hours, then remove the thick top layer of cream (use the leftover loose cream as heavy cream).

CREAM, DOUBLE/CRÈME DOUBLE (European cream containing 48% butterfat) – 1 cup
- 1 1/2 cups heavy whipping cream, gently boiled in a large pan until reduced to 1 cup, about 20 minutes (Whisk the cream for a few seconds every couple of minutes, and be careful it doesn't boil over.)

- 1 cup canned double cream, such as Nestlé Double Cream
- 1 1/2 cups crème fraiche, drained overnight in a sieve lined with dampened cheesecloth (or 2 basket-type paper coffee filters) set over a bowl in the refrigerator (cover the sieve with a plate or plastic wrap)

CREAM, HEAVY (35 to 40% butterfat) – 1 cup
- 1 (8-ounce) carton unsweetened coconut cream, or 1 cup thick cream that rises to the top of canned or homemade coconut milk after chilling several hours (for cooking and whipping)
- 2/3 cup undiluted icy-cold evaporated milk (for whipping)
- 1 cup undiluted evaporated milk (for cooking)
- 3 tablespoons powdered heavy cream mixed with 1 cup water
- 2/3 cup whole milk or soy milk plus 1/3 cup melted unsalted butter, vegan butter/margarine, or coconut oil (for cooking)
- 1 cup dairy-free alternative, such as Mimic Crème, So Delicious Creamer, or Silk or Mocha brand soy creamer
- 1 cup brown rice cream (for cooking)
- 1 cup raw cashews, soaked in water to cover for 8 to 10 hours, drained, then pulverized in a blender with 1/2 cup water

CREAM, LIGHT/SINGLE CREAM (18 to 30% butterfat) – 1 cup
- 1 cup canned table cream, all-purpose light cream, or Mexican *media* cream, such as Nestlé
- 1/2 cup whipping cream and 1/2 cup whole milk (18% butterfat)
- 1/2 cup heavy cream and 1/2 cup half-and-half (25% butterfat)
- 3 tablespoons melted unsalted butter and enough whole milk to make 1 cup (for cooking)
- 1 cup canned or homemade coconut milk (dairy- and casein-free)
- 1 cup coconut milk creamer (nonfat and dairy-free)

CREAM OF COCONUT (cocktail ingredient, such as Coco López) – 1 cup
- 1 cup unsweetened coconut cream, whisked before measuring, plus 1/3 cup confectioners' sugar
- 1 cup sweetened condensed milk plus 1/2 teaspoon coconut extract

CREAM OF COCONUT, UNSWEETENED – 1 cup

Make Your Own Heat 2 cups shredded or flaked coconut with 1 (12-ounce) can evaporated milk until small bubbles appear around the edge, 6 to 7 minutes. Cool, then cover and refrigerate for 8 to 12 hours; strain in a cheesecloth-lined sieve, pressing firmly to extract all the liquid, then keep refrigerated. It will stay, tightly sealed, for up to 2 weeks.

CREAM OF TARTAR (potassium hydrogen tartrate/potassium bitartrate) – 1/4 teaspoon

- 1/2 teaspoon distilled white vinegar (for stabilizing egg whites)
- 1/4 teaspoon xanthan gum (for stabilizing egg whites)
- 3/4 teaspoon distilled white vinegar or lemon juice (for acidifying liquids)
- 1/8 to 1/4 teaspoon tartaric acid (for acidifying liquids)
- Few drops distilled white vinegar (for preventing cooked sugar from crystallizing)

CREAM SAUCE – 1 1/2 to 2 cups

- 1 (10.5-ounce) can condensed cream of mushroom, cream of chicken, or cream of celery soup whisked with 1/3 to 1/2 cup milk
- 1 (12-ounce) package silken tofu, pureed to a creamy consistency with a little soymilk, then seasoned to taste
- 2 to 3 cups tender steamed cauliflower florets, pureed to a creamy consistency with a little water, then seasoned to taste

CREAM SHERRY – 1 cup

- 4 teaspoons dark brown sugar stirred into 1 cup dry sherry (for recipes only)

CRÈMA MEXICANA/MEXICAN CRÈMA – 1 cup

- 1 cup crème fraîche (richer; less salty)
- 1 cup *crema Salvadoreña, crema Centroamericana,* or *crema Hondureña* (darker-hued and tangier)
- 3/4 cup sour cream thinned with 1/4 milk or water plus salt to taste, about 1/8 teaspoon

☞ 1 cup heavy cream (for cooking)

CRÈME FRAÎCHE (French cultured cream with 48% butterfat) – 1 cup (8 ounces)
☞ 1 cup Mexican *crema/crema Mexicana* (will separate if boiled)
☞ 1 cup double cream (less tart; will not separate if boiled)
☞ 1 cup sour cream and 2 tablespoons heavy cream whisked together (will separate if boiled)
☞ 1 cup *labna* (more sour; will not separate if boiled)

Make Your Own Combine 1 tablespoon buttermilk or crème fraîche with 1 cup heavy cream, then lightly cover and leave in a warm spot until thickened, about 24 hours. Refrigerate, well covered, for up to 7 days (it will continue to thicken).

Or

Whisk together 1/2 cup heavy cream and 1/2 cup sour cream, cover lightly and leave at room temperature until thickened, 2 to 4 hours or longer. Refrigerate, well covered, for at least 4 hours before using. It will keep for up to 1 week refrigerated (it might separate if boiled).

CRÈME FRAÎCHE, LOW-FAT – 1 cup (8 ounces)
☞ Nonfat or 2% Greek-style yogurt, whisked until smooth
☞ 1/2 cup fat-free cream cheese (or fat-free sour cream), 1/2 cup 1% milk, and 1/4 teaspoon sugar whisked together, lightly covered and left at room temperature until thickened, about 8 hours

Make Your Own Whisk together 1/2 cup evaporated nonfat milk, 1/2 cup plain low-fat yogurt, and 1 teaspoon lemon juice; lightly cover and leave at room temperature until thickened, about 8 hours. Will keep in the refrigerator for up to 1 week; whisk before using (might separate if boiled).

CREOLE MUSTARD See MUSTARD, CREOLE

CREOLE SEASONING – 1/4 cup See also CAJUN SEASONING
☞ 2 tablespoons salt, 1 tablespoon cayenne, and 1 teaspoon each ground white pepper, ground black pepper, and garlic powder

CREOLE SEASONING, SALT-FREE – 2 tablespoons
- 1 teaspoon each ground black (or white) pepper, ground cayenne pepper, garlic powder, onion powder, and paprika

CRESS (watercress, curly cress/peppergrass, upland/land cress) – 4 ounces
- 4 ounces young agretti, nasturtium leaves and stems, arugula, young radish greens, purslane leaves and tender stems, or young dandelion greens

CUBEB BERRIES/TAILED PEPPER (Indonesian seasoning) – 1 teaspoon
- 1/2 teaspoon allspice berries

CUCUZZA TENDRILS/VINES/TENERUMI (Sicilian) – 4 ounces
- 4 ounces tender young cucumber, pumpkin, or zucchini vine tendrils

CUITLACOCHE See HUITLACOCHE

CULANTRO See SAWLEAF HERB

CUMIN SEEDS, AMBER OR WHITE/SHAH JEERA – 1 teaspoon whole seeds
- 1 1/2 to 2 teaspoons packaged preground cumin or roasted cumin (in place of 1 teaspoon whole seeds toasted and ground)
- 1 teaspoon chili or taco seasoning (adds other flavors)
- 1/2 teaspoon ground coriander or caraway (for adding to curry or chili powder mix)

CUMIN SEEDS, BLACK/KALA JEERA (Kashmir, Pakistan and Iranian seasoning) – 1 teaspoon
- 1 teaspoon amber or white cumin seeds
- 1/2 teaspoon toasted ground cumin seeds (less sweet)
- 1/2 teaspoon caraway seeds

CURRY LEAF/DAUN KARI/KARI PATTA/KARAPINCHA/KITHA NEEM/BAI KAREE (South Asian seasoning) – 1 fresh sprig (8 to 12 leaves)
- 12 to 16 dried or semidried curry leaves (check for aroma; dried leaves can have little flavor)

- 1 teaspoon curry leaf/*kari patta* powder
- 2 dried salam leaves/*daun salam*
- 2 to 3 dried bay leaves
- 1 tablespoon chopped fresh cilantro leaves (grassier flavor)

CURRY OIL (Indian seasoning) – 1/2 cup

Make Your Own Gently heat 1/2 cup peanut or vegetable oil and 1 tablespoon mild Indian curry powder or paste for 15 minutes (do not let the oil get too hot). Cool, then strain through a small cloth-lined sieve; store, refrigerated, for up to 3 months. Or, rather than heating the oil, dry-toast the curry powder, then mix to a paste with 1 tablespoon of the oil; add the rest of the oil and shake to mix thoroughly; leave at room temperature for 8 to 12 hours, then strain.

CURRY POWDER, JAMAICAN – 1 tablespoon

- 1 tablespoon Madras curry powder plus 1/4 teaspoon each ground allspice and star anise

CURRY POWDER, JAPANESE – 1 tablespoon

- 1 tablespoon Indian-style spice blend, such as S&B Oriental Curry Powder

CURRY POWDER, MADRAS – 1 tablespoon

- 1 tablespoon sweet or mild curry powder plus 1/16 teaspoon ground cayenne pepper

CURRY POWDER/SEASONING, VINDALOO – 1 tablespoon

- 2 teaspoons mild/regular sweet curry powder, 3/4 teaspoon hot paprika, and 1/4 teaspoon ground black pepper
- 1 tablespoon Madras curry powder plus 1/2 to 1 teaspoon crushed red pepper flakes

CURRY POWDER, STANDARD/REGULAR BLEND – 1 tablespoon, or to taste

- 1 tablespoon Madras curry powder (classic all-purpose curry powder, spicier and less bitter than most commercial versions; sometimes contains chickpea flour for less heat)

- 2 tablespoons Thai kari/yellow curry paste or Thai Massaman/ matsaman curry paste (mild sweet/spicy)
- 2 tablespoons Thai Panang curry paste (mellow and moderately hot; contains lemongrass and chilis)
- 2 teaspoons Thai red curry paste (medium-hot)
- 2 teaspoons Thai green or hot Madras green curry paste
- 1 1/2 to 2 teaspoons Vindaloo curry paste or powder/seasoning (Indian; spicy/tangy and hot)
- 4 teaspoons garam masala (Indian; warm spice blend; add at the end of cooking to heighten the flavor)

D

DAIDAI JUICE (Japanese bitter citrus souring agent) – 1 tablespoon
- 1 tablespoon lemon or lime juice

DAIKON GREENS/YOUNG DAIKON LEAVES/MU CHONG – 8 ounces
- 8 ounces watercress, broadleaf cress, curly cress, or arugula

DAIKON SPROUTS/KAIWARE – 4 ounces
- 4 ounces sunflower sprouts
- 4 ounces pea or chickpea shoots

DASHI/ICHIBAN DASHI/NIBAN DASHI (Japanese cooking stock) – 1 cup
- 1/4 teaspoon instant dashi granules, such as *hon-dashi* or *dashi-no-moto*, dissolved in 1 cup hot water (*hon-dashi* contains salt; *dashi-no-moto* contains salt, and some contain MSG)
- 1/3 teaspoon liquid dashi concentrate, such as *katsuo dashi, tsuyu no moto,* or *shiro dashi*, dissolved in 1 cup hot water (contains a little salt)
- 1/3 teaspoon white soy sauce/*shiro shoyu* dissolved in 1 cup hot water
- 1 cup kelp stock (10 grams/1/3 ounce kombu soaked in 1 cup cold water for 8 to 12 hours)
- 1/2 cup each light vegetable and seafood stock
- 1 cup low-sodium or diluted chicken broth (if the recipe contains chicken)

DASHI CONCENTRATE/SHIRI DASHI – 1 tablespoon
- 1 tablespoon white soy sauce/*shiri shoyu*

DASHI, VEGETARIAN/KOMBU DASHI/SHOJIN DASHI (Japanese cooking stock) – 1 cup
- 2 to 3 small squares of kombu/kelp and 1 dried shiitake mushroom soaked in 1 cup cold water for 30 to 60 minutes, then simmered for 10 to 15 minutes
- 1 cup low-sodium vegetable stock

DATE HONEY/SILAN/DEVASH (Israeli sweetener) See DATE MOLASSES

DATE MOLASSES/DATE SYRUP/DIBIS TAMAR (Middle Eastern thick sweetener) – 1 cup
- 1 cup Middle Eastern grape syrup (*dibs/pekmez*) or carob syrup (*harnup pekmezi*)
- 1 cup Italian grape syrup (*vino cotto*) or fig syrup (*miele di fichi/cotto di fichi*)
- 2/3 cup strong-flavored dark honey, such as buckwheat, chestnut, linden, or sage
- 1 cup grade A dark, robust pure maple syrup
- 1/2 cup dark molasses or treacle plus 1/2 cup light-colored corn syrup

Make Your Own Simmer 8 ounces fresh pitted Medjool dates in 2 cups water until the mixture is thick and syrupy, about 1 hour; let cool then process in a blender or food processor until smooth. Store, refrigerated, for up to 2 weeks.

DATE-PALM JAGGERY, LIQUID/JHOLA GUR (Indian sweetener) – 1/4 cup
- 1/4 cup coconut nectar or maple syrup
- 1/4 cup grated cane jaggery or other palm sugar
- 1/4 cup dark brown or maple sugar, moistened to a coarse paste with 1 teaspoon light molasses

DATE PASTE (thick natural sweetener) – 1 1/2 cups
Make Your Own Soak 1 pound fresh pitted Medjool dates in 1 cup warm water for 8 to 10 hours; then process to a smooth paste in a blender or food processor. Store, refrigerated, for up to 2 weeks.
Or
Simmer 1 pound chopped pitted dates with 1/2 cup water gently until the water evaporates and the dates become a soft paste. Store, refrigerated, for up to 2 weeks

DATE SUGAR (dehydrated ground dates) – 1 cup
- 1 1/3 cups light brown sugar

DATE SYRUP See DATE MOLASSES

DENDÊ/RED PALM OIL See PALM OIL, RED

DEXTROSE (finely textured glucose) – 1 tablespoon See also GLUCOSE
- 2 teaspoons granulated cane sugar

DHANIA JEERA POWDER (Indian spice blend) – 1 tablespoon
- 2 teaspoons roasted ground coriander and 1 teaspoon roasted ground cumin

DIBS (Middle Eastern thick sweet syrup) See GRAPE MOLASSES

DILL, FRESH – 1 tablespoon minced
- 1 teaspoon dried dill weed or dill seeds (or more to taste)
- 1/2 teaspoon dill pollen
- 1 1/2 teaspoons each chopped fresh tarragon and fresh Italian or curly parsley
- Fresh fennel fronds/leafy tops (for decoration)

DILL POLLEN – 1 tablespoon
- Dried dill blossoms (shake out the pollen to measure 1 tablespoon); or dry dill flower heads upside down in a paper bag (the pollen will fall out)

☞ 1 1/2 tablespoons dried dill seeds, finely ground with a mortar and pestle or a spice/coffee grinder

DILL SEED – 1 tablespoon
☞ 2 to 3 fresh flowering dill heads
☞ 3 to 4 fresh dill fronds
☞ 1/2 teaspoon dill pollen
☞ 2 teaspoons caraway seeds plus 1/2 teaspoon celery salt; reduce the salt in the recipe by 1/2 teaspoon
☞ 1 1/2 teaspoons each caraway seeds and celery seeds

DIPPING SAUCE *See ASIAN DIPPING SAUCE; CHINESE DIPPING SAUCE; GYOZA DIPPING SAUCE; KOREAN SESAME PASTE DIPPING SAUCE; PEANUT DIPPING SAUCE; TEMPURA DIPPING SAUCE; THAI DIPPING SAUCE; VIETNAMESE DIPPING SAUCE*

DISTILLED WHITE VINEGAR – 1 tablespoon for flavoring
☞ 1 tablespoon lemon or lime juice
☞ 1 1/2 tablespoons dry white wine or dry vermouth
☞ 1 to 2 teaspoons vinegar powder (use dry in cooking or spice rubs)
☞ 1 tablespoon mango powder (for curries and chutneys)
☞ 1 1/2 teaspoons tamarind concentrate (for curries and chutneys)

DISTILLED WHITE VINEGAR – 1 cup for pickling and preserving
☞ 1 cup cider vinegar, white wine vinegar, colorless malt vinegar, or any vinegar with at least 5% acidity level
☞ 1 tablespoon citric acid powder dissolved in 1 cup boiled water (approximates 6% acidity level)

DOENJANG *See KOREAN SOYBEAN PASTE*

DOUGLAS FIR NEEDLES (aromatic base for oven roasting)
☞ Douglas fir organic hydrosol (food-safe essential oil) sprayed very lightly on food right before serving

D

DRY RUB See BARBECUE SEASONING/DRY RUB

DUCK FAT, RENDERED – 1 tablespoon
- 1 tablespoon rendered goose fat, pork fat, tallow, or leaf lard
- 1 tablespoon fruity olive oil, or 1 1/2 teaspoons each olive oil and unsalted butter

DUCK SAUCE/SUÀN MÉI JIÀNG (Chinese condiment) – 1/4 cup
- 1/4 cup plum sauce thinned with a little orange juice See PLUM SAUCE

DULCE DE LECHE See CARAMEL PASTE

DULSE POWDER (red seaweed thickening agent) – 1/4 cup
- 2 (6-inch) dulse sheets, or 1/2 cup tightly packed dulse flakes, crumbled and ground to a powder

E

EGUSI SEED/EPUSI (West African flavoring and thickening agent) – 1 tablespoon
- 1 tablespoon raw hull-less squash seeds or shelled pumpkin seeds (for shelled seeds)
- 1 tablespoon tahini/sesame paste, or mashed navy or pinto beans (for egusi paste)
- 2 teaspoons finely ground raw pumpkin or sesame seeds (for egusi powder)

ENCHILADA SAUCE – 1 cup
- 1 (8-ounce) can tomato sauce (or 1 cup tomato puree) plus 2 teaspoons chili powder/seasoning

ENGLISH PUDDING SPICE/BRITISH MIXED SPICE See MIXED SPICE, SWEET

ENO FRUIT SALT POWDER (Indian leavening agent) – 1 teaspoon
- 1 teaspoon baking soda

ENOKI MUSHROOM/SNOW PUFF/ENOKITAKE – 1 bunch (6 ounces)
- 4 ounces canned enoki mushrooms, drained
- 6 to 7 ounces fresh oyster/shimeji or white cap/button mushrooms

EPAZOTE, FRESH (Mexican seasoning herb) – 1 sprig or 1 tablespoon chopped
- 2 frozen epazote sprigs (leaves only)
- 1 to 2 teaspoons dried epazote leaves, crumbled
- 3 fresh cilantro sprigs, and 1 small sprig fresh oregano (5 or 6 leaves)
- 1 tablespoon chopped fresh oregano leaves, or 1 teaspoon dried, preferably Mexican

☞ 1-inch piece of kombu/kelp (for digestive properties only)

ESPELETTE PEPPER *See PIMENT d'ESPELETTE*

ESPRESSO EXTRACT OR POWDER – 1 teaspoon
- ☞ 1 1/2 teaspoons freeze-dried instant coffee finely ground to a powder

EVAPORATED CANE JUICE (golden unrefined sugar crystals) *See SUGAR, TURBINADO CANE*

EVAPORATED MILK (6.6% butterfat) – 1 cup
- ☞ 1 cup fat-free evaporated milk (0.5% butterfat)
- ☞ 2 1/4 cups whole milk, simmered in a medium pan until reduced to 1 cup, about 20 minutes (be careful it does not boil over)
- ☞ 1/2 cup powdered whole milk blended with 2/3 cup water
- ☞ 1 cup half-and-half or light cream

EVAPORATED MILK, VEGAN – 1 cup
- ☞ 1/2 cup soymilk powder blended with enough water to make 1 cup

EXPANDEX (modified tapioca food starch) – 1 teaspoon
- ☞ 1 teaspoon xanthan gum
- ☞ 1 teaspoon guar gum

F

FAROFA/TOASTED YUCA FLOUR (Brazilian condiment) – 1 cup
- 1 cup coarse gari/toasted manioc meal/*farinha torrada*, sautéed with 3 tablespoons butter or oil until golden and fragrant, 2 to 4 minutes
- 1 cup finely ground whole-wheat breadcrumbs, toasted in a dry skillet until fragrant
- 1 cup coarse almond flour, toasted in a dry skillet until a few shades darker

FATBACK (fresh unsalted pork fat) – 4-ounces (1 cup finely chopped)
- 4 ounces fat trimmed from a pork roast (package and freeze until needed)
- 4 ounces Italian lardo, soaked in water to cover for 8 to 10 hours, then rinsed and blotted dry
- 4 ounces salt pork, slab bacon, or thick presliced bacon, blanched in boiling water for 40 to 60 seconds, then rinsed and blotted dry

FENNEL POLLEN/FINOCCHIETTO (Italian and Sicilian seasoning) – 1 tablespoon
- Dried wild fennel blossoms (shake out the pollen to measure 1 tablespoon), or fennel flower heads placed upside down in a paper bag to dry (the pollen will fall out)
- 2 teaspoons dried fennel seeds, lightly toasted in a dry skillet and then ground with a mortar and pestle or a spice/coffee grinder

FENNEL SEEDS, DRIED – 1 teaspoon whole seeds
- 1 scant teaspoon mature wild black fennel seeds/*Foeniculum vulgare* (more intense flavor)
- 1 1/2 teaspoons fresh green fennel seeds or 1 tablespoon minced fresh fennel leaves

- ⊫ 1/2 teaspoon ground fennel seeds
- ⊫ 1 scant teaspoon anise seeds
- ⊫ 3/4 teaspoon caraway or dill seeds

FENNEL, WILD/FOENICULUM VULGARE (Sicilian seasoning) – 1 cup chopped fronds (1 small bunch)
- ⊫ 1 cup regular chopped fennel fronds plus 1 or 2 fennel seeds
- ⊫ 1 cup chopped dill plus 2 teaspoons ground fennel seeds
- ⊫ 1 finely chopped fennel bulb plus 1/3 cup snipped fresh dill

FENUGREEK LEAVES, DRIED/KASURI METHI (Indian and Pakistani seasoning) – 1 tablespoon
- ⊫ 1 teaspoon fenugreek powder; or a small pinch ground roasted fenugreek seeds (for curries; sprinkle over dish just before serving)

FENUGREEK POWDER (Indian and Pakistani seasoning) – 1 teaspoon
- ⊫ 1 tablespoon dried fenugreek leaves crushed through a medium-mesh sieve; discard stem pieces

FENUGREEK SEEDS/METHI KA BEEJ/METHI DANA (Indian curry flavoring) – 1 tablespoon whole seeds
- ⊫ 1 3/4 tablespoons ground fenugreek seeds
- ⊫ 2 teaspoons brown mustard seeds and 1 teaspoon celery seeds

FERMENTED BLACK BEANS/FERMENTED BLACK SOYBEANS/DOW SEE/DOUCHI (Chinese seasoning) – 1 tablespoon
- ⊫ 1 1/2 tablespoons fermented black bean paste/douchi jiang
- ⊫ 1 to 2 tablespoons Japanese dark miso, such as inaka or hatcho
- ⊫ 1 to 2 tablespoons mashed salt-packed capers
- ⊫ 2 to 3 tablespoons dark soy sauce (usually labeled all-purpose)

FERMENTED BLACK GARLIC – 1 whole head/bulb (1/2 ounce)
- ⊫ 1 well-roasted whole garlic head/bulb plus a little balsamic vinegar or molasses

☞ 1 to 1 1/2 teaspoons fermented black garlic powder plus 2 to 2 1/2 teaspoon water

FERMENTED DRIED LOCUST BEAN/NETETOU/SUMBALA (Senegalese seasoning) – 1 tablespoon
☞ 1 tablespoon Chinese fermented black beans/*dow see*

FERMENTED SOYBEAN PASTE/TUA NAO PBUH/TAO JIAO (South Asian flavoring agent) – 1 tablespoon See also MISO
☞ 1 1/2 teaspoons Japanese dark miso, such as *hatcho*, or Korean soybean paste/*doenjang*
☞ 2 teaspoons Chinese black bean sauce/*douchi jiang* or fermented soybeans/*douchi*

FERMENTED SOYBEAN SAUCE/SALTED SOYBEANS/TAUCHEO/TAUEO (Indonesian and Malaysian seasoning) – 1 tablespoon
☞ 1 tablespoon Thai soybean paste/fermented soybeans/*tao jiao*

FERMENTED TOASTED SOYBEAN DISK/TUA NAO KHAAP (South Asian seasoning) – 1 tablespoon chopped or crumbled disk
☞ 1 tablespoon toasted chickpea flour plus 1 teaspoon Japanese brown miso paste
☞ 2 tablespoons Thai soybean paste/fermented soybean/*dao jiao*

FIG SYRUP/MIELE DI FICHI/COTTO DI FICHI (Italian dark thick sweetener) – 3/4 cup
☞ 3/4 cup grape molasses/*mosto cotto* or dark strong tasting honey
Make Your Own Stem and halve 1 pound dried figs. Simmer in 4 cups water until soft and reduced by half. Strain, then simmer the syrup until thickened and dark.

FIG VINEGAR/BLACK FIG VINEGAR – 1/4 cup
☞ 1/4 cup balsamic vinegar

FILÉ POWDER/GUMBO FILÉ/POWDERED SASSAFRAS LEAVES (thickening and flavoring agent) – 1 tablespoon

- 1/2 to 1 teaspoon each ground anise seeds, ground cloves, and ground ginger (for flavoring only)
- 2 cups sliced fresh okra; or 1 (10-ounce) package sliced frozen okra, or whole frozen okra cut into 1/4-inch rounds (cook okra in gumbo for thickening, adding frozen okra without thawing)
- 1 or more tablespoons mallow powder (tender young mallow leaves/*Malva neglecta* dried then ground to a powder; add at the end for thickening)
- 2 teaspoons cornstarch or potato starch mixed with 1 tablespoon cold water (add at the end for thickening only)

FINES HERBES (French seasoning blend) – 1 heaping tablespoon

- 1 teaspoon each finely chopped fresh parsley, chives, and chervil, plus 1/4 teaspoon chopped French tarragon

FINGER LIME *See LIME, AUSTRALIAN FINGER, PULP/JUICE VESICLES*

FINGERROOT/CHINESE KEYS/CHINESE GINGER/KRACHAI, FRESH (Southeast Asian seasoning) – 1-inch piece (1 tablespoon peeled and finely chopped)

- 2 teaspoons brined fingerroot slivers, well drained and rinsed
- 1 1/2 tablespoons jarred galanga/*Ka Chai* (rinse to remove brine, then finely chop)
- 1 tablespoon finely chopped fresh greater galangal
- 1 1/2 teaspoons kencur powder (ground *Kaempferia galanga*)
- 2 scant teaspoons finely chopped fresh young ginger

FISH FLAKES, DRIED/KATSUOBUSHI (Japanese dried bonito/skipjack tuna flakes) – 1 loosely packed cup *See also DASHI*

- 1 cup dried mackerel flakes/*sababushi* (for soups and stocks; less expensive)
- 1 cup bonito thread shavings/*ito-kezuri katsuo* (for garnish on salads and tofu)

☞ 1 cup dried baby sardines or anchovies/*iniko/niboshi*, dry-roasted until very crisp, 20 minutes, then cooled and ground (stronger tasting; use according to taste)

☞ 1 cup ready-to-use dried baby anchovies or tiny whitebait/*ikan teri/ ikan bilis/jiang yu zi*, rinsed and lightly pounded (stronger; use according to taste)

☞ 1 *ikan bilis* stock cube, or part thereof (for soups and stocks)

FISH MINT/FISH SCALE MINT/RAU DIEP CA/VAP CA (Vietnamese seasoning) – 1 ounce

☞ 1 ounce fresh spearmint, young sorrel, lemon basil, or Thai basil

☞ 1 ounce unsprayed variegated chameleon plant/*Houttuynia cordata* (use the top leaves)

FISH PASTE, FERMENTED *See ASIAN FISH PASTE*

FISH SAUCE, ASIAN *See ASIAN FISH SAUCE*

FISH SAUCE, ASIAN, VEGETARIAN *See ASIAN FISH SAUCE, VEGETARIAN*

FIVE-SPICE POWDER, CHINESE *See CHINESE FIVE-SPICE POWDER*

FIVE-SPICE MIX, INDIAN *See BENGALI FIVE-SPICE MIX*

FLAVOR ENHANCERS *See UMAMI*

FLAX OIL – 1 cup

☞ 1 cup hemp oil

FLAXSEED MEAL/FLAXMEAL – 1 cup for baking

☞ 3/4 cup chia seed meal/chia powder

☞ 1 cup almond meal, walnut meal, pecan meal, pumpkin seed meal, sesame seed meal, or sunflower seed meal (lacks omega-3s and gelatinous property)

FLAXSEEDS (brown or golden) – 1 cup
- 1 cup chia, salba, or hemp seeds
- 1 cup sesame seeds (lacks omega-3s and gelatinous property)

FLEUR DE SEL DE GUÉRANDE (fine-grained finishing salt from Brittany) – 1 teaspoon See also SALT, TABLE
- 1 teaspoon French *fleur de sel de Camargue* (from the Mediterranean coast) or *fleur de sel ile de Ré* (from the Atlantic coast)
- 1 1/2 teaspoons crystalline-flake sea salt, such as Maldon, Cornish, or Halen Môn (finishing salt)
- 1 teaspoon coarse-grain moist French sea salt/*sel gris Marin/sel gris de Guérande,* moist Baja sea salt, Korean sea salt, or Maine sea salt
- 3/4 teaspoon finely ground refined sea salt such as Baja, Atlantic, or Mediterranean

FLOUR, NUT (almond, hazelnut, pecan, walnut) – 1 cup
- 3/4 cups whole nuts, ground at low speed in a blender or in small batches in a spice/coffee grinder (For baking, include a teaspoon of sugar or flour from the recipe to avoid oiliness.)

FLOUR, POPCORN (1% protein) – 1 cup
- 2 cups cold unsalted plain popcorn (preferably hot-air popped), ground in small batches in a blender or food processor until powdery

FRA DIAVOLO SAUCE (Italian chili-spiced tomato sauce) – 1 cup
- 1 cup marinara sauce plus crushed red pepper flakes or ground cayenne pepper to taste

FRENCH FOUR-SPICE MIX See QUATRE-ÉPICES

FRUCTOSE/LEVULOSE – 1 cup
- 1 1/2 cups superfine sugar (or 1 1/2 cups plus 1 tablespoon granulated sugar pulverized in a blender or food processor until fine-textured, 20 to 30 seconds)

FRUIT FRESH (anti-darkening agent for fruit and vegetables) – 1/4 teaspoon
> ⊨ 1/4 teaspoon citric acid or 1/8 teaspoon ascorbic acid
> ⊨ 1 tablespoon lemon juice

FRUIT GLAZE (apricot, cherry, raspberry, strawberry, or red currant) – 1/2 cup
Make Your Own Combine 1/2 cup (6 ounces) jelly (or jam or preserves) and 2 tablespoons water (or citrus juice or fruit-flavored liqueur) and heat over low heat, or microwave on High until bubbling. Strain to remove seeds, if necessary, pressing hard on the solids. (For a thinner glaze add 1 or 2 more tablespoons liquid; for a thicker glaze cook, stirring frequently, until glaze is very sticky; use while warm.

FRUIT SWEET (liquid fruit juice concentrate) – 1 cup
> ⊨ 12 ounces thawed frozen white grape or apple juice concentrate, gently boiled in a large pan until reduced to 1 cup, about 10 minutes (or microwaved on High in a 4-cup glass measuring cup, about 12 minutes)

FURIKAKE (Japanese sesame and seaweed condiment for rice) – 1 tablespoon
> ⊨ 1 tablespoon dried nori shreds with sesame seed/*nori komi furikake*
> ⊨ 1 tablespoon flaked or shredded green nori/*ao-nori*
> ⊨ 1 tablespoon toasted black sesame seeds/*kura goma*
> ⊨ 1 tablespoon powdered purple shiso leaves and sea salt/*yukari/shiso yukari/shiso furikake*
> ⊨ 1 tablespoon toasted sesame seed and sea salt/*gomashio*
> ⊨ 1 tablespoon dried nori, alaria/winged kelp, or dulse, toasted then crushed by hand

G

GALANGAL, GREATER (Southeast Asian seasoning root) – 1 1/2-inch slice fresh or frozen (1 tablespoon peeled and finely chopped)
- 4 teaspoons chopped pickled galangal/*kha*
- 3 or more (1/8-inch) slices dried galangal root/galanga soaked in hot water 30 minutes, then squeezed dry
- 1 tablespoon galangal paste
- 1 1/2 teaspoons (or more) Indonesian Laos powder (dried ground galangal root; less flavorful)
- 1-inch piece fresh young ginger (or 2 or 3 teaspoons finely chopped) plus a few grains of ground black pepper, or a few drops of lemon juice, or a small pinch of finely chopped lemongrass
- 1 (2-inch) piece mature ginger, or 1 1/2 to 2 tablespoons peeled and finely chopped ginger (less pungent)

GANACHE, VEGAN – 1 1/2 cups
Make Your Own Heat 1/2 cup nondairy liquid creamer (such as coconut or soy) and 2 tablespoons vegan margarine to boiling, then pour over 8 ounces vegan chocolate chips; gently stir until the chips are melted and the mixture is smooth. Alternatively, use 1/2 cup canned coconut milk in place of the creamer and omit the margarine.

GARAM MASALA (Indian all-purpose aromatic seasoning) – 1 tablespoon
- 1 teaspoon mild/sweet curry powder
- 1/2 teaspoon each ground toasted coriander and cumin

GARLIC, BLACK FERMENTED *See FERMENTED BLACK GARLIC*

GARLIC BUTTER – 4 ounces (1/2 cup)
Make Your Own Stir 2 finely minced or grated garlic cloves (or 1 teaspoon or more liquid garlic seasoning or instant garlic) into 1/2 cup

(1 stick) room-temperature butter. Let sit for a few minutes to develop flavor. It will keep, well sealed and refrigerated, for up to 1 week.

GARLIC CHIVES, JAPANESE/CHINESE CHIVES – 1 ounce (1/4 cup finely chopped)
- 1 or 2 sliced garlic leaves (cut sparingly when plants are no more than 8 inches tall)
- 1/4 cup snipped Western chives or thinly sliced scallion or green onion greens plus 1 scant teaspoon minced garlic

GARLIC, FRESH – 1 medium clove (1 teaspoon minced or pressed)
- 1 thawed frozen garlic cube, such as Dorot, crushed
- 1 tablespoon green fresh garlic/wet garlic (milder and juicier)
- 1 tablespoon finely minced garlic chives
- 1/2 teaspoon garlic juice, garlic flakes, or instant garlic
- 1 teaspoon garlic paste from a tube, or jarred minced garlic
- 1/4 teaspoon granulated garlic, or dried minced garlic softened in 1 teaspoon water, about 10 minutes
- 1/8 teaspoon garlic powder
- 1/2 teaspoon garlic salt; reduce the salt in the recipe by 1/2 teaspoon
- 1 small shallot or 1 medium shallot lobe, finely minced (1 tablespoon)
- 1/2 medium clove (or 1/2 teaspoon minced) wild/meadow garlic or field/crow garlic
- 1 to 2 teaspoons garlic vinegar (if compatible)

GARLIC, GREEN/YOUNG GARLIC – 2 stalks minced (white and tender green parts only)
- 2 stalks garlic chives, garlic scapes (curly garlic shoots), or Chinese garlic stems
- 3 scallions (white and tender green parts only)
- 2 garlic cloves blanched in boiling water 1 minute, then minced

GARLIC MAYONNAISE/AÏOLI/ALLIOLI (Provençal condiment) – 1/2 cup

Make Your Own Crush 2 to 3 cloves of garlic to a smooth paste with 1/8 teaspoon sea salt, then combine with 1/2 cup mayonnaise and 1 to 3 teaspoons lemon juice. (Alternatively, blend all ingredients until smooth.) Let sit, covered, for 1 hour to develop flavor.

GARLIC OIL (Asian cooking condiment) – 1/4 cup

Make Your Own Crush 2 large garlic cloves and cook in 1/4 cup peanut oil over low heat, stirring occasionally, until light brown, 4 to 5 minutes. (Do not let the garlic become too dark or it will be bitter.) Cool and strain, discarding the garlic. Use immediately, or refrigerate in a small sterilized jar for up to 1 week.

GARLIC PASTE/PUREE, ROASTED – 1/4 cup

Make Your Own Toast unpeeled garlic cloves from 2 large garlic heads in a dry skillet over medium heat for 7 or 8 minutes, then squeeze through a garlic press (remove the peels in the press as needed). Or roast the unpeeled garlic, tightly wrapped in foil, in a preheated 425°F oven for 35 to 45 minutes (slice 1/2 inch from the top of the garlic heads and drizzle with 1 teaspoon olive oil before roasting).

GARLIC PEPPER – 1 tablespoon, ground

- 2 teaspoons black or white peppercorns and 1/8 to 1/2 teaspoon (or more) dried garlic flakes, ground in a pepper mill or spice/coffee grinder (mild garlic flavor)
- 1 1/2 teaspoons each coarse ground black pepper and garlic powder (strong garlic flavor)

GARLIC, PICKLED See CHINESE PICKLED GARLIC

GARLIC POWDER (pulverized dehydrated garlic) – 1/8 teaspoon

- 1/2 teaspoon garlic salt; reduce the salt in the recipe by 1/2 teaspoon
- 1/2 teaspoon instant minced garlic, jarred minced garlic, or garlic flakes
- 1/2 teaspoon garlic juice

- 1 teaspoon garlic paste (or 1 garlic clove mashed to a paste with kosher salt; reduce the salt in the recipe accordingly)
- 1 fresh garlic clove, minced

GARLIC SALT – 4 teaspoons
- 1 small peeled garlic clove pounded together with 1 tablespoon kosher salt or coarse sea salt (spread on a saucer to dry if not using immediately)
- 1 piece dried-out garlic scape pulsed in a spice/coffee grinder with 1 tablespoon kosher salt or coarse sea salt
- 1 teaspoon granulated garlic mixed with 1 tablespoon kosher salt or coarse sea salt
- 1/2 teaspoon garlic powder and 1/2 teaspoon dried crumbled parsley flakes mixed with 1 tablespoon kosher salt or coarse sea salt

GARLIC SHOOTS, YOUNG GREEN/GARLIC SCAPES – 1 cup
- 1 cup thinly sliced young scallions, green garlic/young garlic, or garlic chives
- 2/3 cup finely chopped chives plus scant 1/3 cup finely chopped garlic
- 1/2 cup chopped garlic

GARLIC VINEGAR – 1/2 cup
Make Your Own Combine 1 or 2 peeled and halved garlic cloves with 1/2 cup cider vinegar and heat just to the boiling point. Cover and let sit for 24 hours or more in a cool, dark place; then remove the garlic and store in the refrigerator.

GARLIC YOGURT SAUCE (Greek and Turkish) – 1 cup
Make Your Own Stir 1 to 2 teaspoons crushed garlic into 1 cup plain Greek-style yogurt (or 1 1/2 cups plain regular low-fat or full-fat yogurt drained several hours in a dampened, cheesecloth-lined sieve). Season with salt, then refrigerate for 1 or 2 hours to develop the flavor. For added flavor, stir in 1 to 2 tablespoons minced fresh cilantro or spearmint leaves along with the garlic.

GELATIN, FLAVORED – 1 (3-ounce) package

Make Your Own Whisk 1 packet (1/4 ounce or 1 scant tablespoon) unflavored gelatin powder into 1/4 cup cold fruit juice and let sit until dissolved, 3 to 5 minutes. Microwave for 40 seconds on High, then add 1 3/4 cups more juice and stir until combined. Cool; then chill until set. (For more intense flavor add a little sugar and lemon juice before heating.)

GELATIN, GRANULATED/POWDERED UNFLAVORED – 1 packet (1/4 ounce/1 scant tablespoon)

- 4 to 6 sheets leaf gelatin, depending upon size and grade (usually 4 sheets for silver grade or 225 bloom strength)
- 4 teaspoons (.375 ounce) unflavored vegan gelatin powder (blend of vegetable gums and tapioca starch; not for highly acidic ingredients)
- 1 scant tablespoon kosher gelatin (made from fish or all-beef gelatin)
- 2 1/2 teaspoons apple pectin powder (use following the package directions; reduce sugar as necessary)
- 2 teaspoons agar powder (use 2 1/2 teaspoons for acidic ingredients, such as citrus fruit, lemon juice, vinegar, or wine)
- 2 tablespoons agar flakes, or 1 bar (increase the amount for acidic ingredients)

GELATIN SHEETS/LEAVES, SILVER GRADE – 4 sheets

- 1 package (1/4 ounce/1 scant tablespoon granulated/powdered unflavored gelatin), such as Knox, prepared according to the package directions

GHEE/USLI GHEE (Indian-style clarified butter with a higher smoke point than regular clarified butter) – 1 tablespoon

- 1 tablespoon vegetable ghee/*vanaspati*
- 1 tablespoon refined or virgin coconut oil
- 1 tablespoon extra-virgin macadamia oil
- 1 tablespoon clarified butter (lower smoke point)
- 2 teaspoons unsalted butter plus 1 teaspoon corn or sunflower oil (lower smoke point)

GIANDUJA (chocolate-hazelnut spread, such as Nutella or Noccioata) – 1 cup
- 3 ounces melted chocolate (milk or bittersweet) stirred into 1/2 cup room-temperature nut butter, preferably hazelnut
- 1 cup low-carb vegan chocolate-hazelnut spread

GINGELLY/GINGILI/TIL OIL (Indian and Burmese cooking oil) – 1 cup
- 3/4 cup untoasted sesame oil and 1/4 cup toasted sesame oil
- 2/3 cup vegetable oil and 1/3 cup toasted sesame oil

GINGER, CRYSTALLIZED/PRESERVED – 1/3 cup
- 2 tablespoons grated fresh ginger; add 3 1/2 tablespoons granulated sugar to the recipe
- 1/4 teaspoon powdered ginger

GINGER, DRIED
Make Your Own Cut peeled knobs of ginger into 1/8-inch slices; dry in a dehydrator at 115°F until completely dry, 4 to 8 hours, rotating the trays a few times. Let cool, and then grate.

GINGER EXTRACT – 1 cup
Make Your Own Add 1 teaspoon finely grated lemon zest and 2 tablespoons finely grated fresh ginger to 1 cup brandy or whiskey; seal tightly and leave in a cool place for 10 days, shaking the bottle daily. Strain through a cloth-lined funnel or sieve, and store tightly covered.

GINGER FLOWER/TORCH GINGER/BAO JIANG/BUNGA KANTAN (Southeast Asian seasoning) – 1 cup
- 1 cup ginger bud/*myoga* or fresh young/spring ginger

GINGER, FRESH MATURE TROPICAL – 1-inch peeled segment (1 tablespoon minced or coarsely grated)
- 4 teaspoons fresh or frozen minced young stem ginger (no peeling required)

- 4 teaspoons thawed frozen grated ginger (Flash-freeze teaspoon-size portions of grated ginger, then transfer to a small freezer bag when frozen; will keep for up to 1 year.)
- 1 tablespoon bottled ginger puree/paste
- 1 1/2 teaspoons dried cracked ginger, freeze-dried minced ginger, or dried ginger slices broken into pieces (for marinades, stock, soup, and pickling)
- 1/2 teaspoon ginger juice (for curries, marinades, and stir-fries)
- 2 teaspoons minced or grated fresh galangal (stronger flavor; has pine notes)
- 1/4 to 1/2 teaspoon powdered ginger plus few drops lemon or lime juice (for soups, curries, fruit, and baking)
- 1 tablespoon minced or ground fresh wild ginger rhizome/*Asarum canadense*

GINGER, FRESH YOUNG/SPRING – 2-inch segment

- 1 (1-inch) piece regular ginger, peeled and soaked in salted water 5 minutes (about 1/8 teaspoon salt), then rinsed and dried (harsher, less delicate)
- 1 (2-inch) piece regular ginger, peeled and sliced or julienned, then rinsed repeatedly in cold water until the water runs clear (harsher, less delicate)

GINGER-GARLIC PASTE/ADRAK LEHSUN KA PASTE (Indian seasoning) – 1/2 (scant) cup

Make Your Own Process 1/3 cup coarsely chopped fresh ginger, 1/3 cup coarsely chopped fresh garlic, and 1 tablespoon water in a blender or food processor to a fine paste. Store in a sterilized jar in the refrigerator; it will keep for up to 1 month.

GINGER, GROUND DRIED/POWDERED – 1 teaspoon

- 1 tablespoon grated fresh ginger (freeze ginger for 30 minutes, then use a rasp-type grater)
- 2 tablespoons dried uncrystallized ginger, minced (or 1/4 cup crystallized ginger rinsed to remove sugar, then minced; reduce the sugar in the recipe by 2 tablespoons)

- 1 teaspoon ginger juice (grate fresh ginger, then squeeze to extract the juice; add to liquid ingredients)
- 1/4 teaspoon crumbled or ground mace and 3/4 teaspoon finely grated lemon zest

GINGER JELLY – 1/2 cup
- 1/2 cup apple jelly and 2 to 3 teaspoons ginger juice, gently heated together until the jelly melts; cover, and refrigerate overnight to develop the flavor. (For jam, replace the ginger juice with 3 tablespoons minced uncrystallized ginger and add 1/2 teaspoon ground ginger.) Store in the refrigerator; it will keep for 3 to 4 days.

GINGER JUICE – 1 tablespoon (or more)
Make Your Own Peel a 1 1/2- to 2-inch piece of fresh ginger (about 1 1/2 to 2 ounces), finely grate it, and then press through a garlic press, tea strainer, fine-mesh sieve, or cheesecloth. (Freezing and thawing the ginger will produce more juice.)

GINGER JUICE – 6 tablespoons to 1 scant cup
Make Your Own Wash 1 pound unpeeled fresh ginger then chop or thinly slice (should yield 2 1/2 to 3 cups). Process in a blender or food processor for 3 to 5 minutes, then strain in a cheesecloth-lined sieve, pressing on solids to extract all the liquid. It will keep in the refrigerator for up to 1 week, or freeze for longer storage.

GINGER LIQUEUR/GINGER-FLAVORED SPIRIT (such as Domaine de Canton) – 1 tablespoon for cooking
- 1/4 teaspoon ginger juice plus 1 tablespoon water

GINGER MARMALADE – 1/2 cup
- 1/2 cup orange or lemon marmalade, 1/2 to 1 teaspoon ground ginger, and 2 to 3 teaspoons grated fresh ginger stirred together (Cover and leave at room temperature overnight to develop the flavor; then keep refrigerated.)

GINGER PASTE/PISSA ADRAK/AADA BATA (Indian seasoning) – 1/3 cup
 ⊨ 4 ounces scrubbed fresh ginger grated on a rasp-type grater
Make Your Own Process 1/2 cup peeled chopped ginger and a pinch
of salt in a food processor until reduced to a paste, adding a little water
if necessary. (Cut the ginger lengthwise first, then against the grain.)

**GINGER, PICKLED/GARI/AMAZU SHOGA/BENI SHOGA (Japanese sushi
accompaniment) – 1 cup**
 ⊨ 1 cup matchstick-size pieces of red bell pepper, 1/2 cup rice wine
   vinegar, and 3 tablespoons granulated sugar, marinated for 12
   hours, then drained
Make Your Own Bring to a boil 1 cup peeled and very thinly sliced
fresh ginger (about 4 ounces), 1/2 cup unseasoned rice vinegar, and
1/4 cup granulated sugar (or less if desired); cool, then transfer to a
jar. Cover, and refrigerate for 3 or 4 days before using. It will keep in
the refrigerator for up to 12 months. (For *beni shoga,* shred rather
than slice the ginger and add a little beet juice or a drop of food coloring; for *amazu shoga* use the young tender ginger shoot, which turns
pink automatically.)

GINGER, POWDERED See GINGER, GROUND DRIED/POWDERED

GINGER SOY SAUCE – 1 cup
 ⊨ 1 cup light soy sauce and 1 tablespoon ginger juice

GINGER, STEM, PRESERVED IN SYRUP – 2 tablespoons
 ⊨ 2 teaspoons thinly sliced soft/uncrystallized ginger; or crystallized
   ginger, rinsed (for ginger)
 ⊨ 2 tablespoons ginger syrup (for syrup)

GINGER SYRUP – 1 cup
 ⊨ 1 cup syrup from jarred preserved stem ginger (for 1 tablespoon,
   mix 1 teaspoon honey with 1 tablespoon ginger juice)
Make Your Own Bring to a boil 1/3 cup thinly sliced unpeeled ginger,

1/2 cup firmly packed brown sugar, and 1 cup water, then simmer until reduced and syrupy, about 10 minutes. Cool then strain; store, refrigerated, for up to 1 month. (For more intense flavor, let the syrup sit for 45 to 60 minutes before straining.)
Or
Add 2/3 cup peeled and sliced fresh ginger to 1 cup heated heavy syrup (*See SYRUP, SIMPLE*); cool then steep, covered, for 2 days before straining. Store, refrigerated, for up to 1 month.

GINGER VINEGAR – 1 cup
Make Your Own Bring 1 cup cider vinegar, 1/4 cup peeled sliced fresh ginger, and 1 to 2 teaspoons sugar to a boil; cool, covered, then steep in a cool, dark place for 10 days, then strain. It will keep in the refrigerator for up to 3 months.

GINKGO NUTS, FRESH (Japanese and Korean) – 1 dozen shelled and blanched for cooking
- 1 (3.5-ounce) package gingko nuts, shelled and peeled
- 1 dozen canned ginkgo nuts, rinsed
- 1 dozen fresh wild ginkgo nuts/*Ginkgo biloba*, baked for 1 hour at 300°F, then shelled and any remaining skin rubbed off
- 1/4 cup shelled green peas (lacks bitterness)

GINSENG ROOT, AGED/PANAX (Chinese seasoning and medicinal agent) – 1 ounce (2 tablespoons minced)
- 1 ounce fine side roots, stem bits, shavings, or sun-dried white ginseng (less expensive)
- 1 ounce dried precut bellflower root/vine/codonopsis/*doraji/dang shen* (for soups and other cooked dishes; not as strong but less expensive; soak root overnight then squeeze dry)
- 2 ginseng-root tea bags (for fresh minced or dried ground ginseng)

GLACE DE VIANDE *See MEAT GLAZE*

GLAZE See BALSAMIC GLAZE; CAKE GLAZE; FRUIT GLAZE; MEAT GLAZE; POULTRY GLAZE

GLUCOSE/GLUCOSE SYRUP/DEXTROGLUCOSE – 1 cup
- 3/4 cup light-colored (not "lite") corn syrup brought to a full boil, cooled completely, then mixed with 1/3 cup unheated corn syrup
- 1 cup light-colored (not "lite") corn syrup

GOAT'S HORN PEPPER/AJI CACHO DE CABRA (dried chili pepper) – 1
- 1 dried guajillo, puya/pulla, or New Mexico chili
- 1 1/2 teaspoons New Mexico or guajillo chili powder
- 1/2 teaspoon ground cayenne pepper

GOCHUGARU/KOCHUKARU See KOREAN CHILI FLAKES

GOCHUJANG/KOCHUJANG/KOCHUCHANG See KOREAN CHILI BEAN PASTE

GOJI BERRY/WOLFBERRY, DRIED (Chinese flavoring) – 1 cup
- 2 cups homegrown fresh goji berries
- 1 cup dried jujubes (Chinese red dates)
- 1 cup dried Chilean wineberries/maqui berries
- 1 cup dried cranberries, barberries, or mulberries
- 2 to 3 tablespoons goji berry powder (for drinks and smoothies)

GOLDEN MOUNTAIN SAUCE/TUONG GIA VI (Thai seasoning sauce) – 1 tablespoon
- 1 tablespoon Maggi Seasoning, Healthy Boy Stir Fry Seasoning Sauce, or soy sauce

GOLDEN NEEDLES See LILY BUDS

GOLDEN SYRUP/LIGHT TREACLE (British pure cane sugar syrup with a butterscotch flavor) – 1 cup
- 1 cup Swedish light syrup/*ljus sirap,* coconut syrup, or Steen's pure cane syrup

- 3/4 cup light-colored (not "lite") corn syrup and 1/3 cup dark corn syrup, simmered, uncovered, until syrupy and reduced to 1 cup, about 5 minutes
- 2/3 cup light-colored corn syrup plus 1/3 cup light unsulphured molasses or grade A golden, delicate maple syrup, heated until combined
- 1/2 cup each dark corn syrup and light, mild-flavored honey, heated until combined

GOMASHIO/GOMASIO See SESAME SALT

GOOSE FAT, RENDERED – 1 tablespoon
- 1 tablespoon rendered duck fat, pork fat, tallow, or leaf lard
- 1 tablespoon fruity olive oil, or 1 1/2 teaspoons each oil and unsalted butter

GORAKA/GAMBODGE (Sri Lankan souring agent) – 4 dried segments ground to a pulp (1 tablespoon)
- 1 tablespoon tamarind concentrate
- 1 tablespoon bitter orange juice, lemon juice, or lime juice

GRAIN ALCOHOL/NEUTRAL SPIRITS (151 to 190 proof alcohol) – 1 cup
- 1 cup 100-proof vodka
- 1 cup grappa (for a fruit liqueur base)

GRAINS OF PARADISE/GUINEA PEPPER/MELEGUETA (West African seasoning) – 1 tablespoon ground
- 2 teaspoons each cardamom seeds (from black cardamom pods) and black peppercorns, ground in a mortar or spice/coffee grinder (Alternatively, use 1 1/2 teaspoons each ground cardamom and ground black pepper.)

GRAIN SYRUP See KOREAN GRAIN SYRUP

GRAPE MOLASSES/MUST SYRUP/DIBS/MOSTARDA/PEKMEZ/ PETIMÉSI (Italian, Spanish, and Middle Eastern thick syrup) – 1/4 cup
See also VIN COTTO
- 3/4 cup unsweetened grape juice or prune juice, gently boiled until syrupy and reduced to 1/4 cup, about 10 minutes (Stir constantly and skim the foam as necessary.)
- 1/4 cup thick fig syrup/*miele di fichi/melazzo di fichi*
- 3 tablespoons lemon juice and 4 teaspoons dark molasses (or strong-tasting honey) warmed in the microwave a few seconds, then cooled
- 3 tablespoons dark, strong-tasting/bitter honey thinned with 1 tablespoon warm water
- 1/4 cup sweet, heavy wine, such as Greek Mavrodaphne
- 2 to 3 tablespoons aged balsamic vinegar

GRAPPA (Italian clear distilled spirit) – 2 tablespoons
- 2 tablespoons Chilean or Peruvian pisco, French marc, Portuguese bagaciera, Spanish aguardiente, or very dry vermouth, such as Noilly Prat

GRAVY BROWNING – 1 teaspoon
- 1/2 teaspoon powdered caramel color
- 1/2 teaspoon sugar added to the fat before adding flour, then cooked several minutes to a rich brown color
- 1 teaspoon instant coffee granules or unsweetened cocoa powder, preferably Dutch processed, dissolved in 1 tablespoon of liquid, then stirred into the sauce
- Few drops soy sauce; omit or reduce the salt in the recipe accordingly
- Toast the flour used in making the gravy but use twice as much (toast the flour in a dry skillet until brown)
- Onion slices, caramelized until golden (will also add flavor to the gravy)
- Washed, unpeeled onions when making beef stock/broth (peels will color it a rich brown)

GREATER GALANGAL/GALANGA *See GALANGAL, GREATER*

GREEK OREGANO/RIGANI *See OREGANO, GREEK*

GREEK SEASONING – 1 tablespoon
- ☞ 1 teaspoon dried Greek (or Mediterranean) oregano plus 1/2 teaspoon each dried marjoram, garlic powder, ground black pepper, and finely grated lemon zest
- ☞ 1 teaspoon dried oregano and 2 teaspoons lemon pepper

GREEK SWEET WINE (Mavrodaphne, Samos, Muscat) – 1/4 cup for cooking
- ☞ 1/4 cup Madeira

GEEK VINEGAR, AGED RED WINE – 2 tablespoons
- ☞ 1 tablespoon each balsamic vinegar and red wine vinegar

GREEK VINEGAR, SWEET – 1 tablespoon
- ☞ 1 tablespoon aged sherry vinegar

GREEN GARLIC *See GARLIC SHOOTS, YOUNG GREEN*

GREEN MANGO *See MANGO, GREEN*

GROUNDNUT OIL/PEANUT OIL – 1 cup
- ☞ 1 cup corn oil

GROUND RED PEPPER *See CAYENNE PEPPER, GROUND*

GUANCIALE (Italian salt-cured pork jowl) – 4 ounces
- ☞ 4 ounces jowciale or pancetta (saltier and leaner)
- ☞ 4 ounces lean salt pork
- ☞ 4 ounces unsmoked bacon, blanched in boiling water for 1 or 2 minutes, then rinsed and blotted dry

GUANCIALE, SMOKED – 4 ounces
- 3 ounces regular guanciale or pancetta and 1 ounce (1 or 2 slices) traditional bacon

GUASCA/GALINSOGA/QUICKWEED/HATO GRANDE, DRIED (wild Columbian herb) – 1 tablespoon
- 1 teaspoon dried Mexico oregano plus 2 teaspoons chopped fresh cilantro

GUAVA PASTE/ATE/GOIABADA (Latin American and Portuguese condiment) – 4 ounces
- 4 ounces quince paste/*membrillo*; jellied quince paste/*pâte de co-ing,* plumbrillo, or any tart Mexican fruit paste/*ate*
- 4 ounces strawberry or raspberry paste (Cook 6 to 7 ounces strawberry or seedless raspberry jam until very thick and reduced by at least one-third, then transfer to a shallow greased dish and chill until firm.)

GUAVA PUREE – 1 cup
- 1/2 to 2/3 cups guava paste and 1/2 cup water, pureed in a blender until smooth

GUINDILLA CHILI, DRIED – 1
- 1/2 teaspoon crushed red pepper flakes

GUINDILLA CHILIS, JARRED – 1/4 cup
- 1/4 cup pepperoncini pickled in brine, or any small brined mild green chilis

GUM ARABIC/ACACIA GUM (natural thickening and emulsifying agent) – 1 teaspoon
- 1 teaspoon xanthan gum
- 1 teaspoon guar gum,
- 1 to 2 teaspoons instant ClearJel used following package directions

GVINA LEVANA (Israeli soft white cheese) – 1 cup *See also QUARK*
- 1 cup fromage blanc, plain full-fat quark, or plain full-fat Greek-style yogurt

GYOZA DIPPING SAUCE *See ASIAN DIPPING SAUCE*

H

HAJIKAMI (Japanese sweet pickled young ginger) *See GINGER, PICKLED*

HALLABONG JUICE (Korean citrus fruit) – 1 tablespoon
- ☞ 1 1/2 teaspoons each orange and tangerine juice

HAM HOCK, SMOKED – 1 small meaty hock for seasoning
- ☞ 4 ounces meaty salt pork, rinsed if crusted with salt
- ☞ 3 ounces smoked prosciutto or Italian or German speck scraps or rind
- ☞ 1 or 2 smoked sausages
- ☞ 2 1/2 to 4 ounces smoked ham, or nitrate-free turkey ham or bacon
- ☞ 2 1/2 to 4 ounces smoked pork shoulder butt or smoked pork shank
- ☞ 4 ounces smoked pork neck bones
- ☞ 1 smoked turkey wing, drumstick, thigh, or neck
- ☞ 2-ounce end piece of *prosciutto crudo*
- ☞ Parmesan rind (has a rich, slightly smoky flavor)
- ☞ 3/4 teaspoon ham soup base, such as Better than Bouillon, or ham concentrate, such as Goya
- ☞ 1/4 cup lightly packed smoked dulse (sea vegetable) or smoked dulse flakes, heated in a dry skillet until brown and crunchy, about 5 minutes, stirring several times; add during the last five minutes of cooking
- ☞ 1 or 2 teaspoons smoked salt or a smoky seasoning blend; reduce the salt in the recipe accordingly
- ☞ 2 or 3 drops liquid smoke (for aroma only)

HARISSA (Moroccan thick spicy chili paste) – 1 tablespoon
- ☞ 1 tablespoon berbere seasoning, harissa powder, or peri peri sea-soning (add to oil to make a paste, or use dry for seasoning)

➳ 1 tablespoon hot chili paste, such as sambal oelek, plus 1 or 2 tea-spoons vegetable oil, 1 crushed garlic clove, and 1/2 teaspoon each toasted ground cumin and coriander

HATCHO MISO (Japanese dark brown, soybean-based miso) – 1 tablespoon
➳ 1 tablespoon red miso/*inaka miso/sendai miso*
➳ 1 tablespoon *akadashi miso* (*hatcho* and *saikyo* miso blend; less pungent)

HAZELNUT OIL, ROASTED (finishing oil) – 1 cup
➳ 1 cup roasted walnut oil or extra-virgin olive oil

HAZELNUT PASTE/PASTA DI NOCCIOLA – 1 cup
➳ 1 cup pistachio paste/*pasta di pistachio*, or creamy-type almond butter

HEMP SEED BUTTER – 1 cup
Make Your Own Toast 1 1/2 cups hemp seeds in a dry skillet until fragrant, 3 to 4 minutes, then process in a blender until finely ground; add 2 to 3 tablespoons grapeseed oil, and continue to process to a coarse paste. Store in a small airtight container in the refrigerator; it will keep for up to 1 month.

HEMP SEED OIL – 1 cup
➳ 1 cup walnut or flaxseed oil

HEMP SEEDS (raw or toasted) – 1/4 cup
➳ 1/4 cup sunflower seeds (raw or toasted)
➳ 3 to 4 tablespoons plain hemp powder/hemp protein powder (for smoothies)

HERB BOUQUET See BOUQUET GARNI

HERBES DE PROVENCE (Provençal seasoning mix) – 1 teaspoon
➳ 1/4 teaspoon each dried basil, dried marjoram, dried rosemary, and dried thyme, plus a small pinch lavender if available (or desired)

- 1/2 teaspoon each dried thyme and dried basil
- 3/4 teaspoon Italian seasoning

HERBS, DRIED (lavender, marjoram, mint, oregano, rosemary, sage, tarragon, thyme)

- **Make Your Own** Place washed and dried leaves in a single layer between plain paper towels and microwave on High until thoroughly dry and brittle, 1 to 3 minutes, depending upon the amount and moisture content.

Or

Place sprigs in a single layer on a wire cooling rack or paper towel and cover with cheesecloth; or hang a bundle of sprigs upside down in a mesh produce bag, or paper bag punctured with air holes. Leave in a warm, dry, airy, preferably dark place for 7 to 10 days. Strip the leaves when dry.

HERBS, FROZEN (basil, borage, chives, cilantro, dill, garden cress, lemon balm, lemongrass, marjoram, mint, parsley, savory, young sorrel, kaffir lime leaves)

Make Your Own Put chopped herbs in ice cube trays with a little water or olive oil and freeze until solid. Transfer the frozen cubes to freezer bags. To use oil-based cubes, toss 1 or 2 cubes into the pan; for water-based, place in a fine-mesh sieve until the ice melts, then use immediately.

Or

Blanch herb leaves in boiling water until brightly colored, about 10 seconds, freshen in ice water, and then process in a blender or food processor to a smooth paste. Drain in a small cheesecloth-lined sieve for 1 to 2 hours, then freeze in ice cube trays and transfer to freezer bags when frozen.

HERBS, FRESH, PRESERVED IN SALT(basil, borage, chives, cilantro, dill, garden cress, lemon balm, lemongrass, marjoram, mint, parsley, savory, young sorrel)

Make Your Own Layer washed and dried fresh herb leaves in a glass container between 1/2-inch layers of kosher salt, beginning and ending with salt. Make sure the salt covers the leaves completely and is removed before using the herbs. (The leaves will keep their green color for up to 6 months.)

HIBISCUS FLOWERS, DRIED/ROSELLE/FLOR DE JAMAICA/BISAAP (Caribbean, Spanish, and African seasoning*) – 1 ounce (1 cup)*
- ⊢ 1 ounce dried white hibiscus flowers/*bisaap blanc* (less tart)
- ⊢ 15 hibiscus tea bags (remove leaves from the bags)

HIBISCUS LEAVES/INDIAN SORREL/PULINCHA KIRA/RATA BILINCHA (tangy Asian vegetable) *See SORREL, COMMON GARDEN*

HICKORY SMOKED SALT *See SALT, SMOKED SEA*

HING *See ASAFETIDA*

HOG PLUM/MAKAWK (Southeast Asian souring agent) – 1 pound peeled
- ⊢ 12 ounces tomatillos, green or unripe cherry tomatoes, or gooseberries

HOISIN SAUCE/HÓI SÌN JÌANG (Chinese thick, sweet cooking condiment) – 1/4 cup
- ⊢ 1/4 cup Chee hou sauce plus 1 or 2 teaspoons brown sugar or dark-bodied honey
- ⊢ 2 tablespoons each oyster sauce and thick tomato sauce

Make Your Own Whisk together 2 tablespoons thick barbecue sauce, 1 tablespoon each molasses and dark soy sauce, and 1/2 teaspoon Chinese five-spice powder.

HOJA SANTA/HIERBA SANTA/ACUYO/MOMO (Mexican seasoning) – 1 fresh leaf
- ⊢ 2 dried *hoja santa* leaves
- ⊢ 2 Mexican avocado leaves, toasted
- ⊢ 1/2 cup chopped green fennel fronds/leafy tops plus a pinch of ground black pepper

- 1/2 teaspoon freshly ground anise seed
- 1 tablespoon dried Mexican oregano leaf or dried Mexican or French tarragon

HOLLANDAISE SAUCE – 3/4 cup

- 1/2 cup mayonnaise thinned with 1 or 2 tablespoons water, then gently heated until warm (do not let boil)
- 1/2 cup sour cream, 2 tablespoons mayonnaise, 1 tablespoon lemon juice, and 1/4 teaspoon salt, gently heated until warm (do not let boil)

HONEY – 1 cup

- 1 cup light agave syrup/nectar
- 1 1/2 cups firmly packed light or dark brown sugar plus 1/4 cup liquid
- 3/4 cup unsulphured molasses or dark corn syrup plus 1/2 cup granulated sugar (for baking, increase liquid in recipe by 2 tablespoons)
- 1 cup Just-Like-Honey syrup (vegan, rice-based sweetener)
- 1 cup Italian pine syrup/*mugolio* (expensive; not for cooking)
- 1 cup granulated honey crystals/honey powder, dehydrated maple syrup, or molasses powder (for dry rubs and sprinkling over cereal)

HONEY, AVOCADO – 1 cup

- 1 cup strongly flavored dark honey, such as buckwheat, chestnut, manuka, or pine

HONEY, BITTER/SAVORY HONEY/MIELE AMARO (Sardinian) – 1 cup

- 1 cup robust or strongly flavored honey, such as avocado, buckwheat, chestnut, manuka, or pine

HONEY BUTTER – 4 ounces (1/2 cup/1 stick)

- 1 or 2 tablespoons honey stirred into 4 ounces room-temperature butter (for more honey taste, beat together 1/3 cup honey and 1/2 cup butter until creamy)

HONEY, CHESTNUT (Italian) – 1 cup
- 1 cup strong, earthy honey, such as Sardinian, buckwheat, pine, or eucalyptus

HONEY, GREEK/MELI (wildflower and herbs) – 1 cup *See also HONEY, THYME, WILD/HYMETTUS*
- 1 cup Italian wildflower honey/*millefiori*

HONEY, KIAWE (Hawaiian) – 1 cup:
- 1 cup mild-flavored honey, such as orange blossom or clover

HONEY, LAVENDER (French) – 1 cup
- 1 cup wildflower, orange blossom, or any mild, fragrant honey

HONEY, LYCHEE (Asian) – 1 cup
- 1 cup clover honey, or other mild, fragrant golden honey

HONEY, MILD – 1 cup
- 1 cup acacia, alfalfa, blueberry, clover, kiawe, grapefruit blossom, linden blossom, or orange blossom honey
- 1 cup Tupelo honey (sweeter)

HONEY MUSTARD – 1/4 cup
- 2 tablespoons each Dijon mustard and honey

HONEY MUSTARD SAUCE – 1/2 cup
Make Your Own Stir together 1/3 cup mayonnaise, 1 or 2 tablespoons Dijon or American mustard, and 1 or 2 tablespoons honey until combined. Refrigerate for 3 or 4 hours for the flavors to meld.
Or
Stir together 1/3 cup yellow mustard and 2 1/2 tablespoons honey until smooth; season with salt and pepper.

HONEY, THYME, WILD/HYMETTUS (Greek) – 1 cup
- 1 cup unfiltered, aromatic honey, such as pine tree or sunflower

☞ 1 cup grape must syrup/*petimezi*
☞ 1 cup flavorful dark honey, such as berry, chestnut, or wildflower

HONEY, TIGLI (Tuscan) – 1 cup
☞ 1 cup linden, lavender, or acacia honey

HONEY VINEGAR/CHESTNUT HONEY VINEGAR – 1 cup
☞ 1 cup champagne vinegar and 2 tablespoons honey, gently heated until the honey melts

HOP MARJORAM/CRETAN DITTANY (Cretian and Greek herb) See *MARJORAM, FRESH*

HORSERADISH, BOTTLED – 2 tablespoons
☞ 1 tablespoon dried horseradish powder (or horseradish flakes), mixed with 1 tablespoon each vinegar and water then left, covered, for 10 to 15 minutes to develop the flavor

HORSERADISH CREAM – 2/3 cup (about)
Make Your Own Fold 2 to 3 tablespoons (or more) strained bottled horseradish (or grated fresh horseradish root) into 1/2 cup sour cream, crème fraîche, or full-fat yogurt. Refrigerate for at least 30 minutes to develop the flavor.
Or
Whisk 1/4 heavy cream until softly whipped (should equal 1/2 cup), then fold in 1/2 cup strained bottled horseradish plus 1/2 teaspoon salt. Refrigerate for at least 30 minutes to develop the flavor.

HORSERADISH, FRESH – 1 tablespoon grated (from a peeled 1/2-inch segment)
☞ 2 tablespoons drained bottled horseradish
☞ 1 to 2 teaspoons dried horseradish powder, or horseradish flakes, mixed with 1/2 to 1 tablespoon water then left, covered, 10 to 15 minutes to develop the flavor

➵ 1 tablespoon wasabi paste (or 1 tablespoon wasabi powder mixed with 2 teaspoons cold water then left, covered, 10 minutes to develop the flavor

➵ 1 tablespoon grated black radish (the more pungent the better)

➵ 1 tablespoon grated toothwort rootstock/*Dentaria*, or garlic mustard taproot/*Alliaria petiolata*

HOSRUM *See VERJUICE*

HOT PEPPER SAUCE – 1 teaspoon
➵ 1 teaspoon Louisiana-style hot sauce, harissa, sambal oelek, Sriracha, or chili paste

➵ 1/4 teaspoon ground cayenne pepper

➵ 3/4 to 1 teaspoon crushed red pepper flakes, Korean chili powder/ *kochukaru*, or hot Hungarian paprika

HUACATAY/BLACK MINT/TAGETES GRAVEOLENS, FRESH OR FROZEN (Peruvian seasoning) – 1 tablespoon chopped
➵ 1 tablespoon huacatay powder (ground dried huacatay) or jarred paste

➵ 1 1/2 teaspoons each chopped fresh cilantro (or tarragon) and mint leaves

➵ 1 tablespoon chopped fresh cilantro

HUITLACOCHE/CUITLACOCHE/BLACK CORN FUNGUS/CORN SMUT, FRESH OR FROZEN (Mexican seasoning) – 4 ounces
➵ 1 to 2 tablespoons canned huitlacoche puree

➵ 4 ounces black trumpet/horn of plenty mushroom

➵ 4 ounces morel mushrooms

HUMMUS (Middle Eastern dip) – 2 cups
Make Your Own Drain and rinse 1 (15-ounce) can room-temperature garbanzo beans; process with 2 to 3 tablespoons each fresh lemon juice, tahini, and olive oil and 1 minced garlic clove in a blender or food processor until smooth. (Add water if necessary and season with

salt, cumin, or more lemon juice, if desired.) Alternatively, use cannellini or Fordhook lima beans, adding more garlic and olive oil and omitting the tahini. Another alternative is replacing beans with 1 cup roasted garbanzo/chickpea flour mixed with 2/3 cup cold water then cooking it for a few minutes. Keep the humus refrigerated in an airtight container; it will last for up to 1 week.

HYSSOP/HYSSOPUS OFFICINALIS, FRESH (European seasoning) – 1 tablespoon chopped
☞ 1 1/2 teaspoons each chopped fresh mint and sage

HYSSOP, SYRIAN/ORIGANUM SYRIACUM (Middle Eastern seasoning) – 1 tablespoon dried
☞ 2 teaspoons dried thyme and 1 teaspoon dried marjoram

I

INDIAN DRIED RED CHILI/BEGDI/GUNTUR – 1
- 1 dried Kashmiri chili *See also KASHMIRI CHILI*

INDIAN FIVE-SPICE MIX *See BENGALI FIVE-SPICE MIX*

INDONESIAN SOY SAUCE *See KECAP ASIN; KECAP MANIS*

INDONESIAN VINEGAR/CUKA – 1 tablespoon
- 1 tablespoon distilled colorless malt vinegar or rice vinegar

ITALIAN SEASONING – 1 teaspoon
- 1/4 teaspoon each dried basil, dried marjoram, dried Mediterranean oregano, and dried thyme plus 1/8 teaspoon crushed dried rosemary (optional)
- 1 1/2 tablespoons chopped fresh Italian-type herbs (basil, thyme, or oregano)

J

JAGGERY/PALM SUGAR/GUR (Indian dark, unrefined sugar) – 1 cup grated, shaved, granulated, or jarred
- 1 cup grated or crushed Mexican unrefined sugar/*piloncillo/panela* or *panocha/panucha*
- 1 cup crushed/grated Indonesian palm sugar/*gula jawa* or Malaysian palm sugar/*gula melaka*
- 1 cup dark muscovado/Barbados sugar
- 1 cup dark brown unrefined cane sugar, such as Billington's
- 3/4 cup granulated sugar plus 5 tablespoons molasses
- 1 cup dark brown or maple sugar moistened to a coarse paste with 1 tablespoon light molasses (for jarred palm sugar)

JALAPEÑO JELLY – 1 generous cup
Make Your Own Boil 1/4 cup distilled white vinegar, 1/4 cup granulated sugar, and 1 seeded and finely chopped jalapeño until reduced to a few tablespoons, 3 to 4 minutes. Add 1 cup apple jelly and simmer, stirring, until the jelly melts; cool, then stir before transferring to a sterilized jar. Store in the refrigerator; it will keep for up to 4 months.

JAMAICA See HIBISCUS FLOWERS, DRIED

JAMAICAN JERK SEASONING (dry spice blend) – 1 tablespoon
- 2 teaspoons chili seasoning and 1/2 teaspoon each dried thyme and ground allspice (for food)
- 2 to 3 tablespoons allspice berries, softened in warm water, then sprinkled over hot barbecue coals (for imparting an aroma while food is being grilled)

JAPANESE BLACK SUGAR/KUROZATO/KURO SATO (dark unrefined sugar) – 1 cup chopped
- 1 cup chopped or shaved Mexican unrefined sugar/*piloncillo/panela*

- ☞ 1 cup Indian palm sugar/jaggery/*gur* or Indonesian palm sugar/*gula jawa*
- ☞ 1 cup firmly packed dark brown sugar plus 1 tablespoon unsulphured molasses
- ☞ 1 cup dark brown molasses unrefined cane sugar, such as Billington's

JAPANESE BLACK SUGAR SYRUP/KUROMITSU – 1 cup
- ☞ 1 cup dark corn syrup or blackstrap molasses

JAPANESE BLACK VINEGAR/AGED RICE VINEGAR/KUROZU – 1 tablespoon
- ☞ 1 tablespoon balsamic vinegar or good-quality sherry vinegar

JAPANESE BROWN RICE VINEGAR/GENMAIZU – 1 tablespoon
- ☞ 2 teaspoons cider or balsamic vinegar and 1 teaspoon water
- ☞ 1 tablespoon unseasoned rice wine vinegar

JAPANESE CHILI OIL/RAYU – 1 teaspoon
- ☞ 1 teaspoon toasted sesame oil and 1/2 teaspoon Japanese spice mixture *shichimi togarashi*
- ☞ Chinese chili oil

JAPANESE CHILI POWDER/ICHIMI TOGARASHI – 1 teaspoon
- ☞ 3/4 teaspoon Chinese ground red pepper
- ☞ 1/2 teaspoon Hungarian or Spanish mild paprika, or ground cayenne pepper

JAPANESE CURRY POWDER – 1 tablespoon
- ☞ 1 tablespoon mild, sweet-flavored curry powder, such as S&B Oriental Curry Powder
- ☞ 1 tablespoon mild Madras curry powder (spicier)

JAPANESE DAIKON & RED PEPPER CONDIMENT/GARNISH/MOMIJI OROSHI – 1/4 cup
- ☞ 1/2 teaspoon red chili yuzu paste/*yuzu koshu* mixed with 1/4 cup grated, drained daikon (adds citrus flavor)

☞ 1/4 cup grated daikon tip/*daikon oroshi* (lacks heat)

JAPANESE DIPPING SAUCE *See ASIAN DIPPING SAUCE; PONZU SAUCE; TEMPURA DIPPING SAUCE*

JAPANESE FISH SAUCE/SHOTTSURU/ISHIRI/ISHIRU – 1 teaspoon
  ☞ 1 teaspoon Japanese fermented sweet fish sauce/*ayu* (more mellow)
  ☞ 1 teaspoon Thai fish sauce/*nam pla*, Vietnamese fish sauce/*nuoc nam*, Filipino fish sauce/ *patis*, or any Asian fermented fish sauce
  ☞ 1 to 2 teaspoons anchovy paste or finely chopped anchovies

JAPANESE GOMA PASTE *See SESAME PASTE*

JAPANESE HORSERADISH *See WASABI; WASABI, POWDERED; WASABI, PREPARED*

JAPANESE HOT RED CHILI/SANTAKA/TOGARASHI JAPONES/ TAKANOTSUME, FRESH OR DRIED – 1
  ☞ 1 fresh cayenne, japonés, serrano, or Thai chili
  ☞ 1 dried de árbol, cayenne, serrano, or Thai chili
  ☞ 1 teaspoon ground Japanese chili/*ichimi togarashi*
  ☞ 1 teaspoon ground cayenne pepper; or crushed red pepper flakes
  ☞ 1 1/4 teaspoons seven-spice seasoning/*shichimi togarashi*

JAPANESE MAYONNAISE/TOMAGO-NO-MOTO – 1/4 cup
  ☞ 1 tablespoon Kewpie brand or any light, creamy mayonnaise
  ☞ 1 tablespoon Western-style mayonnaise, 1/2 teaspoon rice vinegar, and 1/8 teaspoon superfine sugar, stirred until the sugar dissolves

JAPANESE MUSTARD/KARASHI *See MUSTARD, JAPANESE*

JAPANESE NIHAIZU SAUCE BASE *See NIHAIZU*

JAPANESE OKONOMIYAKI SAUCE *See OKONOMIYAKI SAUCE*

JAPANESE PICKLED CABBAGE/QUICK PICKLES/TSUKEMONO/SHIO ZUKE – 3 cups

Make Your Own Toss 4 cups coarsely shredded napa cabbage with 2 teaspoons coarse salt in a freezer bag; press out the air, seal, and refrigerate for 2 to 3 days, turning the bag daily. Drain, rinse with water and then squeeze out the water. Use within 2 to 3 days. For quick pickling, refrigerate the salted cabbage until limp and reduced to nearly half, 2 to 24 hours. For instant pickling, rub the cabbage vigorously with salt until tender and reduced to half, about 10 minutes, then squeeze out excess water.

JAPANESE PLUM, SALT-PICKLED See UMEBOSHI; UMEBOSHI PASTE

JAPANESE RICE VINEGAR, PURE/JUNMAI ZU/GENMAI MOCHIGOME ZU/JUN-YOMEZU – 1 tablespoon See also JAPANESE BLACK VINEGAR

- ⊱ 1 tablespoon light yellow rice vinegar/*komezu* (made with rice plus other grains)
- ⊱ 1 tablespoon brown rice vinegar/*genmaizu* (darker color)
- ⊱ 1 tablespoon distilled rice vinegar/*kokumotsu-su* or part synthetic rice vinegar/*gohsei-tursu* (lower cost grain vinegars)
- ⊱ 1 tablespoon organic rice wine vinegar, such as Ka-Me brand
- ⊱ 2 teaspoons Chinese white rice vinegar (or cider vinegar) plus 1/4 teaspoon water (sharper flavor)

JAPANESE RICE VINEGAR, SEASONED/AWASEZU/SUSHIZU/ YAMABUKUSU – 1 cup

- ⊱ 1 cup white rice vinegar plus 1 tablespoon sugar and 1 teaspoon salt; alternatively, use 2 tablespoons sugar and omit the salt

JAPANESE RICE WINE/CHŎNGJU – 2 tablespoons See also SAKÉ

- ⊱ 2 tablespoons dry white vermouth

JAPANESE SEA SALT/ARAJIO (coarse natural sea salt) – 1 tablespoon

- ⊱ 1 tablespoon coarse grain moist French sea salt/*sel gris Marin/sel gris de Guérande*

JAPANESE SEASONED SOUP BASE/MEMMI – *1 generous tablespoon*
- 1 tablespoon Japanese soy sauce, 1 teaspoon unseasoned rice vinegar, 1/2 teaspoon sugar, and 1/4 teaspoon Asian fish sauce
- 1 to 2 tablespoons Japanese light or dark soy sauce

JAPANESE SEVEN-SPICE SEASONING/SHICHIMI TOGARASHI/NANAMI TOGARASHI – *1 teaspoon*
- 3/4 teaspoon ground Japanese chili/*ichimi togarashi* or Chinese ground red pepper (for heat only; lacks flavor)

JAPANESE SOBA DIPPING SAUCE/SOBA-TSUYU *See TEMPURA DIPPING SAUCE*

JAPANESE SUSHI VINEGAR/KASUZU – *1 cup*
- 1 cup Japanese seasoned rice vinegar/*awasezu/sushizu*
- 1 cup red sushi vinegar/*kasuzu/akazu*

JAPANESE SWEET RICE WINE *See MIRIN*

JAPANESE SWEET VINEGAR SEASONING SAUCE/AMAZU – *1/2 cup*
Make Your Own Gently heat 1/2 cup rice vinegar, 3 tablespoons granulated sugar, and 1 1/4 teaspoons sea salt until the sugar dissolves, stirring occasionally; cool to room temperature.
Or
Gently heat 1/4 cup each rice vinegar and water, and 1 1/2 tablespoons granulated sugar until the sugar dissolves, stirring occasionally; cool to room temperature (for sunomono or cucumber salad).

JAPANESE TONKATSU SAUCE *See TONKATSU SAUCE*

JAPANESE TORIGARA BASE/WEIHA *See TORIGARA BASE*

JAPANESE YAKITORI SAUCE *See YAKITORI SAUCE*

JAPANESE YUKARI SHISO SALT – 1 tablespoon
- 1 tablespoon matcha salt (powdered green tea salt)
- 1 tablespoon seasoning for rice/*furikake See also FURIKAKE*

JOCOQUE/LABIN/LABNE (Mexican fermented cream) – 1 cup
- 1/2 cup buttermilk and 1/2 cup Mexican crèma or sour cream

JUJUBES (Chinese red dates) – 1 cup
- 1 cup canned jujubes, drained (for fresh)
- 1 cup hard crisp apple chunks (for fresh)
- 1/2 cup dried jujubes, softened in cold water 30 minutes (for fresh)
- 1 cup dried goji berries/wolfberries (for dried)
- 1 cup chopped dried dates, dried figs, or prunes (for dried)

JUNIPER BERRIES, DRIED – 1 teaspoon (8 crushed)
- 8 to 10 wild fresh juniper berries/*Juniperus communis* (soft and easily bruised)
- 8 or 9 dried black myrtle berries/*Myrtus communis* crushed and seeded (juniper-, rosemary-, and pine-tasting); or 1 or 2 teaspoons chopped fresh myrtle leaves (more juniper-tasting), added toward the end of cooking
- 2 to 3 teaspoons gin, stirred in during the last 5 minutes of cooking

K

KABOSU (Japanese citrus souring agent) – 1
- 2 Key limes or 1 Persian lime

KAFFIR LIME JUICE (Southeast Asian) – 1 tablespoon
- 1 tablespoon sour, unripe Persian lime juice

KAFFIR LIME LEAF/WILD LIME LEAF/BAI MAKRUT/JERUK PURUT, FRESH (Southeast Asian seasoning) – 1 leaf
- 1/4 teaspoon kaffir lime leaf powder/*bai maikrut*
- 1 young, fresh organic lemon or lime leaf
- 3/4-inch strip of kaffir or lime zest; or 1/4 to 1/2 teaspoon finely grated kaffir or lime zest (added toward the end of cooking)

KAFFIR LIME LEAF POWDER/KAFFIR POWDER (Southeast Asian) – 1 teaspoon
- 4 or 5 dried kaffir lime leaves, chopped, then ground to a fine powder

KAFFIR LIME ZEST, FRESH, FROZEN, OR BRINED – 1 teaspoon finely grated
- 2 teaspoons dried zest soaked in water to rehydrate (discard soaking water)
- 1 to 2 tablespoons shredded kaffir lime leaves
- 1 1/2 teaspoons finely grated fresh citron or Persian lime zest

KAHLÚA See COFFEE LIQUEUR

KAKDI MAGAZ (Indian dried cucumber seeds) – 1 tablespoon
- 1 tablespoon Chinese dried melon seeds/*qwa tze*, or other dried melon seeds, such as cantaloupe or honeydew

KALA JEERA *See CUMIN SEEDS, BLACK*

KALAMATA VINEGAR (Greek vinegar from sun-dried grapes) – 1 tablespoon
- 1 tablespoon balsamic vinegar

KALONJI *See NIGELLA SEEDS*

KANZURI (Japanese fermented chili paste) – 1 teaspoon
- 1 teaspoon green yuzu chili paste/*yuzu koshu*
- 1 or 2 drops chili oil

KAPI/GAPI (Thai seasoning) *See SHRIMP PASTE, FERMENTED*

KASHMIRI CHILI POWDER/DEGHI MIRCH (Indian) – 1 teaspoon
- 1/2 teaspoon California or New Mexico chili powder and 1/2 teaspoon mild paprika
- 1 teaspoon medium-hot Hungarian paprika

KATSUOBUSHI *See FISH FLAKES, DRIED*

KAYMAK/KAÏMAK/SER (Middle Eastern water buffalo cream) – 1/4 cup *See also CREAM, CLOTTED*
- 1/4 cup top thick layer from creamline yogurt, such as Brown Cow
- 1/4 cup softened natural cream cheese (no gum added) lightened with a little heavy cream
- 1/4 cup clotted cream, thick crème fraîche, or mascarpone

KECAP ASIN (Indonesian soy sauce) – 1 tablespoon
- 1 tablespoon Chinese light soy sauce or Maggi Seasoning

KECAP MANIS/KETJAP MANIS (Indonesian sweet, thick soy sauce) – 1/3 cup
- 1/3 cup Thai sweet black soy sauce/*see-eu wan*
- 1/3 cup Chinese double dark/double black sweet soy sauce/*yewn she jiang*

- 3 tablespoons Chinese dark soy sauce or Japanese tamari, 2 packed tablespoons palm or dark brown sugar plus a pinch of garlic powder and star anise (if available), gently heated until sugar melts (or microwaved on High for 20 seconds); stir to mix
- 1/4 cup Maggi Seasoning plus 1 1/2 tablespoons unsulphured molasses

KELP POWDER/GROUND KELP GRANULES (powdered seaweed) – 1 tablespoon
- 1 tablespoon dulse powder or granules
- 2 tablespoons dulse flakes

KELP STOCK See DASHI, VEGETARIAN/KOMBU DASHI; KOMBU STOCK

KETCHUP – 1 cup
Make Your Own Combine1 (8-ounce) can tomato sauce, 1/3 cup granulated or brown sugar, 2 tablespoons malt or cider vinegar, and 1/8 teaspoon ground cloves (optional) in a small saucepan and boil gently until thickened.

KEUKENSTROOP (Dutch dark thick syrup) – 1 cup
- 1 cup molasses, treacle, golden syrup, coconut honey, or strong traditional honey
- Appelstroop (fruitier tasting)

KEWRA/KEORA/KEVDA ESSENCE (Indian and Sri Lankan flavoring agent) – 1 or 2 drops
- 1/2 or 1 teaspoon kewra (screwpine) water or rose water
- 1/2 teaspoon pandan powder or paste (will add green color)
- 1 or 2 drops food-grade pure rose extract/essence
- 1/4 to 1/2 teaspoon Tahitian vanilla extract
- 1- or 2-inch section Tahitian vanilla bean, split lengthwise and seeds scraped out (use the bean and the seeds)

KEY LIME JUICE See LIME JUICE, KEY

KHOA/KHOYA/MAWA (East Indian unsweetened solid condensed milk) – 1 cup crumbled
- ⮞ 5 cups full-fat milk heated until reduced to 1 cup, stirring constantly, about 30 minutes
- ⮞ 3/4 cup full-fat dried milk powder

KIKURAGE *See CLOUD EAR/BLACK TREE FUNGUS*

KIMCHI/KIMCHEE/BAECHU KIMCHI (Korean pickled napa cabbage) – 1 cup
- ⮞ 1 cup vegan kimchi, such as Trader Joe's
- ⮞ 1 cup rinsed and drained sauerkraut plus 1 or 2 teaspoons Korean chili bean paste, such as *gochujang or taeyangcho*, stirred until combined

KIMCHI PASTE/GOCHUJANG/TAEYANGCHO *See KOREAN CHILI BEAN PASTE*

KINOME/PRICKLY ASH LEAF SPRIGS, FRESH (Japanese garnish) – 2 tablespoons
- ⮞ 2 tablespoons small sprigs of watercress, flat-leaf parsley, cilantro, or mint (for the color)

KIRMIZI BIBER (Turkish red chili powder) – 1 teaspoon
- ⮞ 1 teaspoon Aleppo chili powder
- ⮞ 3/4 teaspoon crushed red pepper flakes plus 1/8 teaspoon paprika
- ⮞ 1/2 teaspoon mild chili powder, such as ancho, California, or New Mexico, plus a pinch of paprika
- ⮞ 1 teaspoon paprika

KOCHUJANG *See KOREAN CHILI BEAN PASTE*

KOCHUKARU *See KOREAN CHILI FLAKES*

KOKUM/COCUM (Indian and Malaysian souring agent) – 1-inch by 1/2-inch dried slice

- 1 dried tamarind slice/*asam gelugor/asam jawa*
- 1 tablespoon tamarind pulp or paste/*asam jara*
- 1 tablespoon green mango powder/*amchur* (add toward the end of cooking)
- 1 1/2 tablespoons fresh lemon or lime juice (use 1/2 teaspoon for each segment or broken piece)

KOMBU POWDER (Japanese condiment)

Make Your Own Cut dried kombu into small pieces and toast in a dry skillet, stirring constantly, until very crisp, about 5 minutes. Grind to a coarse powder in a spice/coffee grinder or with a mortar and pestle (or rolling pin).

KOMBU STOCK/KOMBU DASHI-JIRU (Japanese) – 1 cup See also DASHI, VEGETARIAN

- 1-inch strip (1/8 ounce) dried kiri kombu/kelp (or kombu strands/ *natto kombu*), soaked in 1 cup cold water 8 to 12 hours, then strained (discard the kombu)
- 1 1/2 teaspoons dulse flakes brought just to boiling in 1 cup water (or water from soaking dried mushrooms); removed from heat; cooled 5 minutes, then strained
- 1 teaspoon powdered kombu dissolved in 1 cup hot water

KOREAN CHILI BEAN PASTE/RED PEPPER PASTE/HOT PEPPER PASTE/ GOCHUJANG – 1 tablespoon

- 1 tablespoon Chinese or Sichuan chili bean paste/*dou ban jiang* plus 1 teaspoon molasses
- 1 tablespoon Japanese red miso/*inaka/Sendai* plus 1/2 teaspoon each corn syrup (or sugar) and ground cayenne pepper
- 1/2 tablespoon each Japanese white miso/*shiro/saikyo* and Asian red chili sauce, such as sambal oelek, plus 1/2 teaspoon molasses

**KOREAN CHILI FLAKES/COARSE RED PEPPER POWDER/KOCHUKARU –
1 teaspoon**
- 1 teaspoon Chinese coarsely ground chili/*la jiao mian*
- 1 teaspoon mild chili powder, such as ancho, California or New Mexico (for chili powder)
- 3/4 teaspoon crushed red pepper flakes (for chili flakes)

KOREAN CHILI THREADS/SILGOCHU
- Mild, red, deseeded chilis, flattened and wrapped in a damp paper towel; left an hour to soften, then rolled and sliced into 2- to 3-inch-long threads

KOREAN DIPPING SAUCE – 3 tablespoons *See also KOREAN SESAME PASTE DIPPING SAUCE*
- 1 tablespoon unseasoned rice vinegar and 2 tablespoons reduced-sodium soy sauce, stirred until combined

KOREAN FERMENTED BEAN AND CHILI SAUCE/SSÄMJANG – 3 tablespoons
- 1 tablespoon soybean paste/*doenjang* stirred into 2 tablespoons chili bean paste/*gochujang/taeyangcho*

KOREAN FERMENTED BEAN PASTE/DOENJANG *See KOREAN SOYBEAN PASTE*

KOREAN GRAIN SYRUP/MALT SYRUP/JOCHEONG/CHOCHONG/MUL YUT – 1 cup
- 1 cup light-colored corn syrup

KOREAN GREEN PEPPER/KOCHU – 1
- 1 large green jalapeño chili
- 1 peeled green bell pepper or Anaheim chili (for mild green pepper)

KOREAN LEEK/DAEPA – 1
☞ 1 large scallion or green/spring onion

KOREAN RICE WINE/CHUNG-JU/YAKJU – 1/4 cup
☞ 1/4 cup Chinese yellow rice wine/Shaoxing/Shao Hsing, or medium dry sherry, such as amontillado

KOREAN RICE WINE, SWEET COOKING/SOJU – 1 tablespoon
☞ 1 tablespoon Japanese sweet rice cooking wine/*mirin*
☞ 1 tablespoon Chinese yellow rice cooking wine/*michiu/mi jiu*
☞ 1/2 teaspoon sugar or honey dissolved in 1 tablespoon white wine, saké, vermouth, sherry, or water

KOREAN ROASTED BARLEY TEA/BORICHA – 1/4 cup
Make Your Own Toast 1/4 cup pearl barley in a dry skillet over medium heat, stirring occasionally, until brown and fragrant, 10 to 15 minutes.

KOREAN SESAME PASTE DIPPING SAUCE/GGAE GANJANG – 1/4 cup
Make Your Own Toast 1/4 cup hulled (white) sesame seeds in a dry skillet over medium heat, stirring constantly, until golden brown, about 2 minutes. Immediately pour onto a plate to prevent overbrowning. Crush the seeds with a mortar and pestle and then add 1 tablespoon soy sauce, 1 tablespoon unseasoned rice vinegar, and 1 1/2 teaspoons sugar and mix well. Store in an airtight container in the refrigerator. It should last a couple of months.

KOREAN SHRIMP, SALTED/FERMENTED MINI/SAEUJEOT/SAEWOO-JEOT – 1 tablespoon
☞ 1 tablespoon dried shrimp
☞ 1 tablespoon Asian fish sauce
☞ 2 teaspoons Asian fermented shrimp paste

KOREAN SOLAR SALT (coarse, crunchy salt) – 1 tablespoon
☞ 1 tablespoon kosher salt

KOREAN SOYBEAN PASTE/DOENJANG – 1 tablespoon
- 1 tablespoon Japanese red miso/*inaka/sendai* or brown miso/*hatcho* (less salty; smoother texture)

KOREAN SOY SAUCE *See SOY SAUCE, KOREAN*

KOREAN UNPOLISHED RICE VINEGAR *See RICE VINEGAR, KOREAN UNPOLISHED*

KOREAN WATERCRESS/MINARI – 1 cup
- 1 cup fresh garden cress stems or flat-leaf parsley stems

KUDAMPULI/GARCIA CAMBOGIA *See KOKUM; TAMARIND CONCENTRATE*

KUDZU/KUZU ROOT STARCH/KO FEN/GOK FUN (Asian thickening agent) – 1 tablespoon powder
- 1 1/2 teaspoons arrowroot powder (Remove from the heat as soon as it reaches a boil.)

L

LABNA/LABNEH/LABNI/LABAN/LEBNEH (Middle Eastern thick yogurt/yogurt cheese) – 8 ounces (1 cup)
- 1 cup thick Greek yogurt

Make Your Own Stir 1/2 teaspoon kosher salt into 2 cups plain full-fat yogurt, preferably Greek-style (without pectin or additives). Transfer to a fine-mesh sieve lined with dampened cheesecloth set over a bowl and drain in the refrigerator for 1 to 3 days. (For low-fat labna, replace full-fat yogurt with low-fat and omit the salt; it will be less smooth.)

LAKSA LEAF *See VIETNAMESE MINT*

LALU (African leavening agent from dried crushed seeds of the baobab tree) – 1 tablespoon
- 1 1/2 teaspoons baking powder

LAOS POWDER (ground galangal root) – 1 teaspoon *See also GALANGAL, GREATER*
- 1/2 inch (2 teaspoons) peeled and finely minced galangal (fresh, frozen, or brined)
- 1 or 2 small (1/8-inch) slices dried galangal root/*galanga* (add whole to soup or stock without soaking)
- 1 1/2 teaspoons grated fresh ginger plus a few grains of ground black pepper, or a few drops of lemon juice

LARDO (Italian salt-cured seasoned fatback) – 8 ounces
- 8 ounces thinly sliced pancetta (for wrapping)
- 8 ounces salt pork or slab bacon (for cooked dishes)

LAVENDER, FRENCH OR ENGLISH – 1 tablespoon dried culinary flowers
- 3 to 4 tablespoons pesticide-free fresh lavender buds (*Lavandula angustifolia* or *L. xintermedia*), stripped from stems and flower heads

☞ 1/2 teaspoon lavender extract

LAVENDER SUGAR (French) – *1 cup*
Make Your Own Pulse 1 cup granulated sugar and 2 teaspoon dried lavender blossoms/culinary lavender buds in a food processor until the lavender is finely chopped; store airtight at room temperature. Alternatively, store bruised or coarsely chopped buds in a tightly sealed container with 1 cup granulated or superfine sugar until the sugar is flavored, 2 to 3 weeks, shaking the container periodically, then sift to remove the buds.

LAVENDER SYRUP – *1/2 cup*
Make Your Own Add 1 tablespoon dried lavender blossoms/culinary lavender buds to 1/2 cup hot simple syrup (*See SYRUP, SIMPLE*) and cool for about 30 minutes. Strain and refrigerate; it will keep for up to 1 week.

LEBANESE CLOTTED CREAM/ASHTAR *See CREAM, CLOTTED*

LEBANESE PEPPER MIX – *1 scant tablespoon*
☞ 1 teaspoon each ground allspice and ground black pepper plus 1/2 teaspoon ground white pepper

LEBANESE SEVEN-SPICE MIX *See* **BAHARAT**

LEBANESE SPICY BEEF SAUSAGE/SOUJOUK/SUJUK/YERSHIG – *1 pound*
☞ 1 pound pepperoni or spicy salami

LEKVAR *See PRUNE PUREE*

LEMON AGRUMATO OIL *See LEMON OLIVE OIL*

LEMON BALM/BALM/SWEET BALM, FRESH – *2 tablespoons chopped (10 to 12 leaves)*
☞ 4 teaspoons chopped fresh spearmint, Moroccan mint, or apple mint and 2 teaspoons chopped fresh lemon basil or lemon verbena

⇒ 1 peppermint tea bag plus 1/4 teaspoon lemon zest (for tisane)

⇒ 1 trimmed lemongrass stalk, cut into pieces and crushed with the side of a knife

⇒ Spearmint or applemint (for garnishes and fruit salads)

LEMON BASIL/KEMANGIE, FRESH – 1 ounce

⇒ 1 ounce fresh Thai lemon basil/green holy basil/*Bai manglak*

⇒ 1 ounce fresh lime basil (darker leaves; lime aroma)

⇒ 1 ounce fresh sweet basil (Italian, French, or California) plus a little lemon balm or lemon zest

LEMON CURD (for cake filling) – 1 cup

⇒ 1 cup lemon pudding, thinned with a little fresh lemon juice

LEMON, DAQ (Turkish thin-skinned lemon) – 1

⇒ 1/2 Meyer lemon

LEMON EXTRACT – 1 teaspoon

⇒ 1/8 teaspoon lemon oil, such as Boyajian

⇒ 2 to 3 teaspoons finely grated lemon zest from a scrubbed lemon, preferably organic

Make Your Own Combine 3 tablespoons lemon zest from a well-scrubbed or organic lemon with 1/2 cup vodka and let steep in a small, dark-colored bottle for 14 or more days in a cool, dark place. Shake the bottle from time to time, then strain and store in the refrigerator. Use 1 generous teaspoon for 1 teaspoon extract.

LEMONGRASS, FRESH – 3- to 5-inch trimmed bottom third of inner core/1 to 3 tablespoons finely chopped

⇒ 1 teaspoon sereh/serai powder (lemongrass powder)

⇒ 2 or 3 teaspoons lemongrass paste/puree

⇒ 2 tablespoons chopped lemon leaves or lemon verbena leaves (added at the last moment)

⇒ 2 teaspoons chopped lemon balm or lemon myrtle leaves (added at the last moment)

- 2 (1-inch) strips lemon peel (white pith scraped away) blanched in boiling water 2 or 3 seconds, then blotted dry
- 1 teaspoon finely grated lemon zest

LEMON JUICE, EUREKA/LISBON – 1 tablespoon

- 1 tablespoon Meyer lemon juice; reduce the sugar in the recipe by 1/4 teaspoon
- 2 teaspoons freshly squeezed lime juice
- 1 teaspoon lemon juice powder (for baking, increase the liquid by 1 tablespoon)
- 1/4 teaspoon citric acid powder mixed with 1 tablespoon warm water
- 1/2 teaspoon finely grated lemon zest from a scrubbed lemon, preferably organic; reduce the liquid in the recipe by 1 tablespoon
- 1 tablespoon white wine (only if lemon flavor is not needed)
- 1 1/2 teaspoons distilled white vinegar or cider vinegar (only if lemon flavor is not needed)
- Tiny drop of acid phosphate (for cocktails and sodas only if lemon flavor is not needed)

LEMON JUICE, MEYER – 1 tablespoon

- 2 1/2 teaspoons regular lemon juice plus 1/2 teaspoon tangerine or mandarin juice
- 1 tablespoon regular lemon juice plus a pinch of sugar

LEMON JUICE, MEYER – 1/4 cup

- 2 tablespoons each regular lemon juice and orange or tangerine juice
- 3 tablespoons regular lemon juice, 1 tablespoon orange juice, and 1/8 teaspoon sugar

LEMON JUICE POWDER – 1 tablespoon

- 2 tablespoons lemon zest
- 1 tablespoon lemon juice (reduce the liquid in the recipe by 1 scant tablespoon)

LEMON, MEYER (cross between a lemon and a mandarin) – 1
  ⊯ 1 large, thin-skinned regular Eureka lemon (more acidic)

LEMON OIL (American flavoring agent) – 1/8 teaspoon
  ⊯ 1/2 teaspoon lemon extract
  ⊯ 1 1/2 teaspoons finely grated lemon zest from a scrubbed lemon, preferably organic
  ⊯ 1/4 cup coarsely grated lemon zest from a scrubbed lemon, preferably organic, squeezed in a piece of cheesecloth

LEMON OIL/DAU CHANH (Asian flavoring agent) – 1/3 cup
Make Your Own Combine 1/3 cup vegetable oil with 1 tablespoon lemon zest from a well-scrubbed lemon (preferably organic) and heat slowly until small bubbles appear, 7 to 10 minutes. Cool and strain; store, tightly covered, in in the refrigerator; it will last for up to 1 week.

LEMON OLIVE OIL/AGRUMATO OIL (Italian flavoring agent) – 1/2 cup
Make Your Own Combine 1/2 cup extra-virgin olive oil with 1 tablespoon lemon zest from a well-scrubbed lemon (preferably organic) and heat to 250°F. Cover and let sit for a day or two to develop the flavor, then strain. (Alternatively, use 2 teaspoons natural lemon flavor, such as Simply Organic, in place of the lemon zest.) Store, tightly covered, in the refrigerator for up to a week.

LEMON OMANI (Middle Eastern dried lime powder) See LIME, DRIED

LEMON PEEL, DRIED See also LEMON ZEST
Make Your Own Finely grate lemon zest from well-scrubbed lemons (preferably organic). Spread in a single layer and dry at room temperature for 1 to 2 days; or in a preheated 200°F oven until crisp, about 20 minutes; or in a microwave on High for 1 to 1 1/2 minutes, stirring every 30 seconds. Use it as is, or crush to a powder just before using. Store in a well-sealed container in a cool, dark place. It will keep for a few months.

LEMON PEPPER SEASONING, DRIED – 1/2 cup (about)
☞ 1 tablespoon ground, dried lemon peel (*See LEMON POWDER*), 1 tablespoon coarse salt, 6 tablespoons ground black pepper, and 1 teaspoon garlic powder. For salt-free lemon pepper, use 1 teaspoon onion powder in place of salt.

LEMON PEPPER SEASONING, FRESH – 1 tablespoon (about)
☞ 1/2 teaspoon finely grated lemon zest, 2 teaspoons coarsely ground black pepper, and 1/4 teaspoon coarse salt

LEMON, PICKLED *See PICKLED LEMONS*

LEMON POWDER
☞ Dried lemon peel crushed to a powder *See LEMON PEEL, DRIED*

LEMON, PRESERVED *See PRESERVED LEMON*

LEMON SALT *See CITRIC ACID; CITRON SALT*

LEMON SEASONING SALT – 1/3 cup
Make Your Own Grind 2 tablespoons dried lemon peel in a spice/coffee grinder until very fine, then mix with 1/4 cup kosher or coarse sea salt. (Alternatively, use 1/4 cup finely grated fresh lemon zest in place of the dried peel; dry the salt mixture in a preheated 200°F oven, then cool before storing.) Keep in an airtight container; it will last for up to 3 months.

LEMON SUGAR – 1 cup
Make Your Own Peel the zest from 1 well-scrubbed lemon (preferably organic), trim any pith from the strips, and bury them in 1 cup granulated sugar; store airtight in a cool, dark place for 2 weeks before using.

LEMON SUGAR, SUPERFINE – 1 cup *See also VANILLA SUGAR*
Make Your Own Mix 2 tablespoons finely grated lemon zest (from a well-scrubbed lemon, preferably organic) with 1 cup granulated sugar;

spread on a baking pan, and dry in a preheated 200°F oven for 20 minutes, stirring occasionally. Cool, then grind in a blender or food processor until fine, 30 to 40 seconds. Store, tightly covered, in the refrigerator. It will keep for several months.

LEMON THYME *See THYME, LEMON, FRESH*

LEMON VERBENA, FRESH – 2 tablespoons coarsely chopped (2 to 4 leaves)
- 1/2 to 1 teaspoon dried lemon verbena
- 1 lemon verbena herbal tea bag
- 2 to 4 sprigs lemon thyme
- 1 fresh lemongrass stalk, trimmed, flattened, and cut into 2-inch pieces (tie together with twine to make removal easier)
- 2 teaspoons shredded lemon zest
- Verbena hydrosol (food-safe essential oil) lightly sprayed on the food before serving

LEMON ZEST – 1 teaspoon
- 1 teaspoon grated Buddha's hand citron (more aromatic)
- 1/2 (scant) teaspoon lemon extract
- 1/3 teaspoon dried minced lemon peel, softened for 15 minutes in 1 teaspoon water (or other liquid from recipe)
- 1/4 (generous) teaspoon lemon juice powder (powdered lemon peel)
- 1 1/2 teaspoons frozen lemon peel (Freeze the peel in strips, then finely mince before using; for a non-organic lemon, dunk it into boiling water and firmly wipe off the wax before freezing.)
- 1/16 to 1/8 teaspoon lemon oil, such as Boyajian (double the amount for a cooked dish)
- 2 teaspoons grated or minced candied lemon peel (Rinse to remove sugar before grating or reduce sugar in recipe by 1/2 teaspoon; for easier grating or mincing, pulse with the flour or sugar called for in the recipe.)
- 1 teaspoon finely grated lime zest

LEMON ZEST, MEYER – 1 tablespoon
- 2 teaspoons regular lemon zest and 1 teaspoon tangerine or orange zest

LENGKUAS (Indonesian and Malaysian seasoning) *See GALANGAL, GREATER*

LICORICE/LIQUORICE ROOT POWDER/GLCYRRHIZA GLABRA (flavoring agent) – 1 tablespoon
- 1 or 2 licorice root tea bags, ground in a spice/coffee grinder until powdery
- 1 tablespoon anise seed or dried star anise, ground in a spice/coffee grinder until powdery

LILY BUDS/GOLDEN NEEDLES/GUM JUM/JIN ZHEN/CAI KIM CHAM/ WONCHURI, DRIED (Asian seasoning and garnish)
- Yellow, unopened common daylily/*Hemerocallis fulva* flower buds), dried in a warm, airy place until brittle, about 7 days (To rehydrate, soak in warm water 30 minutes, then trim off the fibrous end bit.)
- Finely shredded green cabbage (for texture; lacks taste)

LIME, AUSTRALIAN FINGER/DOOJA LIME, PULP/JUICE VESICLES – 1 tablespoon
- 1 1/2 teaspoons each lemon juice and lime juice
- 1 tablespoon Meyer lemon juice or Key lime juice

LIME, BEARSS SEEDLESS – 1
- 1 Meyer lemon (sweeter)
- 2 Persian limes (more acidic)

LIME, BITTER/LIMA/CITRUS LIMETTA (Yucatecan seasoning) – 1
- 1/2 Seville orange
- 1 Persian lime plus a little grapefruit zest

LIME CITRUS OIL/PURE LIME OIL – 1/8 teaspoon
- 1/8 teaspoon food-grade essential oil
- 1/2 teaspoon lime extract
- 1 teaspoon finely grated lime zest

LIME, DRIED/BLACK LEMON/OMANI LIME/LOOMI BASRA/LIMOO AMANI (Persian and Middle Eastern souring agent) – 1
- 2 teaspoons dried lime powder
- 1 tablespoon lime or lemon juice (stirred in when the dish is finished cooking)

Make Your Own Boil 1 Persian lime in salted water for a few minutes, then dry on a rack in a warm sunny spot until light and hollow, about 14 days. Alternatively, dry the lime in a preheated 170°F oven until hard and hollow-sounding, 16 to 18 hours. (Make several at once and store, tightly sealed, in a cool, dry place. They will keep for several months.)

LIME JUICE, KAFFIR (Southeast Asian) – 1 tablespoon
- 1 tablespoon sour, unripe Persian lime juice

LIME JUICE, KEY – 1/2 cup
- 1/2 cup Persian lime juice plus 1 teaspoon finely grated lime zest
- 1/4 cup Persian lime juice and 1/4 cup lemon juice
- 1/2 cup bottled Key lime juice, such as Floribbean, Nellie and Joe's, or Rose's

LIME JUICE, PERSIAN/TAHITI – 1/2 cup
- 2/3 cup lemon juice

LIME JUICE POWDER – 1
- 2 tablespoons lemon zest
- 1 tablespoon lemon juice (reduce the liquid in the recipe by 1 scant tablespoon)

LIME, PERSIAN – 1
- 2 Key limes
- 1 Eureka/Lisbon lemon, or 1/2 Meyer lemon

LIME POWDER (Persian seasoning) – 2 teaspoons
- ⇨ 1 home-dried lime, cracked into pieces, seeds removed, then ground until fine *See LIME, DRIED/BLACK LEMON*
- ⇨ 1 preserved lime or whole dried lime/*loom Omanii*, soaked 15 minutes before adding to dish, then discarded before serving

Make Your Own Finely grate 2 to 3 tablespoons zest from well-scrubbed limes (preferably organic). Spread in a single layer and dry at room temperature for 1 to 2 days; or in a preheated 200°F oven until crisp, about 20 minutes; or in a microwave on High for 1 to 1 1/2 minutes, stirring every 30 seconds. Cool, then finely crush or grind to a powder. Store in a well-sealed container in a cool, dark place. It will keep for a few months.

LIME, RANGPUR, JUICE – 1 tablespoon
- ⇨ 2 teaspoons Key or Persian lime juice and 1 teaspoon tangerine juice

LIME, RANGPUR, ZEST – 1 teaspoon
- ⇨ 1 teaspoon Key lime, tangerine, or tangelo zest

LIME, THAI/MANAO
- ⇨ Key lime (for zest)
- ⇨ Key lime juice plus a dash of Meyer lemon juice (for juice)

LIME ZEST – 1 teaspoon
- ⇨ 1 teaspoon limequat, lemon, or orange zest
- ⇨ 1/3 teaspoon dried lime peel, softened in 2 teaspoons water for 15 minutes
- ⇨ 1/2 teaspoon lime extract
- ⇨ 1/8 teaspoon lime citrus oil

LINGONBERRY JAM/PRESERVES (Scandinavian condiment) – 1 cup
- ⇨ 1 cup cranberry sauce

LIQUID SMOKE (seasoning to replicate the flavor of food prepared in a smoker, grill, or wood-burning oven)
- ⇨ Bottled mesquite spray (for a light misting at the end of cooking)

- Smoky ham powder (Dry thin pieces of lean country-style ham on a baking sheet in a preheated 200°F oven until crisp, about 1 hour; cool and grind to a powder in a spice/coffee grinder. Store, tightly sealed, at room temperature.)
- Lapsang Souchong or Scottish breakfast tea (strongly brewed and added to marinades or liquid ingredients, or finely ground and added to cooking ingredients)
- Smoked salt (plain or seasoned), or smoked black pepper (for recipes calling for salt, seasoning salt, or pepper)
- Smoked olive oil, such as hickory-and-pecan-wood-smoked or Spanish-pine-cone-smoked (for a light smoky finishing touch)
- Smoke-dried tomatoes (for recipes calling for tomatoes)
- Smoked paprika, hot or mild (for recipes calling for paprika)
- Smoked mozzarella/*mozzarella affumicata* or other smoked cheese (for pizza)
- Dried dark morel or black shiitake mushrooms (for recipes calling for mushrooms)
- Homemade cold-smoked butter (for recipes calling for sautéed onions, or a mirepoix)
- Canned smoked oysters (for shellfish chowder recipes calling for salt pork or bacon)
- Chipotle chili powder or paste, or chipotle chili crushed or finely ground, or liquid from canned chipotle in adobo (for recipes calling for heat as well as smoke flavor)

LJUS SIRAP (Swedish light syrup) See GOLDEN SYRUP

LONG PEPPER, INDONESIAN/INDIAN/DIPPLI/PIPPALI/TIEU LOP (Indian and Southeast Asian seasoning) – 1 tablespoon
- 1 tablespoon dried Tasmanian pepperberries or Sichuan peppercorns (red colored)
- 1 tablespoon white peppercorns or 2 teaspoons black peppercorns

LOTUS SEEDS, DRIED/LIEN TZU/LIEN JEE/MED BUA (Chinese and Southeast Asian) – 1 cup
- 1 cup canned lotus seeds or canned whole hominy, drained and rinsed

LOVAGE SEEDS – 1 tablespoon
- 1 tablespoon celery seeds or ajwain/ajowan seeds

LÚCUMA PULP, FRESH OR FROZEN (Peruvian fruit puree) – 1/2 cup
- 3/4 cup lucuma powder mixed with 3/4 cup cool water and left to thicken for 2 to 3 hours

LYLE'S SYRUP *See GOLDEN SYRUP/LIGHT TREACLE*

M

MACAPUNO COCONUT STRINGS (Filipino jarred sweet coconut in syrup) – 1 cup
- 1 cup sweetened shredded coconut

MACE – 1 mace blade (1 teaspoon crumbled/flakes)
- 1/2 teaspoon ground mace
- 1 scant teaspoon freshly grated nutmeg, or 1/2 teaspoon fine-ground nutmeg
- 1/2 teaspoon ground allspice

MADAN/GARCINIA (Southeast Asian sour fruit for flavoring) – 1
- 1 unripe green plum or nectarine

MADEIRA (Portuguese fortified wine) – 2 tablespoons
- 1 tablespoon Banyuls, semi-dry Marsala, port, dry sherry, or dry vermouth

MAGGI SEASONING (rich, salty liquid seasoning) – 1 tablespoon
- 1 tablespoon Golden Mountain Seasoning sauce/*tuong gia vi* (contains MSG)
- 1 1/2 teaspoons each Worcestershire sauce and Chinese dark soy sauce (or Thai sweet soy sauce or mushroom soy sauce)
- 1 tablespoon Japanese tamari
- 1 (or more) teaspoons Marmite or Vegemite

MAHLAB/MAHLEB/MAHLEPI (Turkish, Middle Eastern, and Greek aromatic flavoring) – 1 teaspoon powdered or crushed
- 1 drop each almond extract and cherry extract
- 1 teaspoon ground cardamom

MALAGUETA CHILIS, PICKLED (Brazilian) – 1 ounce
- 1/2 ounce pickled jarred or canned jalapeño chilis

MALAI (Indian clotted cream) *See CREAM, CLOTTED*

MALDIVE FISH/UMBALAKADA (Sri Lankan cooking condiment) – 1 tablespoon pounded, flaked or powdered
- 1 tablespoon coarsely chopped dried shrimp, or 1 1/2 tablespoons shrimp powder/floss
- 1 or 2 tablespoons bonito flakes/*katsuobushi,* crumbled to a powder
- 1 tablespoon flaked or crumbled dried cod

MALT EXTRACT, DRIED (brewing base component) – 2 tablespoons
- 2 tablespoons sorghum extract/syrup (for gluten-free ale/beer)

MALTED WHEAT FLAKES (yeast bread flavoring) – 1 tablespoon
- 1 tablespoon Maltex wheat cereal

MALTOSE/MALT SUGAR (sweetening agent) – 1 cup
- 3/4 cup rice bran syrup, corn syrup, golden syrup, or clear honey (increase the liquid in the recipe by 1/4 cup if necessary)

MALT POWDER, DIASTATIC (amylase enzyme dough improver) – 1 tablespoon
- 1 tablespoon sprouted wheat flour/wheat malt (sprouted wheat berries dried on a tray in a food dehydrator set at 120°F until brittle, then ground; use 1/4 teaspoon per large loaf)
- 1/4 cup sprouted wheat berries, pureed in a blender with part of the liquid called for in the recipe (use 1/4 cup per large loaf)

MALT POWDER, NON-DIASTATIC (flavoring agent and sweetener) – 1 tablespoon
- 1 tablespoon packed light brown sugar (for pretzel, bagel, pancake, or waffle batter)

- ⮚ 1 tablespoon barley malt syrup/plain malt syrup or honey (for boiling water bath for bagels)
- ⮚ 1 tablespoon granulated sugar, honey, or agave syrup/nectar (for yeast or flatbread dough)

MALT SUGAR *See MALTOSE*

MALT SYRUP, BARLEY, NON-DIASTATIC *See BARLEY MALT SYRUP, PLAIN*

MALT VINEGAR – 1 tablespoon
- ⮚ 1 tablespoon distilled colorless malt vinegar (for pickling and preserving)
- ⮚ 1 tablespoon cider vinegar or white wine vinegar
- ⮚ 1 tablespoon vinegar powder (used dry in cooking or spice rubs)

MANGO, GREEN/KACHA AM, FRESH OR FROZEN (Indian and Southeast Asian souring and tenderizing agent) – 1 medium (1 pound) *See also AMCHUR*
- ⮚ 1/3 cup *amchur* slices (sun-dried green mango) soaked in hot water until softened, 30 to 60 minutes
- ⮚ 1 hard green unripe yellow/eating mango plus a few drops lime juice (wear plastic gloves when handling raw green mango)
- ⮚ 1/4 of a green papaya
- ⮚ 1 large unpeeled green tart cooking apple, such as Granny Smith or Bramley's Seedling, soaked in acidulated water after cutting, then patted dry

MANGO, POWDER, GREEN *See AMCHUR*

MAPLE SUGAR CRYSTALS *See SUGAR, MAPLE*

MAPLE SYRUP – 1 cup *See also PANCAKE SYRUP*
- ⮚ 1 cup agave syrup/nectar, birch syrup, brown rice syrup, or Swedish light syrup/*ljus sirap*

- 1 1/4 cups barley malt syrup (reduce the liquid in the recipe by 1/4 cup)
- 3/4 cup plus 2 tablespoons dark honey such as buckwheat, thinned with 2 tablespoons apple juice
- 1/2 cup finely grated maple sugar (increase the liquid in the recipe by 1/4 cup)
- 1 cup homemade maple brown sugar syrup (Simmer 2 cups dark brown sugar and 1 cup water until syrupy, then cool. Add 1 teaspoon maple extract and leave for 24 hours to develop the flavor. Store, refrigerated, for up to 6 months.

MARASCHINO LIQUEUR/MARASCHINO-FLAVORED SPIRIT (Luxardo, Maraska) – 2 tablespoons
- 2 tablespoons cherry liqueur or bottled maraschino cherry juice

MARAS RED PEPPER FLAKES (Turkish) – 1 teaspoon:
- 1 teaspoon mild or hot Turkish, Hungarian, or Spanish paprika
- 1 teaspoon Aleppo or Urfa pepper flakes
- 3/4 teaspoon Aleppo or Urfa chili powder

MARINADE FOR MEAT OR POULTRY – 1/2 cup
- 1/2 cup bottled salad dressing, light vinaigrette, or seasoned yogurt or buttermilk

MARJORAM, FRESH – 3 sprigs or 1 tablespoon finely chopped
- 1 teaspoon dried marjoram, crumbled
- 1 1/2 teaspoons chopped fresh oregano or 1/2 teaspoon dried oregano
- 2 to 3 teaspoons fresh thyme, or 1 scant teaspoon dried thyme
- 1 tablespoon chopped fresh basil
- 1/2 teaspoon dried basil, and 1/4 teaspoon dried Mediterranean oregano
- 1 teaspoon dried Italian seasoning

MARMITE (British yeast extract) – 1 tablespoon
- 1 tablespoon Vegemite (less salty)
- 1 tablespoon Vitamin-R yeast extract
- 1 tablespoon Cenovis spread

MARSALA, COOKING (Sicilian fortified wine) – 2 tablespoons
- 1 tablespoon each sweet vermouth and dry sherry
- 2 tablespoons Madeira or dry sherry, such as Dry Sack
- 2 tablespoons white wine (or white grape juice) and 1/2 teaspoon brandy

MARSALA, SWEET COOKING (Sicilian fortified wine) – 2 tablespoons
- 1 tablespoon dry Marsala sweetened with a little sugar

MATCHA/MACCHA/HIKI-CHA (Japanese culinary-grade green tea powder)
- Japanese new crop green tea/Sincha, ground, pressed through a fine-mesh sieve, then spread on parchment paper to dry, about 1 hour (less colorful)
- Green food coloring powder (for baking; use following package directions; less flavorful)

MATSUTAKE POWDER – 1 tablespoon
- 1 tablespoon porcini powder (or dried porcini mushrooms ground in a spice/coffee grinder)
- 1 cup potato starch

MAYONNAISE – 1 cup
- 1 cup canola or olive oil whisked very gradually into 1/4 cup store-bought mayonnaise, along with a little lemon juice. Season with salt and more lemon juice if required
- 3/4 cup silken tofu, 1 tablespoon each unseasoned rice vinegar, lemon juice, and canola or olive oil, plus 1/2 teaspoon Dijon mustard, blended until smooth, then seasoned to taste with salt

- 1 cup creamed cottage cheese, processed in a blender until very smooth, then seasoned to taste with salt and lemon juice
- 1 cup plain Greek-style yogurt seasoned with 1 tablespoon Dijon mustard
- 1/2 cup plain yogurt or sour cream mixed with 1/2 cup mayonnaise, then seasoned to taste with salt and lemon juice (for reduced-fat mayonnaise)
- 1 cup dairy- and egg-free mayonnaise, such as Mindful Mayo, Nayonaise, or Vegenaise

MAYONNAISE-BASED SAUCE/MAYONNAISE-FLAVORED SAUCE – 1/2 cup (about)

1/2 cup mayonnaise (or 1/4 cup mayonnaise and 1/4 cup sour cream) plus any of the following:

- 2 tablespoons Dijon or whole-grain mustard
- 1 1/2 tablespoons black olive paste or tapenade
- 1 tablespoon strained bottled horseradish or wasabi paste
- 1 tablespoon wasabi powder, 1 tablespoon lemon juice, and 1/4 teaspoon salt
- 1 canned or jarred chipotle in adobo, seeded and finely chopped, 1/2 teaspoon adobo sauce, and 2 (or more) garlic cloves mashed to a paste with a pinch of salt
- 2 teaspoons dark *hatcho* miso, or 1 to 2 tablespoons white *shiro* miso
- 1 tablespoon curry powder, toasted in a dry skillet over medium heat for 20 to 30 seconds
- 1 tablespoon Chinese chili-garlic sauce plus fresh lime juice to taste
- 1 tablespoon hot chili sauce, such as Sriracha
- 2 tablespoons pesto or pistou
- 2 tablespoons each fresh lemon juice and extra-fine capers

MEAT GLAZE/GLACE DE VIANDE – 1/4 cup

- 1 quart fat-free unsalted beef stock gently boiled, uncovered, in a wide-bottomed pan until syrupy and reduced to 1/4 cup; cool and refrigerate, tightly covered; it will keep for up to 1 month

☞ 1/4 cup stock base paste or meat extract, such as Bovril, or yeast extract, such as Marmite, or Vegemite; use a small amount to flavor sauces and reduce the salt in the recipe accordingly

MELEGUETA PEPPER *See GRAINS OF PARADISE*

MEMBRILLO/COTOGNATA *See QUINCE PASTE*

MERKÉN, NATURAL (Chilean smoked chili spice blend) – 1 tablespoon
☞ 2 teaspoons hot smoked paprika or ancho chili powder plus a pinch of salt

MESQUITE POWDER – 1 tablespoon
☞ 1 tablespoon carob powder

MEXICAN SEASONING MIX/SPICE BLEND – 1 tablespoon
☞ 2 teaspoons mild chili powder, such as ancho, California, or New Mexico; 1 teaspoon ground cumin; and 1/8 teaspoon garlic powder

MINT EXTRACT – 1 teaspoon
☞ 4 drops oil of peppermint (for chocolate and candies)
☞ 1 cup fresh mint leaves (for infusing and then straining)

MINT, FRESH (peppermint, spearmint) – 1 tablespoon minced leaves
☞ 1 tablespoon fresh, young minced leaves of wild mint/*Yerba buena*, wild spearmint/*Mentha spicata*, wild Tuscan mint/*Nepitella*, catmint/catnip/*Nepeta cataria*, or mountain mint/*Pycnanthemum* (more bitter)
☞ 1/2 to 1 teaspoon dried peppermint from a mint tea bag
☞ 1 tablespoon whole-leaf dried spearmint leaves, pressed through a fine-mesh sieve to make 1 teaspoon
☞ 1/2 teaspoon Indian sun-dried mint powder/*pudina*
☞ 1/4 teaspoon mint extract (for desserts and confections)
☞ 1 drop oil of peppermint (for chocolate and candies)
☞ 1 tablespoon chopped young mountain mint leaves/*Pycnanthemum* (more bitter)

☞ 1 tablespoon chopped fresh basil mint or Thai basil (for savory dishes)
☞ 1 crushed peppermint candy, such as Altoids (for desserts, confections, and lamb jus)

MINT OIL (Turkish seasoning and condiment) – 1/3 cup
Make Your Own Gently heat 1 tablespoon crushed dried peppermint leaves and 1/3 cup olive oil over very low heat for 10 minutes. Cool, and then strain through a fine-mesh sieve or cheesecloth. The oil can be kept in an airtight container, refrigerated, for up to 5 days.

MINT SAUCE (British condiment for lamb) – 2/3 cup (about)
Make Your Own Stir together 1/2 cup chopped fresh spearmint leaves (or 1 or 2 tablespoons crumbled dried leaves), 1 tablespoon sugar, and 1/4 cup boiling water, then add 1/4 cup malt vinegar. Let sit at room temperature for an hour or more to develop the flavor.

MINT SUGAR (beverage flavoring) – 1/4 cup
Make Your Own Grind 2 tablespoons firmly packed fresh spearmint leaves with 2 tablespoons granulated sugar in a spice/coffee grinder until fine. Cover and let sit for 10 or more minutes to develop the flavor.

MINT SYRUP (beverage flavoring) – 1 cup
Make Your Own Heat 1 cup water, 1 cup sugar, and 1/4 cup finely chopped fresh spearmint leaves to boiling, stirring occasionally; then simmer, uncovered, for 5 minutes. Cool and strain. Store in a sterilized jar in the refrigerator; it will keep for up to 1 month.

MIRIN/HON-MIRIN (Japanese sweetened rice cooking wine containing 14% alcohol, or 8% if sold in the United States) – 1 tablespoon
☞ 1 tablespoon *aji no haha mirin* (more like sake; contains 10% alcohol)
☞ 1 tablespoon *shin-mirin* or *mirin-fuhmi*) (synthetic mirin; contains 1% alcohol)
☞ 1 1/2 tablespoons *aji-mirin* (contains sweetener and salt)

- 2 tablespoons each saké and granulated sugar gently simmered until the sugar dissolves, and the liquid is reduced by half
- 1 teaspoon sugar dissolved in 1 tablespoon saké or sweet sherry
- 2 teaspoons sugar (or 1 teaspoon honey) dissolved in 1 tablespoon unseasoned rice wine vinegar, white wine, vermouth, or hot water

MISO, DARK/KURO/MUGI/ INAKA/SENDAI/ HATCHO (Japanese red or dark brown fermented soybean-based paste) – 1 tablespoon

- 1/2 teaspoon beef bouillon (stock) granules or 1/2 beef bouillon cube
- 2 teaspoons Chinese fermented black beans/*dow see*, rinsed
- 1 tablespoon fermented soybean paste: Chinese *dou jiang*, Korean *doenjang*, or Filipino *tausi*
- 1 teaspoon Japanese organic whole-bean soy sauce/*marudaizu shoyu*, organic tamari, or other thick soy sauce

MISO, GLUTEN-FREE – 1 tablespoon

- 1 tablespoon rice *kome* miso, brown rice *genmai* miso, garbanzo bean miso, soybean *hatcho* miso, or golden millet miso

MISO, LIGHT/SHIRO/SHINSHU/SAIKYO (Japanese mild white or yellow fermented soybean-based paste) – 1 tablespoon

- 1 tablespoon (or more) low-sodium saikyo miso (contains 5% salt)
- 1 tablespoon *awase* miso (a mixture of white and red miso)
- 1 tablespoon Chinese yellow soybean paste/*mien see*, Vietnamese *tuong ot*, or Thai *tao jiaw*
- 1 1/2 teaspoons anchovy paste and 1/2 teaspoon tahini or sesame paste
- 1/2 scant teaspoon coarse sea salt

MISO, SOY-FREE – 1 tablespoon

- 1 tablespoon azuki miso, chickpea miso, or sweet brown rice miso

MITSUBA/JAPANESE PARSLEY/JAPANESE CHERVIL/TREFOIL, FRESH – 1 chopped tablespoon

- 2 teaspoons chopped fresh Italian flat-leaf parsley and 1 teaspoon chopped fresh celery leaves (for seasoning)

- ☞ 1 tablespoon chopped fresh cilantro or parsley (for garnish)
- ☞ 1 tablespoon watercress sprigs or daikon sprouts/*kaiware* (for garnish)
- ☞ 1 tablespoon chervil, or young stems and leafy tops of honewort/ wild chervil/*Cryptotaenia canadensis*

MIXED SPICE, SWEET (British spice blend) – 4 teaspoons
- ☞ 1 teaspoon each ground allspice, cloves, and coriander plus 1/2 teaspoon each grated nutmeg and ground Ceylon cinnamon
- ☞ 4 teaspoons pumpkin pie spice

MIYOGA *See MYOGA/GINGER BUD*

MIZUAME *See RICE MALT SWEETENER/RICE SYRUP/MIZUAME*

MOJO SAUCE (Cuban and Latin American condiment) – 1/3 cup (about)
Make Your Own Crush 4 minced garlic cloves to a paste with 1/2 teaspoon salt; then combine with 2 tablespoons olive oil, 1/2 teaspoon crumbled dried oregano (or ground cumin), and 1/3 cup sour orange juice. (Alternatively, use 1/4 cup lemon juice and 1 1/2 tablespoons orange juice in place of the sour orange juice.)

MOLASSES, DARK/REGULAR UNSULPHERED – 1 cup
- ☞ 1 cup cane syrup, dark honey, dark corn syrup, dark treacle, palm syrup/kithul treacle, or very dark, strong maple syrup

MOLASSES, LIGHT/MILD UNSULPHERED – 1 cup
- ☞ 1 cup *yacón* syrup, sorghum syrup, or Swedish dark syrup/*mörk sirap*
- ☞ 1/2 cup dark molasses and 1/2 cup light-colored corn syrup
- ☞ 3/4 cup dark brown sugar dissolved in 1/4 cup hot water (or other liquid in the recipe)

MOLASSES, MIDDLE EASTERN *See DATE MOLASSES; GRAPE MOLASSES; POMEGRANATE MOLASSES*

MOLASSES VINEGAR (dark, heavy vinegar) – 1 tablespoon
- ☞ 1 tablespoon balsamic vinegar

MOLE NEGRO SAUCE (Oaxacan-style seasoning) – 8 ounces
- ☞ 1/4 cup black mole paste/*mole negro* mixed with 3/4 cup beef broth
- ☞ 8 ounces brown poblano sauce
- ☞ 1/4 cup poblano paste/*mole poblano* mixed with 3/4 cup beef broth

MONGOLIAN FIVE-SPICE POWDER *See CHINESE FIVE-SPICE POWDER*

MORA CHILI *See CHIPOTLE MORA*

MORITA CHILI *See CHIPOTLE MORA*

MOSCATEL VINEGAR (Spanish) – 1 tablespoon
- ☞ 1 tablespoon white balsamic vinegar, champagne vinegar, or white wine vinegar

MOSTO COTTO/SABA/SAPA *See GRAPE MOLASSES*

MULATO CHILI (type of dried poblano) *See ANCHO CHILI*

MULBERRIES, WHITE, DRIED – 1 cup
- ☞ 1 cup red or black mulberries (larger and tarter)
- ☞ 1 cup golden raisins/sultanas or chopped dried figs

MUSCATEL SWEET WHITE WINE VINEGAR – 1 tablespoon
- ☞ 1 tablespoon sherry vinegar, champagne vinegar, or seasoned rice vinegar

MUSCOVADO SUGAR *See SUGAR, MUSCOVADO*

MUSHROOM BROTH – 1 quart
- ☞ 1 quart reduced-sodium vegetable broth plus 4 to 8 ounces cut-up mushrooms (portobello, cremini, shiitake) simmered partly covered for 20 to 25 minutes, then strained

☞ 2 to 3 teaspoons mushroom base added to 1 quart boiling water

MUSHROOM ESSENCE – 1/3 to 1/2 cup
☞ 1 pound fresh porcini or shiitake mushrooms frozen, thawed, and squeezed to extract the liquid (reserve the juiced mushrooms for another use)
☞ 1 pound fresh porcini or shiitake mushrooms and 2 cups water cooked for 15 minutes in a covered saucepan; strained, then gently boiled until reduced to one-quarter the volume

MUSHROOM POWDER/POWDERED MUSHROOMS – 2 tablespoons
See also PORCINI POWDER
☞ 6 tablespoons crumbled dried mushrooms, ground in a spice/coffee grinder or blender until powdery
☞ 8 ounces fresh mushrooms
☞ 1 (4-ounce) can whole or sliced mushrooms, drained

MUSHROOM POWDER, WILD – 1 teaspoon
☞ 1 ounce ground dried mushrooms

MUSHROOM SALT/BOT NEM (Vietnamese seasoning) – 1 teaspoon
☞ 1/2 teaspoon kosher salt (less flavor)

MUSHROOM SOUP, CANNED CREAM OF (for recipes) – 1 (10.5-ounce) can
☞ 1 cup thick homemade white sauce plus 1/2 cup chopped sautéed mushrooms (or 2 tablespoons mushroom powder)
☞ 8 ounces reduced-fat cream cheese stirred into 1/2 cup chopped sautéed mushrooms until smooth

MUSHROOMS, DRIED – 3 ounces
☞ 1 pound fresh mushrooms
☞ 10 ounces canned mushrooms, drained
Make Your Own Slice 1 pound fresh mushrooms, spread in a single layer on a baking sheet, and dry at 170°F until dry and crisp, about 2

hours, flipping halfway through. Store thoroughly dried mushrooms, tightly sealed, in the refrigerator or freezer for up to 12 months.

MU SHU/MOO SHU SAUCE (Chinese condiment) – 1 tablespoon
☞ 1 tablespoon hoisin sauce

MUSTARD, CHINESE/PAI-CHIEH – 1 tablespoon
Make Your Own Stir together 1 tablespoon mustard powder (Chinese *gai lat* or European Colman's) and 1 tablespoon cool water to form a paste. Cover and let sit for 15 minutes to develop the flavor.

MUSTARD, CREOLE – 1 tablespoon
☞ 1 tablespoon horseradish mustard
☞ 1 tablespoon whole-grain Dijon mustard plus a little horseradish or a dash of hot pepper sauce

MUSTARD, ENGLISH – 1 tablespoon
Make Your Own Stir together 1 tablespoon mustard powder (such as Colman's) and 2 1/2 teaspoons cold water (or flat beer) to form a paste. Cover and let sit for 15 minutes to mellow and develop the flavor.

MUSTARD, FLAVORED – 1/2 cup
☞ 1/2 cup prepared mustard plus one or more of the following: fresh or strained bottled horseradish; ground or cracked peppercorns; chili powder or minced fresh chili; grated fresh ginger; honey; or minced herbs such as tarragon, chives, parsley, or cilantro

MUSTARD, JAPANESE/NERIGARASHI – 1 tablespoon
☞ 1 tablespoon Chinese or English prepared hot mustard
Make Your Own Stir together 2 teaspoons Japanese powdered mustard/*konakarashii* (or Chinese or English mustard powder) and 1 tablespoon cold water to form a paste. Cover and let sit for 15 minutes to mellow and develop the flavor.

MUSTARD MAYONNAISE – 1 cup
- 1 cup mayonnaise plus 2 (or more) teaspoons prepared mustard, according to taste

MUSTARD OIL/MUSTARD SEED OIL/SHORSHER TEL (Indian seasoning) – 1 tablespoon
- 1 tablespoon vegetable oil plus 1/4 teaspoon dry mustard (add the powder when adding the recipe's liquid)

MUSTARD POWDER – 1 teaspoon
- 1 1/2 teaspoons yellow mustard seeds, ground with a mortar and pestle or a spice/coffee grinder until powdery
- 1 tablespoon prepared mustard; reduce the liquid called for in the recipe by 1 teaspoon (for wet mixtures)

MUSTARD, PREPARED – 1 tablespoon
Make Your Own Stir together1 tablespoon mustard powder, 1 teaspoon vinegar, 1 teaspoon cool water, and 1/4 to 1 teaspoon sugar or honey (optional) until smooth. Cover and let sit for 30 minutes to mellow and develop the flavor.
- 1/8 teaspoon (0.5 gram) xanthan gum (used as a vinaigrette emulsifier)
- 3/4 teaspoon mustard powder (used as a vinaigrette emulsifier)
- 1 tablespoon paprika paste or mayonnaise (used as a vinaigrette emulsifier)

MUSTARD, RUSSIAN/SAREPTSKAJA – 1 tablespoon
Make Your Own Stir together1 tablespoon mustard powder, 1 teaspoon sugar, 1/2 teaspoon ground black pepper, and 2 teaspoons hot water to form a paste. Cover and let sit for 15 minutes to mellow and develop the flavor.

MUSTARD SEEDS, YELLOW – 1 teaspoon
- 3/4 teaspoon mustard powder
- 1 tablespoon prepared mustard; reduce the liquid in the recipe by 1 teaspoon (for wet mixtures)

MYOGA/GINGER BUD/ZINGIBER MIOGA (Japanese and Korean seasoning) – 1 tablespoon shredded myoga
- 1 tablespoon minced young ginger with a pinch of minced lemongrass
- 1 tablespoon minced scallions with a pinch of grated fresh ginger
- 1 tablespoon shredded pickled ginger, rinsed

MYRTLE (Corsican and Sardinian seasoning) – 1 teaspoon
- 1 teaspoon crushed juniper berries

N

NAARTJIE PEEL, DRIED See TANGERINE/MANDARIN PEEL, DRIED

NAM PLA See THAI FISH SAUCE

NAM PRIK See THAI DIPPING SAUCE

NARANJA AGRIA See ORANGE, SOUR/BITTER/SEVILLE

NARANJILLA/LULO JUICE, FROZEN (Ecuadorian fruit juice) – 1 (14-ounce) package
- Pulp from 2 pounds thawed frozen naranjillas (about 8 large fruits), blended with 1 cup water and strained
- 14 ounces passion fruit juice

NARANJILLA/LULO PUREE, FROZEN (Ecuadorian fruit puree) – 1 (7-ounce) package
- Pulp from 6 thawed frozen naranjillas, lightly mashed
- 1 cup frozen passion fruit puree/*maracuyá*

NATTO (Japanese fermented soybean condiment) – 1/4 cup
- 1/4 cup fermented black beans or bean paste (less pungent)

NEEM LEAF See CURRY LEAF

NEPITELLA/CALAMINT/WILD TUSCAN MINT/CALAMINTHA NEPETA, FRESH (Italian seasoning) – 1 tablespoon chopped
- 2 teaspoons chopped fresh marjoram or oregano and 1 teaspoon chopped fresh mint

NEW MEXICO CHILI POWDER – 1/3 cup (about)

⊯ 2 1/2 tablespoons each Hungarian sweet and hot paprika

Make Your Own Toast 3 medium dried New Mexico chilis (about 3/4 ounce) in a preheated 350°F oven until puffed, about 6 minutes. Cool, remove the stems and seeds and process in a food processor to a powder. (Wear plastic gloves, avoid inhaling the fumes, and wear a mask if available.)

NIGELLA SEEDS/KALONJI/KALIJEERA/CHARNUSHKA (Indian and Middle Eastern seasoning) – 1 teaspoon

⊯ 1 teaspoon ajwain/ajowan seeds, black cumin seeds, black sesame seeds, caraway seeds, or cracked black pepper (for garnish, not taste)

NIGER OIL (Ethiopian) – 1 tablespoon

⊯ 1 tablespoon melted ghee, or browned clarified butter

NIHAIZU (Japanese base for dressings and marinades) – 1/4 cup

⊯ 2 tablespoons rice vinegar and Japanese soy sauce; or equal parts rice vinegar, soy sauce, and dashi

ÑORA PEPPERS, DRIED (Spanish smoked peppers) – 2 or 3

⊯ 2 or 3 dried choricero peppers
⊯ 1 dried ancho chili
⊯ 1 1/2 teaspoons smoked mild/sweet Spanish paprika

NORI FLAKES, SHREDS, OR POWDER/AO NORI/AO-NORIKO (Japanese seaweed seasoning and garnish for salads and raw vegetables)

⊯ Nori or wakame sheets, shredded and toasted in a dry skillet for 1 minute, then crushed or ground in a spice/coffee grinder
⊯ Roasted and seasoned nori/*ajitsuke-nori*, or nori with sesame seeds/*nori komi furikake*, shredded
⊯ Powdered sea lettuce/green laver powder
⊯ Buckwhip kelp, lightly crushed

NUOC CHAM *See VIETNAMESE SWEET-AND-SOUR DIPPING SAUCE*

NUOC NAM *See VIETNAMESE FISH SAUCE*

NUT BUTTER, PURE (no added fat) – 1 cup
Make Your Own Toast 2 cups nuts on a baking sheet in a preheated 350°F oven until fragrant, 7 to 10 minutes, stirring halfway through. Transfer the warm nuts to a food processor or high-powered blender and process until reduced to a paste. Cool, then put in a sterilized jar and store in the refrigerator; it will keep for up to 1 month. *See also ALMOND BUTTER; CASHEW BUTTER; COCONUT BUTTER; HEMP SEED BUTTER; PEANUT BUTTER; PECAN BUTTER; SOY NUT BUTTER; SUNFLOWER SEED BUTTER*

NUTELLA *See GIANDUJA*

NUT-FLAVORED LIQUEUR (such as Frangelico, Nocciole, or Noisette) – 1 tablespoon for cooking
⊳ 1/4 teaspoon almond, hazelnut, or walnut extract, plus 1 tablespoon water

NUTMEG, EAST INDIAN – 1 teaspoon fine ground
⊳ 2 teaspoons freshly grated East Indian nutmeg
⊳ 1 1/3 teaspoons freshly grated Grenadian West Indian nutmeg
⊳ 2/3 teaspoon fine ground Grenadian West Indian nutmeg
⊳ 3/4 teaspoon crumbled mace blade, or 1/2 teaspoon ground mace
⊳ 1 teaspoon ground allspice or cinnamon
⊳ 1 teaspoon apple pie spice or pumpkin pie spice

NUTMEG, GRENADIAN WEST INDIAN – 1 teaspoon fine ground
⊳ 2 teaspoons freshly grated Grenadian nutmeg
⊳ 1 tablespoon freshly grated East Indian nutmeg
⊳ 1 1/3 teaspoons fine ground East Indian nutmeg

O

OKONOMIYAKI SAUCE (Japanese condiment) – 1 tablespoon
- 1 tablespoon tonkatsu sauce or yakisoba sauce

OLD BAY SEASONING (seafood seasoning mix) – 1 tablespoon
- 1 tablespoon crab boil spice mix
- 1 tablespoon Cajun seasoning
- 1 teaspoon celery salt, 1/2 teaspoon paprika, 1/2 teaspoon ground coriander, and a scant teaspoon each of ground cayenne pepper and ground cinnamon

OLIVE OIL, EXTRA-VIRGIN, COLD PRESSED (free oleic acid no more than 0.8%) – 1 cup
- 1 cup unrefined avocado oil
- 1 cup virgin olive oil (higher in acidity)

OLIVE OIL, REGULAR/MILD/PURE (free oleic acid no more than 3%) – 1 cup
- 1 cup green olives or olive pits added to 1 cup canola oil and left, covered, 2 or 3 days for the oil to develop flavor (Use immediately or store it, tightly covered, in the refrigerator for no more than a few days.)
- 3/4 cup canola oil, or other neutral tasting oil, plus 1/4 cup extra-virgin olive oil

OLIVE PASTE, BLACK/KALAMATA OLIVE SPREAD/OLIVADA – 1/2 cup
Make Your Own Pulse in a food processor 1 cup brine-cured pitted black olives, such as Gaeta, Alfonso, or Kalamata, and 2 tablespoons (or more) extra-virgin olive oil until reduced to a paste. Transfer to a small, sterilized jar, top with a thin layer of olive oil and store, tightly covered, in the refrigerator; it will keep for up to 3 weeks.

OLIVE POWDER, KALAMATA – 1 cup (about)
Make Your Own Spread 2 cups pitted Kalamata olives on a parchment-lined baking sheet and dry in a preheated 200°F oven until hard and crisp, about 8 hours. Alternatively, microwave the olives on High at 2-minute intervals until brittle. Cool, then grind in a spice/coffee grinder. Store in an airtight container for up to 2 weeks.

OLIVES, OIL-CURED
Make Your Own Place black or green unpitted olives in a small, sterilized jar and cover with olive oil. Store, tightly covered, in the refrigerator; they will last for up to 2 months.

ONION JUICE
- Fresh onion squeezed through a garlic press, or grated on large holes of a box grater then pressed through a fine-mesh sieve

ONION POWDER – 1 teaspoon
- 2 1/2 tablespoons jarred minced onion
- 1/2 cup chopped fresh onion
- 1 tablespoon dried minced onion, onion flakes, or instant minced onion
- 1 teaspoon onion salt; reduce the salt in the recipe by 1 teaspoon

ONION SALT – 1 tablespoon
- 1 teaspoon onion powder mixed with 2 teaspoons kosher or coarse sea salt

ONION SOUP MIX, DRY – 2 scant tablespoons (1/4 packet soup mix)
- 1 teaspoon instant beef bouillon granules (or crumbled bouillon cube), mixed with 1 tablespoon instant minced onion and a pinch of parsley flakes (optional)

ONION SOUP, CANNED – 1 (10.5-ounce can)
- 1 (15-ounce) can beef broth plus 3 tablespoons dried onions, simmered until the onions are soft

ONIONS, FRIED, CANNED – 1 cup for casserole topping

⊨ 1 cup Vietnamese packaged fried shallots/*hahn phi/chiên hahn huong*
⊨ 1 cup crushed onion-flavored soy crisps

ORANGE BITTERS (Fee Brothers, Pomeranzen, Regans', or Angostura Orange) – 1 dash

⊨ 1/16 teaspoon orange extract

ORANGE, BLOOD, JUICE – 1 cup

⊨ 1 cup Florida orange juice plus 1 tablespoon grenadine
⊨ 3/4 cup plus 2 tablespoons Florida orange juice and 2 tablespoons unsweetened pomegranate juice

ORANGE CITRUS OIL/PURE ORANGE OIL – 1/8 teaspoon

⊨ 1/2 teaspoon orange extract
⊨ 1 or 2 teaspoons finely grated orange zest

ORANGE FLOWER WATER/ORANGE BLOSSOM WATER – 1 tablespoon

⊨ 1/2 teaspoon orange extract
⊨ 1/16 to 1/8 teaspoon orange citrus oil, such as Boyajian (double the amount for a cooked dish)
⊨ 2 teaspoons finely grated orange zest
⊨ 1/3 teaspoon Sicilian flower essence/*Fiori di Sicilia* (has vanilla and orange aroma)

Make Your Own Steep 2 teaspoons crushed or minced dried orange peel (preferably sour) for 2 days in 1 cup sweet, nonsparkling white wine. Strain through a fine-mesh sieve; discard the peel. Use 1 tablespoon for each tablespoon in the recipe. Store in a sterilized jar in the refrigerator up to 7 days. Makes 1 cup.

ORANGE JUICE CONCENTRATE – 2 tablespoons

Make Your Own: Gently boil 1 cup fresh orange juice until reduced to 2 tablespoons, 10 to 12 minutes; or microwave it on High in a 4-cup glass measuring cup coated with cooking spray until reduced to 2 tablespoons.

ORANGE JUICE POWDER – 1 tablespoon
- 2 tablespoons orange zest
- 1 tablespoon orange juice; reduce the liquid in the recipe by 1 scant tablespoon

ORANGE LIQUEUR/ORANGE-FLAVORED SPIRIT (Bauchant, Citrónge, Cointreau, Curaçao, Gran Torres, Grand Marnier, Leopold Bros., triple sec) – 1 tablespoon for cooking
- 1/2 teaspoon orange extract and 2 1/2 teaspoons water
- 1 1/2 teaspoons frozen orange juice concentrate and 1 1/2 teaspoons water
- 1 tablespoon fresh orange juice and 1/2 teaspoon finely grated orange zest (or 1/4 teaspoon orange extract)
- 1 teaspoon finely grated orange zest

ORANGE PEEL, DRIED GRANULATED – 1 tablespoon
- Strips of orange peel (removed with a paring knife or vegetable peeler and any white pith scraped away) dried at room temperature for 3 to 7 days, or in the microwave on High for 2 to 3 minutes; crushed or ground as needed
- 1 tablespoon finely grated fresh orange zest
- 2 teaspoons grated candied orange peel; remove sugar in recipe by 1/2 teaspoon
- 1/2 teaspoon orange extract
- 1 tablespoon grated lime zest

ORANGE, SOUR/BITTER/SEVILLE (high-acid orange) – 1
- 1 calamondin/*kalamansi*, or 3 kumquats

ORANGE, SOUR/BITTER/SEVILLE, JUICE – 1 tablespoon
- Juice of 3 large kumquats
- 1 teaspoon each lemon juice, grapefruit juice, and sweet orange juice
- 1 1/2 teaspoons each lime or lemon juice and sweet orange juice
- 2 teaspoons sweet orange juice and 1 teaspoon distilled white vinegar (for savory dishes only)

ORANGE, SOUR/BITTER/SEVILLE, ZEST – 1 tablespoon
☞ 2 teaspoons grated orange zest, and 1 teaspoon grated lemon zest

ORANGE ZEST – 1 tablespoon
☞ 1 teaspoon dried minced orange peel, softened for 15 minutes in 1 tablespoon water
☞ 1 1/2 teaspoons orange extract
☞ 2 tablespoons fresh orange juice
☞ 1/2 teaspoon orange citrus oil, such as Boyajian (Double the amount for a cooked dish.)
☞ 1 tablespoon grated or minced candied lemon peel (Rinse to remove the sugar before grating or reduce the sugar in the recipe by 1/2 teaspoon; for easier grating or mincing, pulse with the flour or sugar called for in the recipe.)

OREGANO, CUBAN/INDIAN BORAGE/SPANISH THYME (Caribbean seasoning) – 1 tablespoon fresh or dried
☞ 1 tablespoon fresh or dried sage

OREGANO, GREEK/RIGANI/ORIGANUM HERACLEOTICUM, FRESH – 1 tablespoon chopped
☞ 2 to 3 teaspoons cultivated dried rigani, crumbled
☞ 2 tablespoons dried Italian oregano, preferably wild mountain, crumbled (milder)

OREGANO, MEDITERRANEAN, FRESH – 3 sprigs (1 tablespoon chopped)
☞ 1 teaspoon crumbled dried Mediterranean oregano (Italian, Sicilian, Turkish)
☞ 1/2 teaspoon powdered Mediterranean oregano
☞ 1 scant tablespoon chopped fresh Mexican oregano, or 1 scant teaspoon dried (more pungent)
☞ 1 1/2 tablespoons chopped fresh sweet marjoram, or 1 1/2 teaspoons dried (milder and more delicate; add towards the end of cooking)
☞ 2 teaspoons chopped fresh thyme, or 1/2 teaspoon dried

☞ 1 teaspoon dried Italian or Greek seasoning
☞ 3 tablespoons chopped fresh bee balm/*Monarda didyma*

OREGANO, MEXICAN/OAXACAN/PUERTO RICAN, DRIED – 1 sprig (1 teaspoon broken leaf, crumbled)
☞ Scant 1/2 teaspoon powdered (ground) Mexican oregano
☞ 1 tablespoon fresh Greek or Spanish oregano
☞ 1 tablespoon chopped fresh pot/Sicilian marjoram, or 1 teaspoon dried
☞ 1/2 teaspoon each dried Mediterranean oregano and dried marjoram

ORGEAT SYRUP (cocktail flavoring) – 1/4 cup
☞ 1/4 cup simple syrup (*See SYRUP, SIMPLE*) flavored with 1/4 teaspoon almond extract, plus a few drops of rose water or orange-flower water, if available

OYSTER SAUCE (Chinese cooking condiment) – 1 tablespoon
☞ 1 tablespoon Thai oyster sauce/*nam man hoi* (less salty; more oyster flavor)
☞ 1 tablespoon vegetarian oyster-flavored sauce or Lee Kum Kee Vegetarian Stir-Fry Sauce (contains mushrooms and vegetable proteins)
☞ 1 1/2 teaspoons mushroom or dark soy sauce and 1 1/2 teaspoons black bean sauce
☞ 1 teaspoon Asian fish sauce mixed with 2 teaspoons kecap manis or Chinese or Thai sweet black soy sauce
☞ 1 tablespoon teriyaki sauce (sweeter)
☞ 1 teaspoon Maggi Seasoning

P

PALM KERNEL OIL (Southeast Asian mild, light-colored oil) – 1 cup
- ☞ 1 cup refined melted coconut oil or mild-flavored olive oil

PALM OIL, RED/ PALM FRUIT OIL/DENDÊ (Brazilian and West African reddish colored oil) – 1 cup
- ☞ 1 cup achiote-infused oil (Heat 1 cup corn, coconut, or peanut oil with 1/4 cup achiote seeds until beginning to bubble; cool and strain, discarding the seeds. Alternatively, color the oil with achiote powder, mild paprika, or ground turmeric; let it sit for 30 minutes, then strain off the oil.)
- ☞ 1 cup coconut oil (for baking)
- ☞ 1 cup strong-flavored olive oil or creamy unsweetened peanut butter (for finishing)

PALM SUGAR, LIGHT/COCONUT PALM SUGAR (Southeast Asian unrefined sugar) –1(1-inch) piece chopped or shaved See also JAGGERY
- ☞ 2 tablespoons coconut sugar crystals or Sucanat
- ☞ 1 tablespoon each maple sugar and light brown sugar
- ☞ 2 tablespoons firmly packed light brown sugar
- ☞ 4 teaspoons granulated sugar

PALM SUGAR SYRUP, HEAVY – 1 cup
- ☞ 2 cups light palm sugar, melted over very low heat until liquefied (add a little maple syrup if desired)
- ☞ 1 cup each shaved palm sugar and water, simmered until thick and syrupy
- ☞ 1 cup golden syrup, such as Lyle's

PALM SUGAR SYRUP, LIGHT – 1 cup
- ☞ 1 cup each shaved (or jarred) palm sugar and water heated until sugar is dissolved

☞ 1 cup simple/stock syrup

PALM SYRUP *See COCONUT NECTAR*

PALM VINEGAR/COCONUT PALM VINEGAR/SIRKA/SUKA NG NIYOG (Indian, Filipino, and Southeast Asian) – 1 tablespoon
☞ 1 tablespoon unseasoned mild rice vinegar, such as Japanese
☞ 2 teaspoons champagne vinegar, coconut vinegar, or white wine vinegar and 1 teaspoon water
☞ 1 1/2 teaspoons each cider vinegar and water

PANANG CURRY PASTE (Thai seasoning) – 1 tablespoon
☞ 1 tablespoon red curry paste (stronger-tasting)

PANCAKE SYRUP – 1 cup *See also MAPLE SYRUP*
☞ 1 cup firmly packed brown sugar, 2/3 cup water plus a pinch of salt, simmered until syrupy, 15 to 20 minutes, stirring occasionally (cool before serving)
☞ 1 cup dark corn syrup, brown rice syrup, barley malt syrup, birch syrup, golden syrup, light or dark agave syrup/nectar, or cane or sorghum syrup, microwaved until warm and pourable
☞ 1 cup jam, jelly, preserves, or fruit spread, melted in the microwave with a little juice or water
☞ 1 1/2 to 2 cups juice from canned fruit, gently boiled until syrupy
☞ 1 1/2 to 2 cups apple cider, gently boiled until syrupy
☞ 2 cups maple sugar and 1 cup water, simmered until the sugar is dissolved and the mixture is syrupy

PANCH PHORON *See BENGALI FIVE-SPICE MIX*

PANDAN/PANDANUS FLOWER ESSENCE *See KEWRA/KEVDA*

PANDAN/PANDANUS LEAF/US/BAI TOEY/LA DUA/DAUN PANDAN (Southeast Asian flavoring and coloring agent) – 1 fresh, frozen, or dried leaf *See also KEWRA ESSENCE*
☞ 1/2 teaspoon pandan syrup, powder, or paste

☞ 2 or 3 drops pandan extract or *kewra* essence and 1 small drop green food coloring (optional)

PANDAN/PANDANUS WATER (Southeast Asian flavoring agent) – 1 tablespoon
☞ 1 or 2 drops pandan essence (or food-grade pure rose extract/essence) and green food coloring
Make Your Own Cut 2 or 3 fresh or frozen pandan leaves into pieces and pulverize in a blender with 1/3 cup water. Strain through a fine sieve, then measure out 1 tablespoon liquid.

PANELA (Latin American loaf sugar) See PILONCILLO

PAPAYA LEAF/PAPALO/PAPALOQUELITE (Mexican seasoning herb) – 1 small leaf (1 tablespoon minced)
☞ 2 teaspoons finely minced cilantro and 1 teaspoon finely minced watercress
☞ 1 generous tablespoon finely minced *pipicha*

PAPELÓN (Venezuelan unrefined loaf sugar) See PILONCILLO/PANELA/PANOCHA

PAPRIKA OIL (South American seasoning and coloring oil) – 1/4 cup
Make Your Own Heat 1/4 vegetable oil and 4 teaspoons sweet Spanish paprika over medium-low heat until hot, 2 to 3 minutes. Strain through a cheesecloth-lined sieve; discard the solids. (For a zestier oil, add 1/2 teaspoon ground cayenne pepper.)

PAPRIKA PASTE (Turkey) – 1 tablespoon
☞ 1 tablespoon mild red pepper paste (or 2 jarred roasted red piquillo peppers drained and pureed) plus mild/sweet smoked paprika to taste

PAPRIKA, GENERIC – 1 teaspoon for garnish and color only
☞ 3/4 teaspoon New Mexico chili powder

☞ 1/2 teaspoon ground turmeric, preferably Alleppey, plus a small pinch of ground cayenne pepper

☞ 1 teaspoon dried tomato powder or Australian dried bush tomato/ *akudjura* powder

☞ 1 teaspoon Asian fermented black bean powder (darker color)

PAPRIKA, HUNGARIAN HOT – 1 teaspoon

☞ 3/4 teaspoon mild/sweet paprika and 1/4 teaspoon ground cayenne pepper, or another hot chili powder

☞ 1 teaspoon Aleppo or Maras chili powder

☞ 1/2 teaspoon ground cayenne pepper

PAPRIKA, HUNGARIAN MILD/SWEET/KULONLEGES – 1 teaspoon for garnish

☞ 1 teaspoon Spanish unsmoked sweet paprika/*pimentón dulce,* mild Basque chili powder/*piment d'espelette,* or Indian paprika/*kashmiri mirch*

PAPRIKA, SPANISH HOT SMOKED/PIMENTÓN DE LA VERA PICANTE – 1/2 teaspoon

☞ 1/4 teaspoon each chipotle chili powder and Hungarian mild/sweet paprika

☞ 1/2 teaspoon Hungarian hot paprika (replace all or part of the salt in the recipe with smoked salt, if available)

☞ 1/2 teaspoon Spanish mild/sweet smoked paprika and 1/8 teaspoon ground cayenne pepper

☞ 1/4 teaspoon ground cayenne pepper or chili de árbol powder

PAPRIKA, SPANISH MILD SMOKED/PIMENTÓN DE LA VERA DULCE – 1/2 teaspoon

☞ 1/2 teaspoon choricero powder

☞ 1/4 teaspoon smoked salt and 1/2 teaspoon mild/sweet California, Hungarian, or Indian paprika; reduce the salt in the recipe by 1/4 teaspoon

☞ Small pinch of ground Lapsang Souchong or Scottish breakfast tea leaves added to Hungarian mild/sweet paprika

☞ 1 teaspoon mild smoked paprika paste

PARMESAN CHEESE (Italian and domestic hard, dry, cow's milk cheese) – 1 ounce
☞ 1 ounce Grana Padano, aged Asiago, or Pecorino Romano (sharper-tasting)

PARMESAN CHEESE, VEGAN – 1 cup
☞ 1 cup nutritional yeast powder or flakes (has a cheesy taste)
☞ 5 ounces hazelnuts, 1 chopped garlic clove, plus a pinch of sea salt pulsed in a food processor until finely chopped (has a savory taste; store, tightly sealed, in the refrigerator)

PARMIGIANO-REGGIANO (Italian hard aged cow's milk cheese) – 1 ounce
☞ 1 ounce Grana Padano (milder, less expensive)
☞ 1 ounce Pecorino gran cru, Pecorino Romano, Pecorino Toscano, Kefalotyri Reggianito (sheep's milk cheeses; sharper)
☞ 1 ounce aged Asiago, aged Cotija/*queso añejo*, aged Gouda, aged *mizithra*, dry Jack, domestic Parmesan, Romano, or Sbrinz (milder)
☞ 1 ounce gluten-free Parmesan, such as Soyco

PASILLA CHILI/PASILLA NEGRO (Mexican dried chilaca pepper) – 1
☞ 1 dried ancho, mulato, or New Mexico chili
☞ 1 tablespoon ancho or New Mexico chili powder
☞ 1 tablespoon ancho paste
☞ 1/2 teaspoon ground cayenne pepper

PASILLA DE OAXACA CHILI/PASILLA OAXAQUEÑO, DRIED – 1
☞ 2 dried mora chilis/*chipotles moras* (purplish-red color)
☞ 1 teaspoon chipotle chili powder or paste
☞ 2 canned or jarred chipotles in adobo

PASSATA/SUGOCASA (Italian jarred tomato pulp) – 16 ounces
☞ 32 ounces whole canned tomatoes, blended or processed, then strained (Alternatively, drain the tomatoes, then puree or crush them.)

- 2 pounds large fresh plum tomatoes, halved, seeded, excess juice expelled, then rubbed against the coarsest holes on a box or sheet grater; skins discarded
- 2 cups thick tomato sauce

PEANUT BUTTER, SMOOTH – 1 cup
- 1 cup sunflower butter/sunbutter/sunflower seed spread
- 1 cup smooth almond butter, cashew butter, hemp butter, or toasted sesame tahini
- 1 cup soy nut butter or golden peabutter (legume flavor)
- 2 cups dehydrated peanut butter powder mixed with 1 cup water (less calories and fat)

Make Your Own Toast 2 cups skinless peanuts on a baking sheet in a preheated 350°F oven until fragrant, 7 to 10 minutes, stirring halfway through. Transfer to a food processor while warm and process until reduced to a paste, about 15 minutes, scraping down the sides of the bowl as needed. (For chunky butter, stir in 1/4 cup chopped peanuts.) Store it in a sterilized jar in the refrigerator; it will keep for up to 3 months.

PEANUT DIPPING SAUCE (Southeast Asian condiment) – 2/3 cup
Make Your Own Stir together 1/4 cup peanut butter, 1/4 cup warm water, and 1 tablespoon each soy sauce, seasoned rice vinegar, and Chinese chili-garlic sauce.
Or
Heat 1/3 cup smooth peanut butter, 1/3 cup well-shaken canned coconut milk, and 1 teaspoon Sriracha over low heat, stirring until smooth, about 5 minutes.

PEANUT OIL, ROASTED – 2 tablespoons
- 2 tablespoons virgin peanut oil (has a roasted flavor)
- 1 tablespoon toasted sesame oil/Chinese sesame oil (has a stronger flavor)
- Cold-pressed peanut oil (has a milder flavor)

PEANUTS – *1 cup*
➻ 1 cup wild jungle peanuts (heirloom variety from the Amazon; does not contain aflatoxin found in American peanuts)

PEANUTS, DRY-ROASTED – *1 cup*
Make Your Own Roast 1 cup raw peanuts on a baking sheet in a preheated 325°F oven until fragrant, 5 to 6 minutes; then rub in a cotton kitchen towel to remove the skins.

PECAN BUTTER – *1 cup*
Make Your Own Process 2 cups raw or toasted pecans in a food processor until reduced to a paste, 10 to 15 minutes, scraping down the sides of the bowl as needed. Store, refrigerated, in a sterilized jar for up to 1 month.

PECTIN, INSTANT, POWDERED – *0.6 ounce (enough for two 1/2-pint jars)*
➻ 1 (0.4-ounce) packet regular powdered pectin, 1 1/3 cups sugar, and 1 tablespoon lemon juice; cooked until jam reaches the desired jel (will be sweeter)

PECTIN, REGULAR, POWDERED – *0.4 ounce (enough for two 1/2-pint jars)*
➻ 1 1/2 ounces regular liquid pectin (Add after the mixture is brought to a full boil, bring again to a full boil, and boil for 1 minute to activate the pectin.)
➻ 1 (0.6-ounce) packet instant powdered pectin (Reduce the sugar by half and prepare following the package directions.)
➻ 4 teaspoons powdered apple pectin (Add after the mixture is brought to a full boil, bring again to a full boil, and boil for 3 minutes to activate the pectin.)
➻ 1/4 cup bottled lemon juice, if not already included in recipe (for jams and preserves; will also reduce the amount of sugar required)
➻ 1 slightly underripe quince, peeled and chopped (for jams and preserves)
➻ 1 crab apple or small tart green apple, peeled and grated (for jams and preserves)

☞ One-quarter of the fruit underripe and three-quarters fruit fully ripe (for jams and preserves)
☞ Increase the cooking time until the jam reaches the desired gel (will result in reduced volume).

PEKMEZ/PETIMEZI (Turkish sweetener) *See GRAPE MOLASSES*

PEPPERCORNS, BLACK (Malabar or Tellicherry) – 1 teaspoon/34 to 60 peppercorns
☞ 1 teaspoon white peppercorns (Muntok or Sarawak), or 1 1/2 teaspoons ground white pepper (for Chinese food, light-colored food, sauces, and soups; less aromatic)
☞ 1 teaspoon French *mignonette* pepper (a mix of black and white pepper)
☞ 2 dried Indian/Indonesian long peppers/*pippali* (milder and larger; use whole in cooking)
☞ 1/8 to 1/4 teaspoon dried Tasmanian pepperberries/mountain pepper (best for slow-cooked dishes; hotter; dark red color)
☞ 1 teaspoon ground papaya seeds (well-washed and well-dried papparsaya seeds ground in a pepper mill)
☞ 1/4 teaspoon ground cayenne pepper (hotter)

PEPPERCORNS, CRACKED – 1 tablespoon
☞ 1 to 1 1/2 tablespoons whole peppercorns split or cracked into 2 or 3 pieces with a pestle or heavy food can

PEPPERCORNS, CRUSHED – 1 tablespoon
☞ 1 1/2 tablespoons whole peppercorns crushed coarsely with a pestle; or folded in plastic wrap and crushed with a meat tenderizer, rolling pin, or heavy skillet (sift to remove the pepper dust)

PEPPERCORNS, CUBEB/TAILED PEPPER (Indonesian seasoning) – 1 tablespoon
☞ 1 tablespoon allspice berries

☞ 2 teaspoons coarsely crushed black peppercorns mixed with a few toasted crushed Sichuan peppercorns

PEPPERCORNS, GREEN BRINED – 1 tablespoon
☞ 2 teaspoons air-dried green peppercorns, softened for 30 minutes in 1 tablespoon hot meat stock (or water) and 1 tablespoon distilled white vinegar
☞ 1 tablespoon rinsed brined capers
☞ 1 tablespoon dried pink peppercorns

PEPPERCORNS, GREEN, FRESH – 1 tablespoon
☞ 1 tablespoon freeze-dried green peppercorns (roast to enhance the aroma)
☞ 1 tablespoon canned or brined green peppercorns, drained and rinsed
☞ 1 teaspoon black peppercorns (more pungent)

PEPPERCORNS, SICHUAN/SZECHUAN – 1 teaspoon
☞ 1/4 teaspoon sansho powder/*kona-zansho* and 1/4 teaspoon ground black pepper
☞ 1 teaspoon *timur* (Nepali peppercorns)
☞ 1/4 teaspoon crushed dried Tasmanian pepperberries/mountain pepper
☞ 1/2 teaspoon black peppercorns and 1/8 teaspoon finely grated lemon zest

PEPPER, MELEGUETA See GRAINS OF PARADISE

PEPPERMINT, FRESH – 1/4 cup chopped
☞ 1 tablespoon dried peppermint, or leaves from 2 to 3 peppermint tea bags

PEPPERONCINI/PEPERONCINI/TUSCAN PEPPER, DRIED (Italian mild chili pepper) – 1 or 2
☞ 1/2 to 1 teaspoon crushed red chili, such as piquin; or crushed red pepper flakes

PEPPER PASTE *See RED PEPPER PASTE, HOT; RED PEPPER PASTE, MILD*

PEPPER-PEPPER SAUCE (West African condiment) – 1 tablespoon
- 1 teaspoon olive oil added to 2 teaspoons Louisiana-style hot sauce, such as Tabasco, Trappey's, or Crystal

PEPPER, ROASTED RED – 1 large (1 cup roasted, peeled, and chopped)
- 1 cup jarred pimientos, drained and blotted dry
- 2 jarred roasted red peppers (bell, Italian frying, or Hungarian)

PEPPER VINEGAR (Southern U.S. condiment) – 1 cup
Make Your Own Wash and dry 2 to 4 ounces small fresh red or green chilis, such as cayenne, de árbol, Korean finger-hot, serrano, Tabasco, or Thai. Pack into a sterilized jar and add 1 cup distilled white vinegar plus a pinch of salt. Cover tightly and keep in a cool, dark place for at least 3 weeks, then strain and refrigerate. It will keep for up to 1 year.

PEQUÍN/PIQUÍN CHILIS, DRIED (Mexican) – 3 or 4
- 3 or 4 tepín/chiltepín, cayenne, serrano, or de árbol chilis
- 1 teaspoon ground cayenne pepper or chiltepín powder

PERILLA LEAF *See SHISO, GREEN*

PERI PERI SEASONING (North African-style hot chili spice blend) – 1 tablespoon
- 1 tablespoon berbere or harissa powder
- 1 tablespoon ground cayenne pepper

PERSILLADE (French seasoning) – 1/4 cup
- 3 tablespoons finely chopped flat-leaf parsley mixed with 2 finely minced garlic cloves

PICKAPEPPA SAUCE (Caribbean condiment) – 1 tablespoon
- 1 tablespoon steak sauce or ketchup plus a dash of Louisiana-style hot sauce, such as Tabasco, Trappey's, or Crystal (for the thick sauce)
- Tabasco or habañero pepper sauce (for the thin hot sauce)

PICKLE RELISH – 2 tablespoons
➢ 2 tablespoons finely chopped pickles plus a little pickle brine if necessary

PICKLED LEMONS/LAMOUN MAKBOUSS/MAKDOUS (Middle Eastern condiment) See also PRESERVED LEMON
Make Your Own Slice lemons, preferably organic, into 1/2-inch slices and freeze overnight. Sprinkle heavily with kosher salt, then let drain in a colander until softened, about 8 hours. Layer in a glass jar, sprinkling each layer with mild/sweet paprika; cover with olive oil and refrigerate; they will keep for at least 5 days.

PICKLED PORK (Creole seasoning) – 8 ounces
➢ 8 ounces ham hocks or pickled pig's feet

PICKLES
Make Your Own Add thinly sliced cucumbers to the boiled leftover brine from a jar of pickles, then refrigerate for 24 hours; they will keep for up to 1 week.

PICO DE GALLO (Mexican relish) – 1 cup
➢ 1 cup chunky bottled salsa

PICO DE GALLO SEASONING (Mexican) – 1 tablespoon
➢ 1 tablespoon chili-lime powder or mild chili powder, such as New Mexico or ancho

PILONCILLO/PANELA/PANOCHA (Mexican and South American unrefined cane sugar) – 1 (8-ounce) cone or 8 (1-ounce) cones See also JAGGERY
➢ 1 1/4 cups Indian palm sugar/jaggery/gur
➢ 1 cup dark brown sugar and 2 tablespoons unsulphured molasses
➢ 3/4 cup granulated sugar and 5 tablespoons molasses

PIMENT d'ESPELETTE (mild red Basque chili powder) – 1 teaspoon
➢ 3/4 teaspoon Chilean smoked chili powder/merquén
➢ 1/2 teaspoon Basque chili paste/crème de piment d'Espelette

- ⇝ 1 teaspoon Aleppo, Urfa, ancho, or New Mexico chili powder
- ⇝ 1 teaspoon medium-hot California, Hungarian, or Spanish paprika/ *pimentón*
- ⇝ 1/2 teaspoon ground cayenne pepper

PIMENTO BERRIES, DRIED *See ALLSPICE, JAMAICAN*

PIMENTÓN *See PAPRIKA, SPANISH HOT SMOKED; PAPRIKA, SPANISH MILD/SWEET SMOKED*

PIMIENTO, CANNED OR JARRED – 4 ounces (1/2 cup)
- ⇝ 1 fresh red bell pepper, roasted, peeled, cored, and cut into thin strips
- ⇝ 2 tablespoons red bell pepper flakes softened in 1/4 cup warm water, about 15 minutes
- ⇝ 1/2 cup bright red tomato slivers from a peeled and seeded plum tomato (add just before serving)

PINEAPPLE VINEGAR – 1 tablespoon
- ⇝ 2 teaspoons cider vinegar and 1 teaspoon water or rice vinegar

PINE NUTS/PIGNOLI/PINYON/PIÑON – 1 cup shelled
- ⇝ 1 cup sunflower seed kernels, pumpkin seed kernels/*pepitas*, hemp-seeds, or slivered blanched almonds

PIPIÁN (Mexican cooking sauce) – 1 cup
- ⇝ 1 ounce pipián powder/*pipián rápido* added to 1 cup chicken broth
- ⇝ 1 cup Mexican red chili sauce or enchilada sauce, and 1 1/2 teaspoons smooth peanut butter

PIPICHA (Mexican herb) – 1 tablespoon finely minced leaf
- ⇝ 1 tablespoon finely minced cilantro
- ⇝ 1 (scant tablespoon finely minced papaya leaf/*papalo*

PIPPALI *See LONG PEPPER, INDONESIAN*

P

PIQUILLO PEPPERS, FIRE-ROASTED (Spanish deep red sweet peppers) – 2
- 1 roasted and peeled sweet red pepper, preferably Greek Florina, and a small pinch of mild/sweet smoked paprika
- 1 roasted and peeled red bell pepper or pimiento chili, and a small pinch of smoked salt (or 1 or 2 drops liquid smoke)
- 2 jarred roasted red peppers and a small pinch of ancho chili powder

PIRI-PIRI CHILI POWDER – 1 teaspoon
- 1 teaspoon cayenne, tepin/chiltepin, Thai, or other hot chili powder

PIRI-PIRI CHILIS, DRIED (African and Portuguese) – 3 or 4
- 3 or 4 cayenne, bird's eye, pequin/piquin, or tepín/chiltepín chilis
- 1/2 to 1 teaspoon piri-piri powder, ground cayenne pepper, or crushed red pepper flakes

PIRI-PIRI SAUCE (African and Portuguese condiment) – 1 cup
- 1/2 cup each Sriracha and Louisiana-style hot sauce, such as Trappey's, Tabasco, or Crystal

Make Your Own Combine 1 cup heated olive oil, 1/4 cup chopped fresh red chilis, such as piri piri or bird's eye, 2 minced garlic cloves, and 1/2 teaspoon salt. Cover and let sit at room temperature for 24 or more hours. Strain the oil and discard the solids. Store, refrigerated, in a sterilized bottle or jar; it will keep for up to 2 months. (Wear plastic gloves when handling the chilis.)

PISTACHIO OIL – 1 cup
- 1 cup almond oil or extra light olive oil

PISTACHIO PASTE/PASTA DI PASTACCHIO (Italian nut paste) – 1 cup
- 1 cup hazelnut paste/*pasta di nocciola*
- 1 cup smooth-style almond butter; or creamy, unsweetened peanut butter

Make Your Own Process 1 1/4 cups raw shelled pistachios and 1/4 cup neutral-tasting vegetable oil in a high-speed blender until smooth.

PISTOU (French pesto) – 2/3 cup
Make Your Own Process 2 cups fresh basil leaves, 2 or 3 garlic cloves, 1/3 cup olive oil, and 1/4 teaspoon kosher salt in a food processor or blender until nearly smooth. (For more color add a few tablespoons fresh parsley to the basil, and for more texture fold in 2 tablespoons Parmesan cheese at the end.)

PIXIAN CHILI BEAN SAUCE See SICHUAN CHILI BEAN PASTE

PIZZA SAUCE – 1 cup
Make Your Own Combine 1 (15-ounce) can crushed tomatoes with 1 1/2 to 2 teaspoons pizza seasoning, or 1 teaspoon Italian seasoning plus 1/8 teaspoon garlic powder. (For a thicker sauce, puree the mixture until almost smooth, then simmer, uncovered, until thickened, about 30 minutes.)
Or
Drain half of 1 (28-ounce) can whole peeled tomatoes (preferably San Marzano), then press through a food mill, and combine with 2 to 3 teaspoons olive oil, 1/4 teaspoon each salt and crumbled dried oregano, and 1 minced garlic clove (optional).

PIZZA SEASONING – 1 tablespoon
- 1 teaspoon Italian seasoning
- 1 teaspoon each dried thyme and granulated garlic, and 1/2 teaspoon each ground fennel and dried oregano

PLUM SAUCE/DUCK SAUCE/MEI JIANG (Chinese condiment) – 1/2 cup
- 1/2 cup mango chutney, thinned with a little vinegar
- 1/4 cup apricot or peach jam, 1/4 cup plum jam, 1 tablespoon cider vinegar, and 1/2 teaspoon sugar simmered until slightly thickened, about 5 minutes (the sauce will thicken further as it cools)
- 1/2 cup Chinese lemon sauce

PLUM WINE/UMESHU (Japanese) – 1 cup
- 1 cup Chinese plum wine/*mui jow*, or sweet sherry, preferably Oloroso

POMEGRANATE CONCENTRATE/ROBB-E ANAR (Middle Eastern souring agent) – 1/4 cup

- 3 tablespoons pomegranate molasses

Make Your Own Boil 2 cups fresh or bottled pure unsweetened pomegranate juice gently over medium heat in a wide, uncovered pan, stirring occasionally, until thickened and reduced to 1/4 cup, 20 to 30 minutes. Use immediately, or store in a small sterilized jar in the refrigerator; it will keep for a couple of weeks.

POMEGRANATE JUICE, SOUR (Middle Eastern souring agent) – 1/3 cup

- 1/3 cup pure unsweetened pomegranate juice and 1 teaspoon lemon or lime juice
- 1 tablespoon pomegranate concentrate added to 4 1/2 tablespoons water
- 1/3 cup pure 100% unsweetened cranberry or sour/tart cherry juice

POMEGRANATE MOLASSES (Middle Eastern seasoning and souring agent) – 1/4 cup

- 2 cups fresh or bottled pure pomegranate juice, 2 tablespoons granulated sugar, and 1 tablespoon lemon juice, gently simmered until syrupy and reduced to 1/4 cup, 30 to 50 minutes
- 3 1/2 tablespoons pomegranate concentrate plus 1 teaspoon fresh lemon juice
- 1/4 cup cherry syrup (for brining)
- 3 tablespoons lemon juice and 1 generous tablespoon unsulphured molasses (or strong flavored honey), warmed in the microwave a few seconds then cooled
- 1 to 2 tablespoons aged balsamic vinegar

POMEGRANATE SEEDS/ARILS, FRESH – 1 tablespoon

- 1 tablespoon fresh papaya seeds (for salad; silvery-black and peppery tasting)
- 1 tablespoon snipped dried barberries or cranberries (for salad or garnish)
- 1 tablespoon pomegranate molasses, applied in tiny drops (for garnish)

POMEGRANATE SEEDS, DRIED SOUR/ANARDANA (Indian and Middle Eastern souring agent) – 1 tablespoon
- 1 tablespoon pomegranate molasses, lemon juice, or lime juice (for souring agent)
- 1 tablespoon snipped dried barberries or cranberries (for garnish)

POMEGRANATE SYRUP See POMEGRANATE MOLASSES

POMEGRANATE VINEGAR – 1 tablespoon
- 1 tablespoon raspberry vinegar, blackcurrant vinegar, or any fruit-flavored vinegar

PONZU SAUCE (Japanese citrus shoyu sauce) – 1/3 cup
Make Your Own Stir together 2 tablespoons each Japanese soy sauce, dashi or kombu stock (optional), and yuzu juice (or lemon or lime juice), and sweeten to taste with mirin (about 1 tablespoon) or sugar.

POPPY SEED OIL (salad oil) – 1 cup
- 1 cup almond oil

POPPY SEEDS, BLUE/BLACK – 1 cup
- 1 cup black amaranth grain, softened in hot water for 8 to 12 hours (for muffins, cakes, and pastries)
- 1 cup packaged ground black poppy seeds or canned poppy seed paste (for pastry filling)
- 1 cup nigella seeds; sesame seeds, preferably black; hulled hemp seeds; chia seeds; dark flaxseeds; salba seeds; or lamb's quarters seeds (as topping for baked goods)

POPPY SEEDS, GROUND – 1 cup
- 1 1/4 cups dark/blue/black poppy seeds, toasted in a dry skillet until fragrant, then ground in a spice/coffee grinder until fine

PORCINI POWDER – 1/3 cup See also MUSHROOM POWDER
Make Your Own Break up 1/2 ounce (3 or 4) smooth or cleaned dried porcini mushrooms and grind to a fine powder in a coffee/spice grinder.

Sift out large pieces, then regrind and sift again. Store in an airtight container in a cool, dark place; it will keep for up to 3 months.

PORCINI SALT – 1/2 cup
Make Your Own Thoroughly combine 1 tablespoon porcini powder and 1/2 cup kosher salt. Store in an airtight container in a cool, dark place; it will keep for up to 2 months.

PORT, RUBY OR TAWNY (sweet fortified wine) – 2 tablespoons
➣ 2 tablespoons Banyuls, Madeira, Moscatel, or sweet vermouth

POULTRY GLAZE/GLACE DE VOLAILLE – 1/4 cup
Make Your Own Gently boil 2 cups degreased unsalted chicken stock, uncovered, in a wide-bottomed pan until syrupy and reduced to 1/4 cup (or 2 tablespoons for a thicker glaze). Cool and store, refrigerated, for up to 1 month, or freeze for longer storage.

POULTRY SEASONING – 1 tablespoon
➣ 1 teaspoon each dried sage, thyme, and marjoram, plus a dash of black pepper

PRESERVED LEMON/CITRON CONFIT/L'HAMD MARKAD, QUICK (North African seasoning) – 1
➣ 1 Asian pickled lemon
➣ Lemon zest (use 1 teaspoon minced for each tablespoon minced preserved lemon)

Make Your Own Cut 1 large lemon (well scrubbed; preferably organic) into 12 crosswise slices. Bring to a boil in a small pan with 1/2 cup lemon juice and 1 tablespoon kosher salt, then cover and simmer until the rind is clear and transparent, about 10 minutes. Cool and transfer to a small covered container. Store in the refrigerator for up to 1 week.
Or
Cut 1 large lemon (well scrubbed; preferably organic) into 8 lengthwise wedges. Rub with 1/4 cup kosher salt, then place in a small sealable freezer bag (or a jar with a nonmetal lid) along with the juice

from another lemon (about 3 tablespoons). Refrigerate for 6 to 7 days, shaking the bag or jar daily. This will keep in the refrigerator for up to a month.

PRESERVED LEMON JUICE (Moroccan seasoning) – 1/4 cup
  ☞ 1/4 cup fresh lemon juice mixed with 1 1/2 teaspoons kosher salt

PRICKLY PEAR FRUIT/XOCONOSTLE (Mexican souring agent) – 1
  ☞ 1 small fresh underripe plum, such as damson or Italian/prune

PRUNE PUREE/PRUNE BUTTER (butter alternative for lowfat baking) – 3/4 cup
  ☞ 3/4 cup baby food prunes
  Make Your Own Process 6 ounces pitted prunes (1 cup packed) with 1/2 cup boiling water to a smooth paste in a blender or food processor. Store in the refrigerator for up to 6 months.

PULQUE, PLAIN (Mexican fermented sap from maguey cactus) – 1 cup
  ☞ 1 cup dry white wine

PUMMELO/POMELO BLOSSOM ESSENCE/KAO PAN (Thai flavoring agent) – 1 teaspoon
  ☞ 1 teaspoon lemon extract

PUMPKIN PIE SPICE – 1 teaspoon
  ☞ 1/2 teaspoon ground cinnamon, 1/4 teaspoon ground ginger, 1/8 teaspoon ground nutmeg, and 1/8 teaspoon ground allspice (or cloves)

PUMPKIN SEED MEAL/FLOUR – 1 cup
  ☞ 1 1/4 cups pumpkin seeds, ground in batches in a spice/coffee grinder until powdery

PUMPKIN SEED OIL (salad and flavoring oil) – 1 cup
  ☞ 1 cup extra-virgin olive oil, preferably deeply colored and flavorful

PUMPKIN SEEDS/PEPITAS – 1 cup

- 1 cup butternut or acorn squash seeds
- 1 cup winter melon seeds
- 1 cup Lady Godiva, Triple Treat, or Hungarian Mammoth squash seeds (hull-less green seeds, three times the size of regular hulled pumpkin seeds)
- 1 cup sunflower seeds

Q

QUAIL EGGS, HARD-BOILED – 4
- ☞ 1 large hen egg, hard boiled, shelled and quartered (or 2 small eggs, halved)

QUARK/QUARGEL (German soft fresh cheese containing 9 to 10% fat) – 1 cup
- ☞ 1 cup Magerquark (low-fat quark), fromage blanc, or plain Greek-style yogurt
- ☞ 2/3 cup ricotta and 1/3 cup sour cream blended until smooth (for cream quark/*Sahnequak)*
- ☞ 1 1/2 cups full-fat yogurt drained 1 hour in a dampened cheese-cloth-lined sieve

Make Your Own Scald 2 cups whole milk; cool, then whisk in 1/2 cup cultured buttermilk. Lightly cover with a cloth or waxed paper and let sit at room temperature until lightly thickened, 12 to 24 hours. Transfer to a sieve lined with dampened cheesecloth and set over a bowl. Cover the sieve with a plate or plastic wrap, place in the refrigerator, and let drain for 8 to 12 hours Use immediately, or keep refrigerated in a covered container for up to 1 week.

QUATRE-ÉPICES/FRENCH FOUR-SPICE MIX/SPICE PARISIENNE – 1 teaspoon
- ☞ 1/2 teaspoon ground white pepper, 1/4 teaspoon grated/ground nutmeg, 1/8 teaspoon ground cloves, and 1/8 teaspoon dried ginger (For sweet dishes substitute ground cinnamon for ground pepper.)
- ☞ 3/4 teaspoon pumpkin or apple pie spice and 1/4 teaspoon ground white pepper
- ☞ 1/2 teaspoon ground allspice

QUESO LLANERO *(Venezuelan salty white grating cheese)* – *1 ounce*
 ⊱ 1 ounce Mexican cotija, aged Asiago, aged ricotta salata, dry feta, dry Jack, Romano, or domestic Parmesan

QUESO PANELA *(Mexican fresh crumbly cheese)* – *8 ounces*
 ⊱ 8 ounces queso fresco, young ricotta salata, hoop cheese, or well-drained farmer cheese

QUILLQUIÑA/KILKIÑE *(Bolivian seasoning herb)* – *1 tablespoon finely chopped*
 ⊱ 1 tablespoon finely chopped Mexican *papaloquelite* or cilantro

QUINCE PASTE/MEMBRILLO/COTOGNATA/PÂTE DE COINGS *(Latin American cheese accompaniment)* – *1 ounce*
 ⊱ 1 ounce guava paste, such as Goya, homemade plum paste/*plumbrillo*, or any tart Mexican fruit paste/*ate*

R

RAITA (Indian condiment) – 9 ounces
- 1/3 cup finely chopped fresh mint, or shredded and drained cucumbers, stirred into 1 cup plain yogurt (full fat, lowfat, or nonfat)

RAPADURA (Brazilian evaporated cane sugar) – 1 cup
- 1 cup Sucanat, organic cane sugar, pre-grated *panela*, or finely grated or shaved *piloncillo/panela*

RAS EL HANOUT (Moroccan spice blend) – 1 teaspoon
- 1 teaspoon Baharat/Lebanese seven-spice blend
- 1 teaspoon garam masala
- 3/4 teaspoon mild/sweet curry powder
- 1/4 teaspoon each ground allspice, coriander, cumin, and ginger, preferably roasted
- 1/8 to 1/4 teaspoon ground cumin, preferably roasted

RASPBERRY LIQUEUR/RASPBERRY-FLAVORED SPIRIT (Chambord, DeKuyper) – 1 tablespoon for cooking
- 1 tablespoon raspberry brandy/framboise, cranberry liqueur, or raspberry balsamic vinegar
- 1/2 teaspoon raspberry extract plus 2 1/2 teaspoons water

RASPBERRY VINEGAR – 1 cup
- 1 cup red wine vinegar plus a little raspberry liqueur, such as Chambord
- 1 cup cranberry vinegar or other red fruity vinegar

Make Your Own Lightly mash 1 pint/12 ounces fresh ripe raspberries, combine with 1 cup red wine vinegar, cover, and let sit at room temperature for 1 week. Strain in a cloth-lined sieve, then bottle and refrigerate for up to 6 months.

RAYU See JAPANESE CHILI OIL

RED PEPPER/CRUSHED RED PEPPER See CAYENNE

RED PEPPER FLAKES, HOT – 1 teaspoon
- 1/2 teaspoon ground cayenne pepper or very hot crushed red pepper flakes
- 1/4 teaspoon hot pepper sauce, such as Tabasco or Crystal (not for Asian dishes)
- 2 teaspoons Asian chili paste

RED PEPPER PASTE, HOT/ACI BIBER SALÇASI (Turkish condiment) – 1 tablespoon
- 1 tablespoon red pepper paste (or 1 or 2 jarred roasted piquillo pepper, drained and pureed) plus few drops hot pepper sauce
- 1 tablespoon tomato paste plus 1/8 teaspoon ground cayenne pepper
- 1 1/2 teaspoons harissa paste

RED PEPPER PASTE, MILD/SWEET PEPPER PASTE/BIBER SALÇASI (Turkish condiment)
- Jarred roasted red peppers, blotted dry, roughly chopped, then processed in a blender until smooth; season with salt and pepper

RED PEPPERS, ROASTED – 1 (12-ounce) jar
- 2 large red bell peppers, roasted, cored, seeded, and peeled (for peppers packed in oil, cut into strips and marinate in olive oil for 1 to 2 days)

RED RICE VINEGAR See CHINESE RED RICE VINEGAR

RED WINE VINEGAR – 1 tablespoon
- 2 teaspoons cider vinegar plus 1 teaspoon red wine
- 1 tablespoon Zinfandel vinegar
- 1 1/2 teaspoons each balsamic vinegar and water

RESHAMPATTI CHILI POWDER (Indian seasoning) – 1 teaspoon
- ⇨ 1 teaspoon ground cayenne pepper

RICE BRAN, ROASTED/IRI NUKA (Japanese preserving medium for nuka pickles/nukazuke) – 1 pound
- ⇨ 1 pound wheat bran, toasted (Toast in a dry skillet over low heat, stirring frequently, until toasty-smelling, 10 to 12 minutes. Cool completely.)

RICE BRAN OIL/KOME-NUKA ABURA (Asian cooking oil with a high smoke point) – 1 cup
- ⇨ 1 cup peanut, corn, or canola oil

RICE MALT SWEETENER/RICE SYRUP/MIZUAME (Japanese glucose/syrup) – 1/4 cup
- ⇨ Scant 1/3 cup light-colored (not "lite") corn syrup, brought to a full boil then cooled
- ⇨ 2 tablespoons pale, mild-tasting honey (such as clover or alfalfa)

RICE MEAL (Indian) – 1 cup
- ⇨ 3/4 cup plus 2 tablespoons white or brown rice, ground until fine in a blender, or in small batches in a spice/coffee grinder

RICE PADDY HERB/NGO OM/MA OM/PHAK KHAYANG (Southeast Asian seasoning) – 4 or 5 sprigs (1 tablespoon chopped)
- ⇨ 5 or 6 fresh cilantro sprigs (for flavor or for garnish)
- ⇨ 1/4 teaspoon whole cumin seeds, or 1/8 teaspoon ground cumin (for flavor)

RICE POWDER, ROASTED/KAO KUA PON/THINH/TEPUNG BERTIH (Southeast Asian thickener) – 1/2 cup
- ⇨ 1/2 cup uncooked sticky rice (or long-grain rice) toasted in a dry skillet over medium heat, stirring frequently, until golden, 8 to 10 minutes; cooled, then ground in small batches in a spice/coffee grinder until sandy-textured. Store, tightly covered, in the refrigerator (for

best flavor store toasted rice and grind just before using). For Chinese brown rice powder/*chau mi fen,* use brown rice
- 1/2 cup toasted chickpea/garbanzo flour

RICE SYRUP *See BROWN RICE SYRUP*

RICE VINEGAR – 1 tablespoon *See also JAPANESE, RICE VINEGAR*
- 1 tablespoon champagne vinegar, cava vinegar, or white wine vinegar
- 2 teaspoons cider vinegar or distilled white vinegar, 1 teaspoon water, and 2 or 3 grains sugar

RICE VINEGAR, KOREAN UNPOLISHED/HYUNMI SIKCHO – 1 tablespoon
- 1 tablespoon cider vinegar

RICE WINE *See CHINESE YELLOW RICE COOKING WINE; JAPANESE RICE WINE; KOREAN RICE WINE; KOREAN RICE WINE, SWEET COOKING; MIRIN; SAKÉ; SHAOXING*

ROCK SUGAR *See SUGAR, BROWN ROCK; SUGAR, YELLOW/CLEAR ROCK*

ROCOTILLO/ROCOTO CHILI, FRESH (Peruvian) – 1
- 1 fresh *aji dulce* or Cuban cachucha chili
- 1 to 2 teaspoons chopped red bell pepper
- 1 to 2 teaspoons rocoto chili paste or milder *pasta de panca* (Peruvian red chili paste)

ROSE EXTRACT/ESSENCE (food flavoring agent) – 1 teaspoon
- 1 1/2 tablespoons rose water (reduce the liquid in the recipe by 1 tablespoon)

ROSE GERANIUM LEAF – 1 fresh or dried leaf
- 1 drop orange flower water

ROSE GERANIUM SYRUP – 1 cup
Make Your Own Add 2 or 3 unsprayed rose geranium sprigs (including leaves) to 1 cup hot simple syrup (*See SYRUP, SIMPLE*). Cool, then remove the sprigs and store, tightly covered, in the refrigerator; it will keep up to 7 days.

ROSE HIP SYRUP – 1 cup
Make Your Own Halve, seed, and rinse 8 ounces fresh unsprayed rose hips. Simmer, uncovered, with 1 cup water until softened, 20 to 30 minutes. Strain, discard the hips and then boil the liquid with 1 cup sugar until clear, about 2 minutes. Cool and store, refrigerated, in a sterilized jar for up to 6 weeks. (Wear plastic gloves when handling the rose hips, and remove the seeds with a small demitasse spoon.)

ROSEMARY, FRESH – 4-inch sprig (10 leaves/needles/1 tablespoon finely chopped)
- 1 tablespoon frozen rosemary leaves/needles, crushed (frozen sprigs will keep 6 months to a year)
- 1 to 2 teaspoons whole or cracked dried rosemary leaves/needles (crush in a mortar, pepper grinder, or with the back of a spoon)
- 1/2 to 3/4 teaspoon powdered rosemary

ROSEMARY OIL – 1/2 cup
Make Your Own Slowly heat 2 or 3 sprigs fresh rosemary and 1/2 cup olive oil to 190°F. Cool, then store in a sterilized container. It will keep for up to 1 month.

ROSE PETALS, WILD FRESH/DOK GULAB (Southeast Asian aromatic garnish) – 1 cup
- 1 cup fresh, pesticide-free Rugosa or pink damask rose petals (cut off the white part at the base of each petal; it is bitter)
- 1 cup fresh, pesticide-free nasturtium petals, or other colorful petals *See FLOWERS/BLOSSOMS/PETALS, FRESH EDIBLE*

ROSE WATER (food flavoring agent) – 1 tablespoon
☞ 1/2 teaspoon food-grade pure rose extract/essence (reduce the liquid in the recipe by 1 tablespoon)

Make Your Own Simmer 3/4 cup purified water and 1/2 cup trimmed, fresh, pesticide-free rose petals, covered, for 30 minutes. Cool, strain, then add 1 or 2 teaspoons vodka. Store in a sterilized bottle in the refrigerator. Makes 1/3 cup; use 1 tablespoon for each tablespoon in the recipe. Use within 7 days.

RUM – 2 tablespoons for cooking
☞ 1/2 teaspoon imitation rum extract plus 1 1/2 tablespoons vodka or water
☞ 2 tablespoons bourbon or brandy
☞ 1/8 to 1/4 teaspoon butter-rum flavor/extract (if the recipe contains butter)

RUM EXTRACT – 1 teaspoon
☞ 2 tablespoons rum; omit 2 tablespoons liquid from the recipe

RUSSIAN DRESSING – 1 cup
☞ 2/3 cup mayonnaise and 1/3 cup ketchup-based chili sauce

Make Your Own Stir together 1/3 cup each plain yogurt, mayonnaise, and ketchup. Add 1 tablespoon strained bottled horseradish and stir until thoroughly combined.

RUTABAGAS/SWEDES – 1 pound
☞ 1 pound parsnips or turnips (drier texture)

S

SABA/SAPA/MOSTO COTTO (Italian grape must syrup) *See GRAPE MOLASSES*

SACHA INCHI NUTS, ROASTED (large Peruvian oil-rich nuts) – 1 ounce
  - 1 ounce macadamia nuts

SACHA INCHI OIL (Peruvian oil high in omega-3 fatty acids) – 1 tablespoon
  - 1 tablespoon hemp or flaxseed oil

SAEUJOT/SAEWOO-JEOT *See KOREAN SHRIMP, SALTED*

SAFFLOWER/SAFFRON THISTLE/FALSE SAFFRON/TURKISH SAFFRON/ MEXICAN SAFFRON (coloring agent) – 1 teaspoon dried compressed petals
  - 1 teaspoon pesticide-free dried marigold petals, preferably pot marigold/*Calendula officinalis*, steeped in a little warm water for about 5 minutes (use the liquid for color and discard the petals)
  - 1/2 teaspoon ground annatto seeds
  - 1 teaspoon whole annatto seeds, steeped in a little hot water for about 5 minutes (use the liquid for color and discard the seeds)
  - 1/4 teaspoon sweet California or Hungarian paprika plus 1/2 teaspoon ground turmeric, preferably Madras

SAFFRON/COUPÉ/SARGO – 1/2 teaspoon (10 to 15 threads)
  - 1/8 teaspoon ground/powdered saffron
  - 2 or 3 drops saffron extract
  - 1 1/2 teaspoons safflower stigmas/Mexican saffron/*azafrán,* soaked in 1 tablespoon warm water for 20 minutes, then added to the dish along with the water (for color)

- ☙ 1 teaspoon pesticide-free dried marigold petals, preferably pot marigold/*Calendula officinalis*, steeped in 1 or 2 tablespoon warm water for 5 minutes (use the liquid for color and discard the petals)
- ☙ 1/2 teaspoon ground annatto seeds (for color)
- ☙ 1 teaspoon whole annatto seeds, steeped in a little hot liquid (use the liquid for color and discard the seeds)
- ☙ 1/4 to 1/2 teaspoon powdered Madras turmeric, or just enough for color

SAGE, COMMON, FRESH – 2 (3-inch) sprigs, or 3 to 5 leaves, or 1 table-spoon chopped
- ☙ 2 or 3 whole dried sage leaves, crushed
- ☙ 1 to 2 teaspoons rubbed sage, or 1/2 teaspoon ground/powdered sage
- ☙ 1 1/2 teaspoons chopped fresh Greek sage, or scant 1/2 scant teaspoon dried (more aromatic)
- ☙ 3/4 teaspoon dried marjoram or summer savory
- ☙ 1 teaspoon poultry seasoning

SAHLAB/SALEP (Greek and Turkish ground orchid root thickener) – 1 tablespoon pulverized
- ☙ 2 teaspoons cornstarch (lacks flavor; for flavor add 1/2 teaspoon rose water, orange blossom water, or even a drop or two of elder-flower cordial)

SAKÉ/JAPANESE RICE WINE/BEER/SEISHU/FUTSU-SHU – 1/4 cup for cooking
- ☙ 2 to 3 tablespoons sake-based mirin, such as *aji no haha* or *aske mirin*; reduce the sugar in the recipe accordingly
- ☙ 1/4 cup Chinese yellow rice wine/Shaoxing
- ☙ 1/4 cup dry sherry, such as Dry Sack, or dry vermouth
- ☙ 1/4 cup white wine plus a pinch of brown sugar

SALAD BURNET, FRESH – 1 ounce
- ☙ 1 ounce fresh borage

SALAD CREAM (British creamy salad dressing) – 1/2 cup
- ⊵ 1/2 cup honey-mustard dressing, or ranch dressing

SALAD DRESSING, CREAMY TYPE – 1/2 cup
- ⊵ 1/4 cup mayonnaise and 1/2 cup sour cream or plain yogurt; thinned with wine vinegar, lemon juice, or pickling liquid from jarred pepperoncini, giardiniera, or pickles

SALAD DRESSING, RUSSIAN *See RUSSIAN DRESSING*

SALAD DRESSING, THOUSAND ISLAND *See THOUSAND ISLAND DRESSING*

SALAD OIL – 1 cup for vinaigrette
- ⊵ 1 cup oil from jarred marinated artichoke hearts, sun-dried tomatoes, or olives

SALAM LEAF/INDONESIAN BAY LEAF/DAUN SALAM/ (Indonesian seasoning) – 1 (3-inch) dried leaf
- ⊵ 2 or 3 fresh curry leaves plus a few drops of lime juice

SALEP/SALAP/SAHLAB/ORCHIS MASCULA (Middle Eastern mucilaginous thickening powder for stretchy ice cream) – 1 teaspoon
- ⊵ 1/2 teaspoon *konjac* flour/*konjac glucomannan* (whisk into cold liquid until thoroughly combined)
- ⊵ 1 teaspoon locust bean gum or guar gum (for jelling only; not for stretchy properties)
- ⊵ 1 teaspoon arrowroot powder or cornstarch (for thickening only; not for stretchy properties)

SALMON, SALTED, FLAKES/SHIO ZAKE (Japanese) – 1 pound
- ⊵ 1 pound poached salmon, flaked and lightly sprinkled with salt

SALMON, SMOKED OR CURED – 1 pound
- ⊵ 1 pound gravlax (dill flavor)

☞ 1 pound smoked arctic char, bluefish, haddock, mackerel, sablefish, trout, or whitefish (bones and skin removed as necessary)

SALONICA PEPPERS (Greek hot pickled peppers) – 1 cup
☞ 1 cup jarred Italian pepperoncini

SALSA, FRESH/SALSA CRUDA (Mexican condiment) – 1 cup
☞ 1 cup canned or jarred salsa freshened with chopped cilantro, chopped white or red onion, and a little lemon or lime juice

SALSA GOLF/MARIE ROSE SAUCE/SALSA ROSADA (Argentine table condiment) – 1 cup
Make Your Own Combine 1/2 cup each ketchup-based chili sauce (or ketchup) and mayonnaise, plus a little lime juice, Worcestershire sauce, or sweet pickle relish

SALT COD/BACALAO/BACCALÀ/BACALHAU/KLIPFISH (Spanish, Italian, Portuguese, and Norwegian salted and dried cod) – 8 ounces
Make Your Own Completely bury 1 pound skinned and boned cod in kosher or sea salt in a small container. Cover tightly and refrigerate until firm, 6 to 7 days, pouring off any brine that accumulates and adding fresh salt as needed.

SALT PORK (fatty, salt-cured flavoring agent) – 4 ounces
☞ 4 ounces thick slice of slab bacon (or fatty end piece of cured ham) soaked in boiling water 2 minutes to reduce smoke flavor
☞ 4 ounces fatback plus salt to taste
☞ 4 ounces pancetta (leaner)
☞ 4 ounces guanciale (less salty)
Make Your Own Completely submerge small, uniform pieces of pork shoulder in pickling or kosher salt in a small container. Refrigerate for 2 weeks, adding more salt after 7 days. Rinse, blot dry, and package in plastic wrap. It will keep refrigerated for up to 1 month.

SALT SUBSTITUTION CONTAINING SODIUM CHLORIDE – 1 teaspoon
- 1 teaspoon Biosalt, LoSalt, or Lite Salt (usually two-thirds potassium chloride with one-third sodium chloride)
- 1 teaspoon powdered kelp, or salt substitute containing kelp, such as Herbamare
- 1 teaspoon Japanese soy sauce crystals (light flaky salt crystals)
- 2 teaspoons Japanese tamari, or 1 tablespoon soy sauce/*shoyu* (for prepared dishes)
- 2 teaspoons Japanese fermented rice/*shio-koji* (for adding an umami taste to dishes)
- 1 to 2 tablespoons dark *hatcho* miso containing 12% salt (softened with a little liquid and added to a dish just before removing from heat)
- 1 tablespoon Japanese sesame salt/*gomashio* or seaweed *gomashio* containing sesame seeds, dulse, nori, kombu, and sea salt (for lower-sodium finishing salt)
- 2 teaspoons dried and ground glasswort/salicornia

SALT SUBSTITUTION, SODIUM-FREE/POTASSIUM CHLORIDE – 1 teaspoon
- 1 or 2 teaspoons salt-free herb-and-spice seasoning blend, such as Mrs. Dash or Vege-Sal
- 1/2 teaspoon lemon juice, unseasoned rice vinegar, or white wine vinegar

SALT, BLACK/KALA NAMAK (Indian unrefined salt) – 1 tablespoon
- 1 tablespoon Hawaiian coarse-grain black lava sea salt (slightly smoky flavor)
- 1 tablespoon Cyprus medium-grain black lava sea salt flakes (for finishing)
- 4 teaspoons table salt or sea salt (for cooking; lacks sulphuric aroma and flavor)

SALT, CHEESE (coarse non-iodized, additive-free flake salt) – 1 tablespoon
- 1 tablespoon Diamond Crystal kosher salt

SALT, CHILI – 1 tablespoon
- ↠ 1 teaspoon chili seasoning mixed with 2 teaspoons coarse kosher or sea salt

SALT, CHIPOTLE – 1 tablespoon
- ↠ 1/8 teaspoon chipotle chili powder mixed with 1 tablespoon kosher or sea salt

Make Your Own Toast 1 dried chipotle chili in a dry skillet, 2 to 3 minutes each side. Cut into pieces, then grind in a spice/coffee grinder. Mix with 2 teaspoons kosher or sea salt.

SALT, CURING/PINK SALT See SALTPETER/ POTASSIUM NITRATE/ SODIUM NITRATE

SALT, FLEUR DE SEL See FLEUR DE SEL DE GUÉRANDE

SALT, HIMALAYAN PINK (rose-colored, mineral-rich salt) – 1 tablespoon
- ↠ 1 tablespoon Bolivian Rose, Hawaiian Haleakala Ruby, Hawaiian Red Alaea Volcanic, Australian Murray River (peach or rose-color), or Peruvian Pink (pinkish-beige color)

SALT, KOSHER/KOSHERING SALT (additive-free salt with irregular coarse grains) – 1 teaspoon Diamond Crystal or 3/4 teaspoon Morton
- ↠ 1/2 teaspoon non-iodized table salt
- ↠ 1 teaspoon coarse or extra-coarse sea salt (non-iodized and additive-free)
- ↠ 3/4 teaspoon pickling, canning, or cheese salt (non-iodized and additive-free)

SALT, LAVENDER (French seasoning) – 1 tablespoon
- ↠ 1 teaspoon French dried lavender blossoms and 1 tablespoon coarse sea salt, pulverized until fine, then left several days to develop flavor

SALT, PICKLING, GRANULATED (fine-grain non-iodized, additive-free salt) – 1 tablespoon
- ↠ 1 1/2 tablespoons flaked pickling salt

- 1 tablespoon non-iodized and additive-free (no anti-caking agent) table salt
- 1 1/2 tablespoons Morton kosher salt
- 2 tablespoons Diamond Crystal kosher salt (takes longer to dissolve)

SALT, POPCORN – 1 cup
- 1 1/4 cups kosher or sea salt, ground in a blender or food processor, or in batches in a spice/coffee grinder, until very fine
- 1 cup table salt

SALT, PRETZEL (large-grain, bright white salt; used for soft pretzels, salt bagels, or focaccia) – 1 cup
- 1 cup extra-coarse sea salt; margarita salt; or kosher salt, preferably Diamond Crystal

SALT, ROCK (food-grade coarse salt)
- Crumpled foil, raw rice, dried beans, or well-washed small beach or river pebbles (as a bed for oysters and clams on the half shell)
- Kosher salt, preferably Diamond Crystal, or extra-coarse sea salt (for an ice cream maker)

SALT, SEA, FINE-GRAIN – 1 teaspoon See also SALT, TABLE
- 1 teaspoon table salt
- 1 1/2 teaspoons coarse-grain sea salt, pulsed in a spice/coffee mill until fine, then measured (Clean the mill immediately after use to prevent corrosion.)
- 1 1/2 teaspoons Morton kosher salt or Morton coarse sea salt
- 2 teaspoons Diamond Crystal kosher salt, Morton extra-coarse sea salt, or coarse gray sea salt

SALT, SEASONING – 1 generous tablespoon
- 1 tablespoon kosher salt and 1/8 teaspoon each garlic powder, onion powder, and paprika (or turmeric) plus a few grains of sugar (For a smoky version use smoked paprika or smoked sea salt, or both.)

SALT, SMOKED SEA – *1 cup* *See also SALT, CHIPOTLE*
- ⊨ 1 cup sea salt and 1/4 to 1/2 teaspoon (or more) hickory smoke powder
- ⊨ 1 cup sea salt and 3 or 4 drops liquid smoke, kneaded together in a sealable plastic bag, then spread out on a baking sheet and dried in an oven with a pilot light, or at warm room temperature for 2 or 3 hours

SALT, SOUR *See CITRIC ACID/CITRIC SALT*

SALT, TABLE/GRANULAR, IODIZED AND NON-IODIZED (*fine-grained, free-flowing salt with anti-caking additives*) – *1 teaspoon*
- ⊨ 1 teaspoon finely ground Baja, Atlantic, or Mediterranean sea salt (include a few dry rice grains in the salt shaker for the free-flowing feature)
- ⊨ 1 1/4 teaspoons coarse moist sea salt from Brittany, Baja, Camargue, or Ibiza
- ⊨ 1 1/2 teaspoons Morton kosher salt
- ⊨ 2 teaspoons Diamond Crystal kosher salt or Morton extra-coarse sea salt
- ⊨ 2 teaspoons English Maldon or Welsh Halen Môn crystal-flake sea salt (for finishing)

SALTPETER/POTASSIUM NITRATE/SODIUM NITRATE (*meat curing agent*) – *1 ounce*
- ⊨ 1 ounce sodium nitrate–based curing salt, such as DQ Curing Salt #2 or Insta Cure #2, used following the package directions

SAMBAL MANIS (*Indonesian dipping sauce*) – *1 tablespoon*
- ⊨ 1 tablespoon sambal oelek (hotter)

SAMBAL OELEK (*Indonesian hot chili paste*) – *1 tablespoon* *See also CHILI PASTE, HOT*
- ⊨ 3 stemmed fresh bird's eye chilis (or other small red chilis), simmered in 1/4 cup water for 5 minutes; drained, cooled, and crushed to a

coarse paste with a pinch each of salt and brown sugar (Wear plastic gloves when handling the chilis and avoid touching your face.)

⇨ 1 (or more) tablespoons Indonesian dipping sauce/*sambal manis* (milder)

⇨ 1 tablespoon harissa, Sriracha, Vietnamese chili sauce/*tuong ot toi*, Chinese hot chili paste/*la jiao jiang*, or Japanese chili yuzu paste/*yuzu koshu*

⇨ 1 to 2 teaspoons hot pepper sauce, such as Tabasco, or hot chili powder, such as cayenne

SÂMNA/SAMNEH/SMEN (Middle Eastern and North African preserved butter) – 1 cup

⇨ 1 tablespoon toasted sesame seed oil combined with 3/4 cup plus 2 tablespoons room-temperature clarified butter

⇨ 1 1/2 teaspoons creamy blue cheese combined with 1 cup room-temperature salted butter (or unsalted butter plus 1/2 teaspoon salt)

⇨ 1 cup ghee, clarified butter (preferably tangy, cultured-milk butter), or solidified coconut oil

SANAAM CHILIS/LONG CHILIS, DRIED (Indian) – 3 or 4

⇨ 3 or 4 dried de árbol, cayenne, or Thai red chilis

⇨ 1/3 to 1/2 teaspoon ground cayenne pepper, Thai chili powder, or very hot crushed red pepper flakes

SANSHO POWDER/PRICKLY ASH POWDER/KONA-ZANSHO/SANSYO (Japanese seasoning) – 1 teaspoon

⇨ 1 teaspoon lemon pepper seasoning; reduce the salt and pepper in the recipe accordingly

SATAY SAUCE See PEANUT DIPPING SAUCE

SAUSAGE, BREAKFAST PORK, SEASONING – 1 scant tablespoon

⇨ 1 teaspoon kosher salt and 1/2 teaspoon each ground white pepper, thyme, and sage

⇨ 1 teaspoon kosher salt and 2 teaspoons poultry seasoning

SAVORY, SUMMER, DRIED – 1 teaspoon
- ☞ 1/2 teaspoon dried winter savory (spicier and sharper)
- ☞ 3/4 teaspoon dried thyme and 1/8 teaspoon dried marjoram

SAVORY, SUMMER, FRESH – 1 tablespoon finely chopped leaves
- ☞ 1 1/2 to 2 teaspoons fresh winter savory (spicier and sharper)
- ☞ 1 1/2 teaspoons finely chopped fresh thyme and 1/2 teaspoon finely chopped fresh mint

SAVORY, WINTER, FRESH – 1 tablespoon finely chopped leaves
- ☞ 1 1/2 teaspoon dried winter savory leaves, crumbled
- ☞ 1 1/2 tablespoons chopped fresh summer savory, or 1 1/2 teaspoons dried summer savory (milder)
- ☞ 2 teaspoons chopped fresh thyme and 1 teaspoon chopped fresh mint
- ☞ 1/2 teaspoon dried thyme and 1/4 teaspoon dried marjoram (or sage)
- ☞ 1/2 teaspoon dried sage or oregano

SAWLEAF HERB/SAWTOOTH HERB/FITWEED/CULANTRO/RECAO/ NGO GAI/PAK CHI FARANG (Latin American and Southeast Asian seasoning) – 1 fresh leaf
- ☞ 1 large sprig fresh cilantro or 1 scant tablespoon minced
- ☞ 1 teaspoon each fresh minced cilantro, mint, and basil leaves

SAZÓN (Spanish spice blend) – 1 tablespoon (about)
- ☞ Scant 1/2 teaspoon each paprika, roasted ground coriander, and ground cumin, plus 1 teaspoon garlic powder and 1 teaspoon salt

SCALLIONS/GREEN ONIONS/SPRING ONIONS – 4 ounces
- ☞ 4 ounces spring onions, Egyptian onions, Mexican onions, ramp bulbs, onion sprouts, young thin leeks, garlic shoots, or young shallot tops

SCAMORZA, SMOKED – 1 ounce
- ☞ 1 ounce *mozzarella affumicata* or *provolone affumicata*

SCHMALTZ (rendered chicken fat) – 2 tablespoons
- ⇝ 2 tablespoons pork fat, goose fat, or duck fat
- ⇝ 2 tablespoons shortening
- ⇝ 1 tablespoon each mild vegetable oil and unsalted butter

SCOTCH BONNET CHILI, FRESH – 1
- ⇝ 1 fresh Fatalii, Red Savina, or habañero chili
- ⇝ 2 or 3 fresh jalapeño or serrano chilis
- ⇝ 2 tablespoons Scotch bonnet hot pepper sauce
- ⇝ **SEA BUCKTHORN JUICE – 1 ounce**
- ⇝ 2 tablespoons orange juice plus a few drops lemon juice (for flavor, not antioxidant properties)

SEAFOOD COCKTAIL SAUCE *See COCKTAIL SAUCE*

SEASONED SALT *See SALT, SEASONING*

SEAWEED SEASONING/GARNISH – 1 tablespoon
- ⇝ 1 tablespoon shredded nori with sesame seeds/*nori komi furikake*
- ⇝ 1 tablespoon crushed wakame or nori (sheets toasted, then coarsely crushed; or pretoasted nori sheets/*yaki-nori* coarsely crushed)
- ⇝ 1 tablespoon crumbled seasoned nori strips/*ajitsuke-nori*
- ⇝ 1 to 2 teaspoons powdered nori/*ao nori/aosa*, or powered sea lettuce/green laver powder

SEED BUTTER *See HEMPSEED BUTTER; SUNFLOWER SEED BUTTER*

SEITAN, FLAVORED (wheat gluten meat substitute) – 4 ounces
- ⇝ 4 ounces tempeh (stronger-tasting)
- ⇝ 4 ounces savory baked tofu (less chewy)
- ⇝ 4 ounces extra-firm tofu, weighted to remove excess water (less flavorful; less chewy)

SERRANO CHILI/CHILI VERDE, FRESH – 1
- ⇝ 1 fresh japoné, cayenne, Fresno, or Thai chili

☞ 1 dried de árbol or cayenne chili

☞ 1 teaspoon sambal oelek or other hot chili paste; reduce the salt in the recipe accordingly

☞ 1/2 teaspoon crushed red pepper flakes or ground cayenne pepper

SERRANO HAM/JAMÓN SERRANO (Spanish salted dry-cured ham) – 1 pound

☞ 1 pound Ibérico ham, Italian proscuitto, Portuguese *presunto*, or French *Haute Savoie*

☞ Iowa organic cured ham, such as La Quercia or Rossa Berkshire proscuitto

SESAME BUTTER *See SESAME PASTE; TAHINI*

SESAME LEAF *See SHISO, GREEN*

SESAME OIL, TOASTED/GOMA ABURA/MA YAU/DAU ME/XIANG YOU (Asian seasoning) – 1 tablespoon

☞ 1 teaspoon peanut oil mixed with 2 teaspoons ground toasted sesame seeds (or untoasted seeds dry-toasted, then ground)

☞ 1 tablespoon Indian sesame oil/*gingelly/til ka tel*

☞ 1 tablespoon roasted peanut oil

SESAME PASTE/GOMA PASTE/ZHI MA JIANG/NERI-GOMA (Chinese and Japanese seasoning) – 1 tablespoon *See also TAHINI*

☞ 1 tablespoon tahini plus few drops toasted sesame oil

☞ 1 tablespoon smooth unsweetened peanut butter plus few drops light/untoasted sesame oil

Make Your Own Toast 1 tablespoon white unhulled sesame seeds in a dry skillet over medium heat, stirring constantly, until golden, 1 to 2 minutes; then grind it in a spice mill/coffee grinder, with 1 teaspoon sesame oil (or soy oil) and a pinch of salt until reduced to a paste.

SESAME SALT/GOMASHIO (Japanese condiment) – 1/3 cup (about)

☞ 1/3 cup packaged smoked sesame seeds/*shirogoma*

Make Your Own Toast 1/2 cup black sesame seeds in a dry skillet over medium heat, stirring constantly, until fragrant, 3 to 4 minutes, (or in a preheated 350°F oven for 5 to 7 minutes). Cool, then coarsely grind it in a spice mill/coffee grinder with 1 tablespoon coarse sea salt (or kosher salt). For 1 teaspoon, grind 1 teaspoon toasted sesame seeds plus few grains of sea salt in a salt mill or mortar.

SESAME SEED FLOUR – 1 cup
- 1 1/4 cups hulled/white sesame seeds, ground in a spice/coffee grinder until fine
- 1 cup pumpkin seed flour/meal, sunflower seed meal, or hempseed meal

SESAME SEEDS, HULLED WHITE/MUKI GOMA (Japanese condiment) – 1 ounce
- 1 ounce white poppy seeds, sunflower seed kernels, golden flaxseeds, hulled hemp seeds, salba seeds, or finely chopped blanched almonds

SEVEN-SPICE SEASONING See JAPANESE SEVEN-SPICE SEASONING

SEVILLE ORANGE See ORANGE, SOUR/BITTER/SEVILLE

SHADO BENI See SAWLEAF HERB

SHALLOTS, ASIAN/HOM DAENG/BAWANG MERAH/BRAMBANG, FRESH – 1 bunch/3 or 4 small
- 2 red pearl onions, halved lengthwise
- 1 medium shallot
- 1 very small red onion

SHALLOTS, FRESH – 3 to 4 small, or 2 medium, or 1 extra-large
- 2 to 3 tablespoons freeze-dried shallots, softened in 2 tablespoons warm water for 10 minutes
- 6 purple Asian shallots (smaller, milder, and less moist) or Egyptian walking onions

- 1 small-to-medium chopped red onion plus a little minced garlic (more pungent)
- 1/2 cup chopped young thin leeks, ramp bulbs, green onions, or scallions (white part only)
- 1/2 to 1 teaspoon shallot salt; reduce the salt in the recipe by 1/2 to 1 teaspoon

SHALLOTS, FRIED, PACKAGED/CHIÊN HAHN HUONG (Vietnamese garnish) – 1 cup
- 1 cup (2 ounces) packaged fried onions, such as Indonesian *bawang goreng*
- 1 cup (2 ounces) canned domestic fried onions, such as French's

Make Your Own Thinly slice 5 or 6 shallots, then fry in 1/3 cup hot oil until crisp and golden, about 4 minutes. Drain on paper towels. (For a more pronounced flavor, add the shallots to cold oil and cook on medium heat until golden.)

SHANGHAI BOK CHOY/BOK CHOY SHOOTS – 1 pound
- 1 pound baby bok choy, or regular bok choy cut into 3-inch pieces

SHAOXING/SHAO HSING/HUANG JIU (Chinese yellow rice wine, 36% proof) – 1 cup
- 1 cup Shaoxing cooking wine/*liao jiu/chiew* (contains salt)
- 1 cup glutinous yellow rice wine/*gnow mei dew*
- 1 cup medium dry sherry, such as amontillado
- 1 cup dry vermouth

SHATTA (Sudanese condiment) – 1/3 cup
- 1 crushed garlic clove and 1 tablespoon ground cayenne pepper stirred into 1/3 cup lemon juice
- 1 teaspoon garlic paste stirred into 1/3 cup hot pepper sauce, such as Tabasco or Frank's RedHot Original

SHEMIJI/SHIMIJI MUSHROOM See OYSTER MUSHROOM

SHERRY, CREAM (sweet, dark fortified wine) – 2 tablespoons for cooking
- ☞ 2 tablespoons dry sherry plus 1/2 teaspoon dark brown sugar
- ☞ 2 tablespoons Madeira
- ☞ 2 tablespoons apple juice plus a few drops mild vinegar

SHERRY, DRY (fortified wine) – 2 tablespoons for cooking (not cooking sherry, which has salt added)
- ☞ 2 tablespoons dry vermouth or saké
- ☞ 2 1/2 tablespoons white wine (regular or nonalcoholic) plus few grains light brown sugar
- ☞ 2 tablespoons unseasoned rice vinegar

SHERRY PEPPER SAUCE (Caribbean hot pepper sauce) – 1 cup
Make Your Own Put 4 or 5 (or more) small hot dried chilis in a sterilized bottle and add 1 cup dry sherry. Cover and let sit in a cool, dark place for 10 or more days, shaking the bottle occasionally. It will keep for up to 6 months.

SHERRY VINEGAR, AGED/VINAGRE DE JEREZ/XERES (Spanish) – 1 tablespoon
- ☞ 1 tablespoon domestic aged sherry vinegar, such as Noble
- ☞ 1 1/2 teaspoons each white wine vinegar (or white balsamic vinegar) and dry sherry
- ☞ 1 tablespoon balsamic vinegar or red wine vinegar
- ☞ 1 tablespoon white wine vinegar or champagne vinegar (milder)

SHICHIMI TOGARASHI *See JAPANESE SEVEN-SPICE SEASONING*

SHIITAKE MUSHROOMS/GOLDEN OAK/PYOGO, FRESH – 1 pound
- ☞ 3 ounces dried shiitake mushrooms, soaked in hot water for 30 minutes, stem sides down and weighted with a saucer, squeezed dry, and stems discarded (The strained soaking water may be reserved for another use. For more deeply flavored mushrooms, soak for 8 to 12 hours in cool water.)

☞ 3 ounces dried flower mushrooms/*hua gu/hana/donko* (thick variety of shiitake with a more potent flavor; soak for 1 hour in hot water)

☞ 1 pound fresh cremini or matsutake mushrooms

SHIITAKE POWDER – 1/3 cup (packed)

☞ 1/2 ounce dried shiitake mushrooms, cleaned and ground in a spice/coffee grinder or blender until fine

☞ 1/3 cup porcini powder

SHISHITO PEPPER/SHISHITO-TOGARASHI, FRESH (small green Japanese pepper) – 3 or 4

☞ 3 or 4 Japanese green fushimi peppers/*fushimi-togarashi*

☞ 3 or 4 Spanish Padrón peppers

☞ 1 green Cubanelle pepper, or Italian frying pepper, cut into 1-inch-wide strips

☞ 1 medium green bell pepper or Anaheim chili, peeled and cut into 1-inch-wide strips

SHISO, GREEN/PERILLA LEAF, FRESH (Korean and Japanese seasoning and garnish) – 1 leaf

☞ 1 to 2 fresh wild shiso leaves/*Perilla frutescens* (smaller leaves; more flavorful)

☞ 1 fresh Vietnamese green/purple perilla/*la tia to* (stronger flavor; less expensive)

☞ 3 fresh holy basil, Thai basil, lemon basil, or anise basil leaves

☞ 2 fresh sweet basil leaves (Italian, French, or California) and 2 mint leaves

☞ 2 to 3 watercress or mint sprigs, baby spinach, baby arugula, or other small fresh leaves (for salad or garnish)

SHISO, RED/PERILLA LEAF/BEEFSTEAK PLANT, FRESH – 1 leaf

☞ 2 or 3 purple basil leaves, such as Dark Opal, Red Rubin, Purple Delight, or Purple Ruffles added just before cooking ends, or for garnish (loses color when cooked)

☞ 1 dried red shiso leaf, or a generous pinch of shiso powder (for coloring)

SHITO/GHANAIAN BLACK SAUCE – 1 tablespoon
☞ 1 tablespoon spicy chili sauce (lacks color and depth of flavor)

SHOYU *See SOY SAUCE, JAPANESE*

SHRIMP, DRIED (Asian and Latin American cooking condiment) – 1/4 cup
☞ 1/4 cup dried crayfish
☞ 1/4 cup smoked salted fish, chopped or flaked
☞ 1/3 pound (27 or 28) small cooked fresh shrimp (used without soaking)
☞ 1 tablespoon minced anchovies

SHRIMP PASTE, FERMENTED/BAGOONG/BLACHAN/BELACAN/KAPI/ MAM TOM/ NGAPI/TRASI/XIA JIANG (Southeast Asian pungent seasoning) – 1/2-inch cube
☞ 2 teaspoons pounded (or finely chopped) preroasted dried shrimp
☞ 1 scant tablespoon fermented fish or fish paste, such as pickled gouramy fish (more pungent)
☞ 1 tablespoon anchovy paste, or 1 1/2 rinsed and mashed salt-packed anchovy fillets
☞ 1 tablespoon Chinese fermented black beans/*dow see,* Burmese fermented soybean paste/*tua nao,* or Japanese dark miso, such as *inaka* or *hatcho*
☞ 1 teaspoon Worcestershire sauce plus 1/2 teaspoon red miso/*inaka miso*

SHRIMP POWDER, DRIED/SHRIMP FLOSS/PAZUN CHAUK (Asian flavoring and thickener) – 1/2 cup (packed)
☞ 1/2 cup toasted chickpea flour plus 1 or 2 teaspoons dark Japanese miso, such as *hatcho,* or Burmese fermented soybean paste/*tuo nao* (for vegan option)

Make Your Own Toast a scant 1/2 cup dried shrimp in a dry skillet over low heat for 4 to 5 minutes, then grind to a fine powder in a blender or spice/coffee grinder. Store, tightly sealed, in the freezer. Alternatively, soak the shrimp to cover until softened, 20 to 30 minutes; pat dry, then pulse in a food processor until flossy.

SHRIMP SAUCE, FERMENTED/HOM HA/HAE KOH/BALICHAO/MAM RUOC/PETIS (Southeast Asian jarred seasoning) – 1 tablespoon

- 1 tablespoon Chinese jarred fermented shrimp/*xia jiang*
- 2 tablespoons Asian fish sauce, such as *nam pla, nuoc nam, patis* or *shottsuru,* plus a dash of oyster sauce
- 1 tablespoon anchovy paste, anchovy essence/syrup, or 1 1/2 rinsed and mashed salted anchovy fillets, thinned with a little soy sauce

SICHUAN CHILI BEAN PASTE/PIXIAN CHILI BEAN SAUCE/ DOUBANJIANG/TOBAN JHAN (Chinese condiment) – 1/3 cup

- 1/4 cup fermented black beans/*dowse*, rinsed briefly in a fine sieve, then mashed with 1 1/2 tablespoons Chinese chili sauce or chili-garlic sauce
- 1/3 cup Korean chili bean paste/*gochujang*

SICHUAN PEPPER/ANISE PEPPER/DRIED PRICKLY ASH/SANSHO/HUĀ JIĀO (Chinese seasoning) – 1 teaspoon ground/powdered

- 1/4 teaspoon each ground anise and allspice
- 1 or 2 teaspoons Sichuan pepper salt/*hu jiao yeni*; reduce salt in recipe accordingly
- 1/2 teaspoon Chinese five-spice powder (only if it contains ground Sichuan/Szechuan peppercorns, not regular peppercorns)

Make Your Own Toast 1 tablespoon Sichuan/Szechuan peppercorns in a dry skillet over low heat until very fragrant and slightly darkened, 4 to 5 minutes. Crush with a mortar or rolling pin while hot, then sift through a fine-mesh sieve and measure (or cool, grind, sift, and measure). Discard the husks.

SICHUAN PEPPERCORNS See PEPPERCORNS, SICHUAN/SZECHUAN

SICHUAN PEPPER OIL/HUĀ JIĀO YOU (Chinese seasoning) – 2/3 cup
Make Your Own Heat 1/4 cup toasted Sichuan peppercorns and 1 cup peanut oil over low heat for 10 minutes. Cool, then strain into a sterilized jar or bottle. Store, tightly covered, in the refrigerator. It will keep for up to 6 months. (Toast the peppercorns in a dry skillet over low heat until fragrant, 4 to 5 minutes.)

SICHUAN RED CHILI OIL/HONG YOU (Chinese chili and spice-infused oil) – 1 teaspoon
- 1 teaspoon Chinese savory chili oil/*chiu chow*
- 1 teaspoon Japanese chili oil/*rayu*

SICHUAN SALT/HUĀ JIĀO YAN (Chinese condiment) – 1/4 cup (about)
Make Your Own Toast 1 tablespoon Sichuan peppercorns and 3 tablespoons coarse sea salt in a dry skillet over low heat until the pepper starts to smoke faintly and the salt is slightly colored, about 5 minutes. Cool, sift, and grind to a powder. (For a coarser texture, toast and grind the peppercorns, then add to the untoasted salt.)

SICHUAN SWEET BEAN PASTE/SAUCE/TIAN MIAN JIANG/TENMENJAN (Chinese condiment) – 1 tablespoon
- 2 teaspoons Chinese cooking sauce (*chee hou* sauce or hoisin) and 1 teaspoon rice vinegar

SICILIAN CITRUS FLAVORING/FIORI DI SICILIA – 1 teaspoon
- 1/8 teaspoon orange citrus oil, such as Boyajian, plus 1/2 teaspoon vanilla extract

SIMPLE SYRUP See *SYRUP, SIMPLE*

SKYR (Icelandic super thick yogurt) – 1 cup
- 1 cup full-fat plain Greek-style yogurt, *fromage blanc*, quark, or *gvina levana* (Israeli soft white cheese)

SMEN See *SÂMNA/SAMNEH/SMEN (Middle Eastern and North African preserved butter)*

SMETANA/SMATANA/SMITANE (Eastern European fermented cream) – 1 cup
- ☞ 1/2 cup heavy cream and 1/2 cup sour cream, whisked together, lightly covered, and left at room temperature for 2 to 4 hours (Store, tightly covered, in the refrigerated for up to 1 week.)
- ☞ 1/2 cup each sour cream and crème fraîche (less fat)
- ☞ 1 cup Mexican sour cream/*crema Mexicana agria* (less fat)

SOBA SAUCE/KAESHI – 1 scant cup
- ☞ 3/4 cup Japanese soy sauce, and 2 tablespoons each mirin and granulated sugar brought to a boil and simmered until sugar dissolves, 2 to 3 minutes; it will keep up to 3 months refrigerated

SOJU See KOREAN RICE WINE, SWEET COOKING

SORGHUM SYRUP/SORGHUM MOLASSES/SWEET SORGHUM (Southern U.S. sweetener with a malty flavor) – 1 tablespoon
- ☞ 1 tablespoon cane syrup, golden syrup, dark honey, light unsulphured molasses, or maple syrup
- ☞ 4 teaspoons dark corn syrup

SORREL, COMMON GARDEN/BELLEVILLE – 1 pound
- ☞ 1 pound baby spinach or young tender spinach, plus a little fresh lemon juice added just before serving (for soups)

SOUP, CANNED See TOMATO SOUP, CANNED

SOUP, CANNED CREAM OF See CELERY SOUP, CANNED CREAM OF; CHICKEN SOUP, CANNED CREAM OF; MUSHROOM SOUP, CANNED CREAM OF

SOUR CREAM (18% butterfat) – 1 cup
- ☞ 1 cup crème fraîche, Mexican *crema*, or Venezuelan *nata* (higher fat; less sour)
- ☞ 1 cup *smetana/smitane* or quark (thinner consistency; lower-fat)

- 1 cup plain full-fat Greek-style yogurt (thicker consistency; more calories)
- 1 tablespoon lemon juice (or distilled white vinegar) stirred into 1 cup heavy cream (or evaporated milk); left at room temperature until slightly thickened, 30 to 40 minutes; and refrigerated for 4 hours before using
- 3/4 cup natural cream cheese, 1/4 cup milk or water, and a dash of lemon juice blended until smooth and creamy
- 1/2 cup each plain yogurt and creamed cottage cheese, blended until smooth and creamy
- 1 cup (8 ounces) firm or extra-firm silken tofu, 1 to 4 tablespoons canola or olive oil, 2 tablespoons lemon juice, and 1 teaspoon salt, processed in a blender until smooth and creamy
- 1 cup soaked cashews, 1/2 cup water, 2 (or more) tablespoons lemon juice, and 1/4 to 1/2 teaspoon sea salt, processed in a high-speed blender until smooth and creamy

SOUR CREAM, FAT-FREE OR LOW-FAT – 1 cup
- 1 tablespoon lemon juice or distilled white vinegar, stirred into 1 cup fat-free evaporated milk and left at room temperature until slightly thickened, about 30 minutes (chill for 4 hours before using)
- 1 cup plain nonfat or low-fat quark (richer texture)

SOUR CREAM, MEXICAN See CRÈMA MEXICANA

SOUR MIX (bottled product for cocktails) – 1 cup
- 1/2 cup heavy simple syrup and 1/2 cup fresh lemon juice (or half lemon, half lime) See also SYRUP, SIMPLE

SOUR PLUM/PRUNE/ALOO BUKHARA (Central Asian souring agent) – 1
- 1 umeboshi (Japanese salt-pickled dried plum) or 3 umeboshi-sa (tiny plum paste balls)
- 2 teaspoons jarred umeboshi puree/sour plum paste/bainiku/neriume, or pomegranate molasses
- 1 regular prune, soaked in white vinegar or umeboshi plum vinegar for 8 to 10 hours

SOUR SALT See CITRIC ACID/SOUR SALT

SOYBEAN PASTE, FERMENTED See FERMENTED SOYBEAN PASTE; KOREAN CHILI BEAN PASTE; MISO

SOY BUTTER – 2 cups

Make Your Own Combine 3/4 cup powdered soy milk, 3/4 cup water, 1 teaspoon salt in a double boiler and cook for 25 minutes; gradually whisk in 1 cup canola oil and beat until thick. Store, refrigerated, in a tightly sealed container. It will keep for up to 1 month.

SOY NUT BUTTER – 8 ounces

Make Your Own Process 8 ounces plain or roasted cooked soybeans, 1/4 teaspoon salt (optional), and 1 to 2 tablespoons vegetable oil in a high-power blender or food processor until reduced to a paste, scraping down the sides of the bowl as needed. It will keep in a sterilized jar in the refrigerator for up to 1 month.

SOY PROTEIN CONCENTRATE (sausage-making binder to improve moisture retention) – 14 ounces for 25 pounds meat

- 1 1/2 ounces concentrated carrot fiber binder/C-Binder (per 25 pounds meat)
- 12 ounces nonfat dry milk powder (per 25 pounds meat)

SOY PROTEIN ISOLATE (sausage-making binder to improve moisture retention) – 1 1/4 cups for 10 pounds meat

- 2 cups soy protein concentrate (per 10 pounds meat)

SOY SAUCE (ALL PURPOSE) – 1 tablespoon

- 1 tablespoon reduced-sodium/lower sodium or lite soy sauce (regular or gluten-free)
- 2 teaspoons tamari soy sauce (contains wheat but naturally brewed and without additives)
- 2 teaspoons gluten-free tamari, such as San-J, Crystal, or Westbrae

- 1 tablespoon citrus-seasoned soy sauce, such as Japanese ponzu-seasoned/*ponzu shoyu* or Filipino calamsi-seasoned/*toyo mansi* (for condiments and dressings)
- 1 tablespoon gluten-free liquid aminos, such as Dr. Bronner's or Bragg's
- 1 tablespoon gluten-free and soy-free coconut aminos, such as Coconut Secret, plus a pinch of salt
- 2 to 3 teaspoons Japanese fermented rice/*shio-koji* or miso (thicker consistency; for cooking)
- 1 tablespoon Maggi Seasoning or oyster sauce (for a small amount)
- 2 teaspoons molasses, 1 teaspoon balsamic vinegar, and a few grains of sugar (for a small amount)
- 1 tablespoon Chinese soy sauce powder/*funmatsu* (for cooking or barbecue dry rubs)

SOY SAUCE, CHINESE DARK/BLACK/TABLE SOY/CHO YO/SEE YAU/LAO CHOU – 1 tablespoon

- 1 tablespoon Japanese organic tamari (wheat-free, naturally fermented, darker, thicker, more flavorful)
- 1 tablespoon Japanese dark soy sauce (darker, slightly sweeter, less salty)
- 1 tablespoon mushroom soy sauce (richer tasting)
- 2 teaspoons Chinese light soy sauce and 1 teaspoon black/dark/sweet soy sauce (Chinese or Thai)
- 1 tablespoon Chinese light soy sauce plus 1/4 teaspoon molasses

SOY SAUCE, CHINESE DOUBLE DARK/DOUBLE BLACK/SWEET/YEWN SHE JIANG – 1 tablespoon

- 1 tablespoon Malaysian sweet, dark soy sauce/*tim cheong*
- 2 teaspoons Chinese dark soy sauce plus 1 teaspoon brown sugar or molasses

SOY SAUCE, CHINESE LIGHT/PALE OR THIN/JIANG JING/JIANG YAO/ SHENG CHOU – 1 tablespoon

- 1 tablespoon Japanese all-purpose soy sauce/*shoyu*, such as Kikkoman; or Korean soy sauce/*ganjang* (darker, less salty, and a touch sweeter)

- 1 tablespoon Chinese white soy sauce/*yin bai jiang,* or Japanese white soy sauce/*shirojoyu* (a little sweeter, but will not add color)
- 1 tablespoon Chinese dark soy sauce/*cho yo* (thicker, stronger, a little sweeter, and less salty)

SOY SAUCE, FILIPINO/TOYO – 1 tablespoon

- 1 tablespoon Japanese-style soy sauce/*soyu* (saltier and thinner)

SOY SAUCE, FILIPINO KALAMANSI/TOYO MANSI – 1 tablespoon

- 1 tablespoon Lu soy/*lu shiu* (spicy lime soy sauce; contains spices, ginger, sugar)
- 1 1/2 teaspoons Filipino soy sauce/*toyo* (or Japanese-style soy sauce) and 1 1/2 teaspoons fresh calamansi juice (or Meyer lemon juice)

SOY SAUCE, INDONESIAN/KECAP ASIN (dark salty soy sauce) – 1 tablespoon

- 1 tablespoon Malaysian soy sauce/*kicap pekat*
- 1 tablespoon Chinese dark/black soy sauce (thinner and less salty)

SOY SAUCE, INDONESIAN/KECAP MANIS (thick sweet soy sauce) See KECAP MANIS

SOY SAUCE, JAPANESE ALL-PURPOSE REGULAR DARK/KOIKUCHI SHOYU (such as Kikkoman) – 1 tablespoon

- 1 tablespoon Japanese organic whole soybean soy sauce/*maruda-izu shoyu,* or unpasteurized/raw soy sauce/*nama shoyu* (contains wheat)
- 1 tablespoon Japanese low-salt/reduced-salt soy sauce/*gen'en shoyu* (contains additives)
- 2 1/2 teaspoons Japanese light-colored soy sauce/*usukuchi shoyu* or Chinese regular/light soy sauce (thinner and saltier)
- 1 tablespoon Japanese white soy sauce/*shiro shoyu* (very light colored, mellow, and relatively sweet)
- 1 tablespoon Japanese strong-flavored rich soy sauce/*saishikomi* (dark brown and thick; for sashimi and sushi)

SOY SAUCE, JAPANESE LIGHT-COLORED/USUKUCHI SHOYU (saltier and thinner than all-purpose regular dark soy sauce) – 1 tablespoon
- ⊩ 1 tablespoon Chinese light/thin regular soy sauce
- ⊩ 1 tablespoon soy sauce wheat-free replacements, such as Dr. Bronner's or Braggs Liquid Aminos; or wheat- and soy-free replacement, such as Coconut Secret Coconut Aminos
- ⊩ 2 teaspoon teriyaki sauce and 1 teaspoon water
- ⊩ 1 teaspoon Maggi Seasoning

SOY SAUCE, KOREAN/GANJANG/KANJANG (medium-bodied) – 1 tablespoon
- ⊩ 1 tablespoon Japanese-style all-purpose dark soy sauce (saltier)
- ⊩ 1 tablespoon Chinese light/thin regular soy sauce (saltier and less sweet)

SOY SAUCE, MALAYSIAN/KICAP CAIR (light soy sauce) – 1 tablespoon
- ⊩ 1 tablespoon Chinese or Japanese all-purpose regular soy sauce

SOY SAUCE, MALAYSIAN/KICAP HITAM (dark sweet soy sauce) – 1 tablespoon
- ⊩ 1 tablespoon Indonesian thick sweet soy sauce/*kecap manis*

SOY SAUCE, MALAYSIAN/KICAP PEKAT (dark soy sauce) – 1 tablespoon
- ⊩ 1 tablespoon Indonesian all-purpose soy sauce/*kecap asin*
- ⊩ 1 tablespoon Chinese dark/black soy sauce (thinner and less salty)

SOY SAUCE, MUSHROOM (dark soy sauce infused with nameko or shiitake mushrooms) – 1 tablespoon
- ⊩ 1 tablespoon dark soy sauce plus a pinch of sugar or drop of honey

SOY SAUCE, THAI SWEET BLACK/NAM PLA SIIW/SIEW DAM – 1 tablespoon
- ⊩ 1 tablespoon Indonesian thick sweet soy sauce/*kecap manis* (thicker)
- ⊩ 1 tablespoon Chinese thick soy sauce/*jee yow* plus a little unsulphured molasses as sweetener

SOY SAUCE, THAI THIN/SEE EIW/SI-EW – 1 tablespoon
- 1 tablespoon all-purpose Chinese light soy sauce

SOY SAUCE, VIETNAMESE/XI DAU
- 1 tablespoon all-purpose Chinese or Japanese light soy sauce

SOY SAUCE, WHITE/YIN BAI JIANG/SHIROJOYU – 1 tablespoon
- 2 teaspoons all-purpose soy sauce plus 1 teaspoon water

SPECK, GERMAN (mildly cured and smoked pork fat) – 1/4 pound
- 1/4 pound Italian *lardo*
- 1/4 pound thinly sliced bacon

SPECK, ITALIAN (cold-smoked seasoned pork product) – 1/4 pound
- 1/4 pound Italian or domestic prosciutto (less firm; unsmoked; lacks juniper aroma)
- 1/4 pound Westphalian ham (hot-smoked; smokier flavor)
- 1/4 pound Serrano ham or Ibérico ham (lacks juniper flavor)

SPLENDA, GRANULATED (sucralose and maltodextrin sweetener) – 1 cup
- 1 cup granulated sugar (has more browning properties)
- 1 cup stevia and maltodextrin sweetener, such as Stevia Extract in the Raw
- 1 1/3 cups erythritol/fermented cane sugar, such as Z-sweet or Organic Zero

SPRINKLES, INDIVIDUAL COLORED – 1 ounce
- 1 ounce white sprinkles shaken with a pinch of powdered food coloring in a tightly closed jar or sealable plastic bag

SPRUCE TIP SYRUP (Norwegian honey-like sweetener) – 1/2 cup (about)
- 1 cup young, tender, unsprayed spruce sprigs/tips/*Picea* species, about 2 inches long (or balsam, Douglas fir, pine, or other fir sprigs),

boiled in a simple syrup (1 cup each water and granulated sugar) until thick and syrupy (strain through a fine-mesh sieve and discard the spruce)

SRIRACHA See THAI HOT CHILI SAUCE

SRIRACHA SALT – 1 cup
Make Your Own Mix 1 cup kosher salt with 1/4 cup Sriracha sauce and spread in a thin layer on a parchment-lined baking sheet. Bake in a preheated 200°F oven until dry, 2 to 3 hours, then cool and pulse in a food processor until finely ground. Store in a tightly sealed container in a cool, dry place; it will keep for several weeks.

STAR ANISE (Chinese seasoning) – 1 whole star (8 points)
- 3/4 teaspoon crushed or broken star anise pieces
- 1/2 teaspoon ground star anise
- 3/4 teaspoon anise seeds (crushed with the side of a knife)
- 1/2 teaspoon ground anise or fennel
- 1/2 teaspoon Chinese five-spice powder (for savory dishes)

STAR ANISE, GROUND – 1 teaspoon
- 2 whole star anise, crushed; or 1 1/2 teaspoons broken pieces
- 1 1/2 teaspoons anise or fennel seeds, ground in a pepper mill or spice/coffee grinder
- 1 teaspoon ground anise
- 1 teaspoon Chinese five-spice powder (for savory dishes)

STEAK SAUCE See BROWN SAUCE, BOTTLED

STEVIA LEAF EXTRACT (liquid herbal sweetener) – 8 ounces (1 cup)
Make Your Own Add 3/4 cup lightly crushed dried stevia leaves/*Stevia rebaudiana* to 1 1/2 cups 180°F water; cover and steep for 40 minutes. Strain and transfer to a dark-colored bottle; it will keep in the refrigerator for up to 2 weeks. (One teaspoon equals 1 tablespoon granulated sugar.)

STOCK SYRUP *See SYRUP, SIMPLE*

STRAWBERRY DUST
- Freeze-dried strawberries, pulverized in a spice/coffee grinder

STRAWBERRY SUGAR
- Equal parts freeze-dried strawberries and granulated sugar, pulverized in a spice/coffee grinder

STURGEON, SMOKED – 4 ounces
- 4 ounces smoked arctic char, bluefish, haddock, mackerel, pollock, sablefish, salmon, trout, or whitefish

SUCRALOSE *See SPLENDA, GRANULATED*

SUDACHI (Japanese lime-like citrus) – 1
- 1 kabosu or yuzu (larger; for juice and zest)
- 1 Key lime or small lemon (for juice and zest)
- Fresh or bottled yuzu juice (for juice)

SUGAR, BROWN ROCK/SLAB/PIAN TANG/PEEN TONG (Chinese large-crystal sugar) – 1 (5 x 1-inch slab) (3 1/4 ounces coarsely grated or finely chopped)
- 1/2 cup firmly packed dark brown sugar plus 1 teaspoon unsulphured molasses

SUGAR, COCONUT PALM *See JAGGERY*

SUGAR, CORN – 3/4 cup
- 2/3 cup granulated sugar
- 3/4 cup malt powder
- 1 1/4 cups dry malt extract

SUGAR, DEMERARA (coarse-grained, pale brown, dry semirefined sugar) – 1 cup
- 1 cup turbinado/semirefined sugar, such as Sugar in the Raw

➻ 1 cup pregrated Brazilian semirefined sugar/*rapadura*
➻ 1 cup pregrated Columbian semirefined sugar/*panela*

SUGAR, FLAVORED *See CINNAMON SUGAR; CITRUS SUGAR; LAVENDER SUGAR; LEMON SUGAR; MINT SUGAR; STRAWBERRY SUGAR; VANILLA SUGAR*

SUGAR, FRUCTOSE *See FRUCTOSE*

SUGAR, GLAZING *See SUGAR, CONFECTIONERS'*

SUGAR, GOLDEN BAKER'S (British fine-grained unrefined sugar) – 1 cup
➻ 1 cup plus 1 tablespoon Demerara or turbinado sugar, pulverized in a blender or food processor until fine-textured, about 20 seconds
➻ 1 cup superfine sugar (lacks color and caramel taste)

SUGAR, LEMON *See LEMON SUGAR*

SUGAR, LUMP – 6 ounces (1 cup)
➻ 3/4 cup granulated sugar

SUGAR, MALT *See MALTOSE*

SUGAR, MAPLE (dried crystallized maple syrup) – 1 cup
➻ 2/3 cup Grade A dark, robust maple syrup (reduce the liquid in the recipe by 2 tablespoons or add 2 tablespoons extra flour)
➻ 1 cup light or dark muscovado/Barbados sugar
➻ 1 cup (or more) birch sugar (less sweet)
➻ 1 cup granulated sugar plus 2 teaspoons maple extract, or 2 tablespoons maple syrup
Make Your Own Boil 1 1/2 cups Grade A dark, robust maple syrup to the soft ball stage (240°F), then stir until thick and creamy. Pour into a greased baking dish, let sit until firm, then break up for coarse crystals or pulverize for medium-fine crystals.

SUGAR, MINT *See MINT SUGAR*

SUGAR, MUSCOVADO/BARBADOS, LIGHT OR DARK (moist, fine-textured unrefined sugar) – 1 cup
- 1 cup dark brown sugar
- 1 cup finely grated *piloncillo/panela* or panocha/*panucha* (Mexican unrefined sugar)

SUGAR, RAW *See SUGAR, TURBINADO CANE*

SUGAR, ROCK *See SUGAR, BROWN ROCK; SUGAR, YELLOW/CLEAR ROCK*

SUGAR, SANDING/PEARL (extra-large-crystal cane or beet sugar) – 1 ounce
- 1 ounce Asian rock sugar, coarsely grated or finely chopped
- 1 ounce sugar pearls or sugar cubes, coarsely crushed
- 1 tablespoon turbinado/semirefined sugar

SUGAR, SUPERFINE/ULTRA FINE/BAKER'S/CASTOR/CASTER (fine-crystal cane or beet sugar) – 1 cup
- 1 cup golden castor sugar/golden baker's sugar
- 1 cup plus 2 teaspoons granulated sugar, pulverized in a blender or food processor until finely textured, 20 to 30 seconds (let the sugar dust settle before opening lid)
- 1 cup granulated sugar (takes longer to dissolve)

SUGAR SYRUP *See SYRUP, SIMPLE*

SUGAR, TURBINADO CANE (coarse-grained light-brown unrefined sugar) – 1 cup
- 1 cup unrefined sugar, such as Sugar in the Raw; or Demerara sugar, such as Florida Crystals
- 1 packed cup light brown sugar (if sprinkled, press through a sieve)

SUGAR, YELLOW/CLEAR ROCK/BING TANG/DUONG PHEN (Asian large-crystal sugar) – 1-inch crystal piece (scant 1/2-ounce) coarsely grated or finely chopped: *See also SUGAR, BROWN ROCK*
- 1 tablespoon granulated or turbinado sugar

SULUGUNI (Russian salt-brined cheese) – 1 ounce
- 1 ounce halloumi or feta cheese

SUMAC LIQUID (Middle Eastern red souring agent) – 1/4 cup
- 1/4 cup whole dried sumac berries, soaked in 1/3 cup hot water for 8 to 12 hours (Strain through a fine-mesh sieve, pressing to extract the liquid, then discard the berries.)
- 1/2 cup fresh sumac berries, such as Dwarf, Squaw Bush, or Staghorn, lightly crushed and soaked in 1/3 cup cold water until the water turns pink, about 30 minutes (Strain through a fine-mesh sieve, pressing to extract the liquid, then discard the berries.)
- 1/4 cup pure pomegranate juice
- 1/4 cup verjuice or lemon juice (lacks color)

SUMAC POWDER/DRIED GROUND SUMAC (Middle Eastern tart, red seasoning) – 1 teaspoon
- 1 1/2 teaspoons dried European sumac berries/*Rhus coriaria* ground in a spice/coffee grinder with a pinch of salt
- 1 1/2 teaspoons ground dried North American wild sumac berries/ *Rhus glabra/Rhus typhina/Rhus hirta* (Dry fresh berries for 2 to 3 hours on a parchment-lined baking sheet at 200°F, then cool and grind.)
- 1 scant teaspoon sour grape powder, lemon powder (dried and crushed lemon zest), green mango powder (*amchur*), or Indian dried and powdered pomegranate seeds (*anardana*)
- 1 teaspoon very finely grated lemon zest plus a tiny pinch of mild paprika or tomato powder spread out to dry slightly (for sprinkling on flatbread or bread salad/*fattoush*)

SUMMER SAVORY *See SAVORY, SUMMER*

SUMO/DEKOPON (Japanese sweet hybrid orange) – 1
- 1 sweet satsuma orange

SUN BUTTER *See SUNFLOWER SEED BUTTER*

SUNFLOWER MILK – 4 cups
Make Your Own Soak 1 cup raw unsalted sunflower seeds in water to cover for 4 to 8 hours; drain, rinse, then blend with 4 cups water until smooth, about 3 minutes. Strain in a nutmilk bag or fine-mesh sieve, pressing firmly on the pulp to extract all the liquid. Keep refrigerated and shake before using. It will keep for up to 3 days.

SUNFLOWER OIL – 1 cup
⊨ 1 cup light peanut oil

SUNFLOWER SEED BUTTER – 1 cup
⊨ Golden peabutter (made from brown peas)
Make Your Own Toast 1 1/2 cups sunflower seed kernels in a dry skillet until fragrant, 3 to 4 minutes. Process with 1/4 teaspoon salt (optional) in a blender or food processor until finely ground, then add 2 to 4 tablespoons grapeseed oil, and process to a coarse paste, scraping down the bowl as needed. Store, refrigerated, in a small sterilized jar. It will keep up to 1 month.
Or
Toast 2 cups sunflower seed kernels on a baking sheet in a preheated 350°F oven until golden, 15 to 20 minutes; cool a few minutes then process in a food processor until reduced to a paste, about 25 minutes, scraping down the sides every 2 to 3 minutes. Add 1/4 teaspoon salt if desired and process a few minutes longer.

SUNFLOWER SEED KERNELS – 1 cup
⊨ 1 cup hulled hemp or pumpkin seeds
⊨ 1 cup pine nuts or slivered almonds
⊨ 1 cup chia or salba seeds

SUPERFINE SUGAR See SUGAR, SUPERFINE

SURE-JELL See PECTIN, REGULAR

SUSHI DIPPING SAUCE (Japanese) – 1/4 cup

Make Your Own Combine 3 tablespoons water, 3 tablespoons Japanese soy sauce/*shoyu*, and 1 tablespoon mirin in a small saucepan and simmer for 1 minute, then cool to room temperature.

SUSHI GINGER *See GINGER, PICKLED*

SUSHI MESHI DRESSING (Japanese sushi rice seasoning) – 1/2 cup
- ⇨ 1/2 cup Japanese seasoned rice vinegar (for sprinkling on hot rice)
- ⇨ 1/2 cup instant powdered sushi vinegar (for sprinkling on hot rice)

SÜZME (Turkish extra-thick yogurt for dips and desserts) – 1 cup
Make Your Own Line a sieve with a double layer of dampened cheesecloth (or 2 basket-type paper coffee filters) and set it over a bowl. Put 2 cups plain full-fat yogurt (without pectin or additives) in the sieve and drain for 8 hours in the refrigerator.

SWEDISH LIGHT SYRUP/LJUS SIRAP *See GOLDEN SYRUP*

SWEET-AND-SOUR SAUCE *See CHINESE SWEET-AND-SOUR SAUCE*

SYRUP, FLAVORED – 1 cup *See also ALMOND SYRUP; CINNAMON SYRUP; CITRUS SYRUP; COCONUT SYRUP, LIGHT; ROSE GERANIUM SYRUP*
- ⇨ 1 cup heavy simple syrup (*See SYRUP, SIMPLE*) flavored with 1/2 to 1 teaspoon extract (such as vanilla, almond, butterscotch, walnut, coffee, or eggnog in season), or 2 to 4 tablespoons liqueur
- ⇨ 1 cup sugar-free, calorie-free flavored syrup, such as Torani
- ⇨ 1 cup syrup from canned fruit packed in heavy syrup

SYRUP, REFINER'S/INVERT – 1 cup
- ⇨ 1 cup golden syrup, such as Lyle's
- ⇨ 1 cup light or dark corn syrup

SYRUP, SIMPLE/STOCK SYRUP, REGULAR – 1 cup
- ⇨ 1/2 cup each honey and boiling water, stirred until combined, then cooled

- 1/2 cup each light agave syrup/nectar and hot water, stirred until combined, then cooled
- 1 cup each superfine sugar and water, shaken in an airtight container until the sugar dissolves

Make Your Own Bring 1 cup granulated sugar and 1 cup water to a gentle simmer over medium heat, then simmer, stirring, until the sugar dissolves, 1 to 2 minutes. Cool and store, refrigerated, for up to 6 months. (For light syrup, reduce the sugar to 1/2 cup; for heavy syrup increase the sugar to 1 1/2 cups.)

SYRUP, SIMPLE/STOCK SYRUP, RICH/DOUBLE STRENGTH – 1 tablespoon for drinks

- 1 tablespoon light agave syrup/nectar

Make Your Own Gently simmer 2 cups sugar, 1 tablespoon corn syrup or glucose, and 1 cup water until the sugar dissolves, 2 to 3 minutes. Or omit the corn syrup or glucose and gently simmer, covered, for 10 minutes. Cool and measure out 1 tablespoon. The syrup will keep in the refrigerator for up to 6 months.

T

TABASCO SAUCE – 1 teaspoon *See also HOT PEPPER SAUCE*
- 3/4 teaspoon pepper vinegar
- 1/4 teaspoon ground cayenne pepper or crushed red pepper flakes

TABIL/TABBIL (Tunisian spice paste) – 1 generous tablespoon
- 2 teaspoons each roasted ground coriander and ground caraway, 1 teaspoon ground cayenne pepper, 1/4 teaspoon garlic powder, and enough vegetable oil to mix to a paste

TACO SAUCE, RED – 1 cup
- 1 cup canned enchilada sauce
- 1 cup refrigerated or jarred mild salsa, or homemade tomato salsa

TACO SEASONING – 1 tablespoon
- 2 teaspoons mild chili powder, such as New Mexico or pasilla; 1/2 teaspoon ground cumin; 1/4 teaspoon garlic or onion powder; and salt and pepper to taste
- 1 tablespoon Chili Seasoning Mix

TAHINI (Middle Eastern sesame paste) – 1/3 cup *See also SESAME PASTE*
- 1/3 cup roasted tahini (less bitter)
- 1/2 cup powdered tahini, rehydrated with water following the package directions
- 1/4 cup smooth unsweetened almond or peanut butter (or other nut butter) mixed with 4 teaspoons untoasted sesame oil (use half the quantity of tahini called for)

Make Your Own Combine 1/2 cup hulled (white) sesame seeds and 3 tablespoons vegetable oil, preferably untoasted sesame oil, in a mortar or blender and grind or process until smooth. Transfer to a small lidded jar and store in the refrigerator; it will keep for up to 6 months; stir before using.

TAJIN CLÁSSICO SEASONING (Mexican) – 1 tablespoon (about)
- 2 teaspoons New Mexico chili powder, 1/4 teaspoon fine sea salt, and 1 teaspoon finely grated lime zest
- 1 tablespoon New Mexico chili powder plus a dash of lemon pepper

TAMARA/IKURA (roe for cod, carp, or mullet) See BOTTARGA DI MUG-GINE (salt-cured, dried gray mullet roe)

TAMARI (Japanese naturally fermented/traditionally brewed dense soy sauce) – 1 tablespoon See also SOY SAUCE
- 1 tablespoon tamari soy sauce (contains wheat but naturally brewed and without additives)
- 1 tablespoon wheat-free tamari, such as Crystal, Eden, San-J, or Westbrae tamari
- 1 tablespoon Japanese premium whole-bean organic soy sauce/ marudaizu, or marudaizu-grade soy sauce
- 1 tablespoon gluten-free soy sauce, such as LaChoy or San-J gluten-free
- 1 tablespoon reduced-sodium/lower-sodium tamari or soy sauce
- 1 tablespoon Bragg Liquid Aminos or Raw Coconut Aminos
- 1 1/2 teaspoons Maggi Seasoning
- Small pinch ground dulse seaweed

TAMARIND CONCENTRATE/EXTRACT/PASTE/PULP (Asian, Indian, and Latin souring agent) – 1 tablespoon
- 1 dried tamarind slice/assam gelugor (for curries, soups, and stews; discard before serving)
- 1 tablespoon pomegranate molasses
- 1 teaspoon molasses mixed with 1 1/2 teaspoons lemon or lime juice (or 1 1/2 teaspoons lime juice plus 1/2 teaspoon Worcestershire sauce)

☞ 1 teaspoon brown sugar dissolved in 2 teaspoons Worcestershire sauce

TAMARIND LEAVES (Asian souring agent) – 1 ounce fresh or frozen
☞ 1 ounce chopped fresh sorrel

TAMARIND POWDER (Asian, Indian, and Latin souring agent) – 1 ounce
☞ 1/3 cup lemon or lime juice

TAMARIND PUREE (Asian, Indian, and Latin souring agent) – 1 cup
☞ 8 ounces (8 to 10) peeled tamarind pods, soaked in boiling water until softened, 1 to 2 hours; strain pulp and discard solids
☞ 1/2 cup (3 1/2 ounces) thawed frozen tamarind pulp, blended with 1/2 cup water; strain and discard solids
☞ 1/4 cup (1 3/4 ounces) tamarind paste/concentrate, blended with 1 cup boiling water until smooth; strain and discard solids

TAMARIND SAUCE (Asian, Indian, and Latin souring agent) – 1/2 cup
☞ 1 tablespoon tamarind concentrate added to 1/2 cup just-boiled water

TAMARIND SYRUP (Latin American concentrate) – 1 cup
☞ 3 tablespoons tamarind concentrate/paste, 1/2 cup sugar, and 1/2 cup boiling water, stirred together until the sugar dissolves

TAMARIND WATER (Asian, Indian, and Latin souring agent) – 1 cup medium-strength
☞ 1 1/2 tablespoons tamarind paste, dissolved in 1 cup hot water
Make Your Own Soak 1 ounce (1 by 1 1/2-inch piece) compressed tamarind (or 6 cracked and peeled tamarind pods) in 1 1/2 cups boiling water until softened, 15 minutes or more. Strain and discard the solids. (For thick tamarind water, simmer the tamarind in the water until reduced by half and then strain.)

TANDOORI COLORING/TANDOORI RANG (Indian seasoning and coloring agent) – 1 teaspoon
- 1 tablespoon mild/sweet Hungarian or Spanish paprika (for coloring only)
- 1 tablespoon ground Madras turmeric, toasted in a dry skillet until fragrant (for coloring only)
- 1 drop red food coloring (for coloring only)

TANDOORI SEASONING (Indian spice blend) – 1 tablespoon
- 1/4 teaspoon each ground cumin (preferably roasted), ground coriander (preferably roasted), ground ginger (preferably roasted), mild paprika, turmeric, and ground cayenne pepper, plus salt to taste (optional)
- 1 tablespoon mild curry powder

TANGERINE/MANDARIN PEEL, DRIED/TSEN PEI/CHEN PI (Chinese and Vietnamese seasoning)
- 1 (2-inch-long) strip orange zest removed with a vegetable peeler, or 1/4 teaspoon grated fresh orange zest will substitute for 1 (1-inch-wide) piece dried tangerine peel

Make Your Own Arrange tangerine peels (preferably organic) on a rack and set in the sun, covered by a food umbrella or tented cheesecloth, until hard and dry. Alternatively, microwave on High for about 2 minutes, sandwiched between paper towels, or dry on a baking sheet in a preheated 200°F oven for about 1 hour. (If the oven has a top heating unit, place a large baking sheet as close to the heating unit as possible to deflect the heat, then place the baking sheet with the peels on a lower rack.) Store the peels in a small container and grind just before using.

TANGERINE/MANDARIN ZEST – 1 teaspoon
- 2 tablespoons tangerine juice; reduce the liquid in the recipe by 2 tablespoons
- 1/2 teaspoon tangerine or orange extract

↠ 1 teaspoon grated orange zest

↠ 1/8 teaspoon tangerine citrus oil, such as Boyajian

TANSY, FRESH – 3 to 4 sprigs (1 tablespoon chopped)

↠ 1 1/2 tablespoons chopped mint leaves

TAPENADE (French condiment) – 1 cup See also OLIVE PASTE, BLACK

Make Your Own Process 1 cup pitted black olives, such as Kalamata or Niçoise; 2 tablespoons rinsed capers; 2 or 3 well-rinsed anchovy fillets; 1 to 2 teaspoons minced garlic; and 1/3 cup (or more) olive oil in a food processor until smooth. Transfer to a small jar, top with a thin layer of olive oil and store, tightly covered, in the refrigerator; it will keep for up to 2 weeks.

TARE (Japanese marinade and glaze) See TERIYAKI SAUCE

TARRAGON, FRENCH – 1 large branch (4 to 6 sprigs or 1 tablespoon finely chopped leaves)

↠ 1 teaspoon dried French tarragon, crumbled

↠ 1 1/4 teaspoons dried Russian tarragon, crumbled

↠ 2 tablespoons chopped fresh Mexican tarragon/Mexican mint marigold/*Tagetes lucida*

↠ 2 tablespoons chopped fresh chervil or flat-leaf parsley

↠ 1 1/2 to 2 teaspoons dried chervil, crumbled

↠ 1/8 teaspoon crushed anise or fennel seeds, or 16 whole seeds

↠ 1 to 2 teaspoons anise-flavored spirits, such as pastis or ouzo

TARTARIC ACID (tart flavoring and acidifying agent) – 1 teaspoon See also CITRIC ACID

↠ 1 teaspoon crystallized or powdered citric acid (not for wine making)

↠ 1/4 cup lemon juice (will give a lemon taste; not for wine making)

TARTAR SAUCE – 3/4 cup

Make Your Own Stir together 1/2 cup mayonnaise, 2 to 3 tablespoons finely chopped pickles (or drained pickle relish), 1 to 2 tablespoons finely chopped shallot or onion, and 1 to 2 teaspoons lemon juice or vinegar.

TARTAR SAUCE, QUICK – 1/4 cup
☞ 3 tablespoons mayonnaise plus 1 tablespoon pickle relish

TASAJO (Cuban smoke-dried salted beef) – 1 pound
☞ 1 pound Brazilian dried beef/*carne seca* or sun-dried beef/*carne de sol*
☞ 1 pound Cajun tasso

TASSO/CAJUN HAM (highly seasoned boneless smoked pork) – 1 pound
☞ 1 pound thick-cut country bacon; smoked ham, such as Black Forest or Westphalian; or country-style cured ham, such as Virginia or Kentucky, rubbed with a little garlic powder and ground cayenne pepper (or Cajun seasoning)
☞ 1 pound Cajun andouille or other fully cooked spicy smoked sausage

TEMPEH, FRESH OR FROZEN (fermented soybean patty) – 1 pound
☞ 2 (8-ounce) packages Organic Savory Baked Tofu/baked bean curd (spicy or smoked seasoned; softer texture)
☞ 1 pound firm tofu, weighted a few hours, then blotted dry and sliced crosswise (softer texture; less flavorful)
☞ 1 pound seitan (chewier)

TEMPURA DIPPING SAUCE/TENTSUYU (Japanese) – 1/3 cup
☞ 1/4 cup dashi (or light vegetable or chicken broth) plus 1 tablespoon each mirin and Japanese soy sauce/*shoyu*, brought to a boil then cooled
☞ 1/4 cup Japanese soy sauce/*shoyu*, 2 tablespoons mild vinegar, 2 teaspoons sugar, and 1 or 2 teaspoons finely grated ginger, stirred until the sugar dissolves
☞ 1 1/2 tablespoons Memmi noodle soup base, such as Kikkoman, mixed with 1/4 cup water

TERASI/TRASI (Indonesian and Malaysian seasoning) *See SHRIMP PASTE, FERMENTED*

TERIYAKI SAUCE/TERIYAKI SOSU/TARÉ (Japanese marinade and glaze) – 1/3 cup
Make Your Own Bring 2 tablespoons each Japanese dark soy sauce, mirin, and saké (or dry sherry) to a boil in the microwave, or in a small saucepan over medium heat, then cool. (For a sweeter sauce, add 1 teaspoon sugar; for a thicker sauce add 1 1/2 teaspoons sugar and simmer until syrupy.)
Or
Heat 1/4 cup soy sauce and 2 tablespoons sugar (or honey) in the microwave until the sugar dissolves, 10 to 20 seconds.

THAI CHILI FLAKES/POWDER – 1/2 cup
Make Your Own Toast 1 cup dried Thai chilis in a dry skillet over medium heat, stirring frequently, until slightly darker, 2 to 3 minutes (or in a preheated 350°F oven until puffed, about 5 minutes). Cool, remove the stems, then pulse in a food processor into coarse flakes or process to a powder. (For less heat remove the seeds and veins; wear plastic gloves and avoid inhaling the fumes.)

THAI CHILI, FRESH OR DRIED – 1
- 1 fresh or dried de árbol, japonés, small serrano, tien tsin, or cayenne chili
- 1/4 to 1/2 teaspoon Thai red pepper flakes or hot red pepper flakes
- 1/8 teaspoon each ground cayenne pepper and paprika

THAI CHILI VINEGAR/NAM SOM – (Pad Thai condiment) – 1/2 cup
- 1/2 cup rice vinegar, 2 to 3 tablespoons sugar, and a few thin slices of serrano chili

THAI CURRY POWDER/PONG GARI – 1 tablespoon
- 1 tablespoon mild Madras curry powder

THAI DIPPING SAUCE/NAM PRIK – 1/4 cup

☞ 2 tablespoons fresh lime juice, 1 tablespoon each sugar and Thai fish sauce (*nam pla* or *pla raa*), 1 teaspoon chopped cilantro, and 1 small minced garlic clove (For chili dipping sauce, add 1 or 2 tablespoons minced or sliced fresh Thai chili.)

THAI FISH SAUCE/NAM PLA (salty liquid seasoning) – 1 tablespoon

☞ 1 tablespoon Vietnamese fish sauce/*nuoc nam/nuoc mam* (slightly stronger), or Vietnamese premium sauce from the first extraction/ *nuoc mam nhi* or *nuoc mam cot* (bolder flavor)

☞ 1 tablespoon Korean fish sauce/*saengseon*, Japanese fish sauce/ *shottsuru*, or Filipino fish sauce/*patis*

☞ 1 tablespoon Vietnamese vegetarian fish sauce/*nuoc mam au chay*

☞ 1 tablespoon anchovy essence/syrup

☞ 2 teaspoons anchovy paste mixed with 1/2 teaspoon soy sauce or Maggi Seasoning

☞ 1 tablespoon oyster sauce

☞ 1 scant tablespoon light soy sauce plus a little salt

THAI FISH SAUCE WITH CHILIS/NAM PLA PRIK – 2/3 (scant) cup

Make Your Own Stir 1/4 cup minced fresh Thai chilis (including seeds) into 1/2 cup fish sauce/*nam pla*. Store, tightly covered, in the refrigerator; it will last for up to 3 months. (Wear plastic gloves when handling the chilis.)

THAI GINGER See GALANGAL, GREATER

THAI GINGER, WILD/GRACHAI/KACHAI/LESSER GINGER – 1 ounce

☞ 1 ounce regular ginger (less pungent)

THAI HOT CHILI SAUCE/SRIRACHA SAUCE/TUONG OT SRIRACHA – 1 teaspoon

☞ 1/2 teaspoon each American-made Sriracha sauce/rooster sauce (thicker, stronger, less sweet) and Thai sweet chili sauce/*nam jim kai*

☞ 1/2 to 1 teaspoon Sriracha dry seasoning (for pizza or rubs)

☞ 1 teaspoon sambal oelek sweetened with a little sugar

☞ 3/4 teaspoon ketchup plus 1/4 teaspoon Louisiana-style hot sauce, such as Tabasco or Crystal
☞ 1/4 to 1/2 teaspoon ground cayenne pepper (for cooking)

THAI ROASTED RED CHILI PASTE/CHILI JAM/NAM PRIK PAO – 1 tablespoon
☞ 1 tablespoon chili-garlic sauce
☞ 2 teaspoons vegetable oil, 1 teaspoon granulated sugar, and 1 teaspoon chili powder

THAI SAUCE BASE – 1/4 cup
☞ 3 tablespoons fish sauce/*nam pla*, 1 tablespoon lime juice, 1 tablespoon brown sugar, and 1/8 teaspoon crushed red pepper flakes, stirred until the sugar dissolves

THAI SEVEN-SPICE POWDER – 1 teaspoon
☞ 1 teaspoon Chinese five-spice powder

THAI SHRIMP PASTE/KAPI *See SHRIMP PASTE, FERMENTED*

THAI SOY SAUCE *See SOY SAUCE, THAI THIN*

THAI SWEET BLACK SOY SAUCE *See SOY SAUCE, THAI SWEET BLACK*

THAI SWEET CHILI-GARLIC SAUCE/NAM JIM KRATIEM – 1/2 cup
Make Your Own Simmer 1 cup distilled white vinegar, 1/2 cup sugar, and 1 teaspoon salt until syrupy, 10 to 15 minutes. Remove from the heat and add 1 teaspoon minced fresh Thai chili and 1/2 teaspoon minced garlic. Cool and transfer to an airtight container. (The sauce will thicken further as it cools, and will keep in the refrigerator for up to 2 months.)

THAI YELLOW BEAN PASTE/DAU JIAO/TAO JIAW *See VIETNAMESE YELLOW BEAN SAUCE*

THOUSAND ISLAND DRESSING – 1 cup
Make Your Own Stir 1/2 cup mayonnaise, 1/4 cup ketchup, and 1/4 cup well-drained pickle relish (or 2 finely minced gherkins) until thoroughly combined; season with salt and thin to the desired consistency with cider vinegar.

THYME, GARDEN/COMMON, FRESH – 3 to 5 whole sprigs, or leaves from 6 to 9 sprigs, or 1 tablespoon minced leaves
- 1 teaspoon dried French or English thyme leaves, crumbled
- 1 to 2 teaspoons finely minced fresh Spanish thyme leaves (stronger, slightly bitter)
- 3 to 4 teaspoons minced fresh wild/creeping thyme leaves/*Thymus serpyllum* (less flavorful)
- 1 tablespoon minced fresh summer savory
- 1 teaspoon poultry seasoning
- 1/2 teaspoon each dried marjoram and oregano leaves, crumbled
- 1 teaspoon ajwain/ajowan seeds

THYME, LEMON, FRESH – 3 to 5 whole sprigs, or leaves from 6 to 7 sprigs, or 1 tablespoon finely minced
- 1 teaspoon dried lemon thyme softened in 1 tablespoon warm water for 10 to 15 minutes
- 1 tablespoon minced fresh garden or French thyme plus 1/8 to 1/4 teaspoon grated lemon zest

TIGER LILY BUDS See LILY BUDS

TIGER NUTS See CHUFA

TOFU, DRIED/FOO JOOK – 1 pound
- 1 pound firm or extra-firm tofu, baked at 375°F until dry, about 25 minutes (or wrapped in a non-terry cotton dishtowel or paper towels and microwaved on High in 30-second increments for about 2 minutes)

TOFU, FERMENTED/FERMENTED BEAN CURD/DOUFU RU/FUYU/ SUFU – 1 pound
- 1 pound firm or extra-firm tofu, sliced or cubed, then marinated for 1 to 2 days in miso or soy sauce
- 1 pound mild French or Greek feta cheese, crumbled

TOFU, FREEZE-DRIED/KOYADOFU – 1 pound
- 1 pound firm or extra-firm tofu, rinsed, weighted for 1 to 2 hours, then frozen in plastic wrap for 8 to 12 hours (rinse in water after thawing)

TOGARASHI See JAPANESE HOT RED CHILI

TOMATO PASTE – 1 tablespoon
- 1 1/2 teaspoons double-concentrated tomato paste or extra-concentrated tomato extract
- 1 1/2 teaspoons tomato powder and 1 1/2 tablespoons water
- 1 tablespoon sun-dried tomato pesto
- 1 tablespoon ketchup (sweeter)
- 2 oil-packed sun-dried tomato halves, drained and pureed
- 3 tablespoons tomato sauce (Reduce the liquid in recipe by 2 tablespoons, or gently boil the tomato sauce until reduced to 1 tablespoon.)

TOMATO PASTE – 1/2 cup
- 1 1/2 cups tomato puree, simmered, uncovered, over low heat, stirring occasionally, until reduced to 1/2 cup

TOMATO PASTE, SICILIAN/STRATTO DI POMODORO – 1 tablespoon
- 1 tablespoon double-concentrated tomato paste (comes in a tube), or tomato extract (comes in a glass jar)

TOMATO PASTE, SUN-DRIED – 1 cup
- 2 ounces sun-dried tomatoes, softened in 1 1/2 cups boiling water 20 to 40 minutes, then puréed until smooth (strain if necessary)

TOMATO POWDER – 1 tablespoon

☞ Peel tomatoes, then dry the skins in a food dehydrator, or in a pre-heated 225°F oven for 45 to 60 minutes. Grind to a powder in a spice/coffee mill. Measure out 1 tablespoon.

TOMATO PUREE OR PULP – 1 cup

☞ 1 (14.5- to 16-ounce) can whole tomatoes with their juice, pureed in a blender or food processor until smooth (measure out 1 cup, then refrigerate or freeze the rest for another dish)

☞ 1/3 cup tomato paste and 2/3 cup water

☞ 1 cup plain tomato sauce

Make Your Own Halve 1 pound tomatoes and then grate on the large holes of a box grater or press through a sieve, discarding the skin and seeds. Cook over high heat until thickened, about 5 minutes. Alternatively, peel and seed the tomatoes and puree them in a blender or food processor until smooth.

Or

Coarsely chop 1 pound plum tomatoes and simmer until softened, 5 to 10 minutes, then press through a sieve or food mill to remove the skins and seeds.

TOMATO SAUCE – 1 cup

☞ 1 (14.5- to 16-ounce) can tomatoes, drained (reserve the juice) and processed in a blender or food processor until smooth (Measure after blending, then add more juice if needed to make 1 cup. Season with salt if needed.)

☞ 2 cups tomato juice, cooked until reduced by half

☞ 8 ounces peeled, seeded and chopped plum tomatoes (3 to 4) plus 1 or 2 teaspoons tomato paste

☞ 1/2 cup tomato paste and 1/2 cup water (season to taste with salt and sugar, 1/4 to 1/2 teaspoon, to duplicate commercial brands)

TOMATO SAUCE, SPANISH-STYLE – 1 cup

☞ 1 cup canned tomato puree

☞ 1 cup canned enchilada sauce

TOMATO SOUP, CANNED (for recipes) – 1 (10.75-ounce can)
- 1 cup tomato sauce plus 1/4 cup water

TOMATOES, SUN-DRIED, ITALIAN – 3 or 4
- 3 or 4 sun-dried wild bush Australian tomatoes/*Solanum centrale*
- 2 or 3 sun-dried, oil-packed tomatoes, drained
- 1 tablespoon sun-dried tomato paste
- **TOMATOES, SUN-DRIED, OIL-PACKED**

Make Your Own Soften dry-packed sun-dried tomatoes in hot water to cover for 30 to 60 minutes. Drain, blot dry, and then marinate them in olive oil for at least 1 hour. (Alternatively, marinate the tomatoes in oil for 12 to 24 hours without prior soaking.)

TONKATSU SAUCE/TON/KATSU SOSHU (Japanese sauce for tonkatsu) – 1/3 cup

Make Your Own Stir 1 tablespoon Worcestershire sauce and 1 teaspoon dark soy sauce into 1/4 cup ketchup until thoroughly combined. (For a more pungent sauce, use 3 tablespoons Worcestershire sauce, 2 tablespoons ketchup, and 1 teaspoon soy sauce.)

TORIGARA BASE (Japanese chicken stock base) – 1 teaspoon
- 1 teaspoon reduced-sodium chicken bouillon cube, 1 envelope instant chicken broth or granules, 1/2 to 3/4 teaspoon chicken extract or soup base, or 2 teaspoons vegetarian-based chicken broth powder (all substitutions will be saltier)

TOYOMANSI See SOY SAUCE, FILIPINO KALAMANSI

TREACLE, DARK (British dark thick syrup) – 1 tablespoon
- 1 tablespoon blackstrap molasses See also MOLASSES

TREE EAR See CLOUD EAR/BLACK TREE FUNGUS

TRIMOLINE/NULOMOLINE (inverted sugar) – 1 cup
- 1 cup liquid glucose

TRUFFLE, BLACK/FRENCH PÉRIGORD/TUBER MELANOSPORUM, FRESH OR FLASH-FROZEN – 1 ounce

- 1 ounce jarred black truffle pieces or shavings, canned black truffle peelings in truffle juice, or canned black truffle juice from the pre-serving process
- 1 to 2 tablespoons black truffle paste or oil (usually synthetic truffle flavoring)
- 1 to 2 ounces Italian hydrated dried cèpes/*Funghi porcini secchi*
- 1 to 2 ounces fresh (or dried rehydrated) black trumpet/horn of plenty mushrooms (for the color only)
- Black truffle butter, if butter is called for in the recipe (add at the last minute)
- Grated truffle cheese, if cheese is called for in the recipe (add at the last minute)
- Black truffle salt, such as Casina Rossa or homemade, if salt is called for in the recipe (reduce the salt in the recipe by 95%)

TRUFFLE BUTTER – 4 ounces (1/2 cup/1 stick)

Make Your Own Place 1 fresh black truffle and 1 stick unwrapped butter in a glass container, seal tightly, and let sit for 12 to 24 hours (or longer). Wrap the truffle butter in plastic wrap and then foil and keep refrigerated if not using immediately. It will last for up to a week.
Or
Stir 1 to 2 tablespoons minced fresh black truffle (or black truffle paste) into 1/2 cup room-temperature unsalted butter until thorough-ly incorporated. Season to taste with coarse salt, if desired, then tight-ly seal and refrigerate for 24 hours before using; it will last for up to a week.

TRUFFLE OIL – 1/2 cup

Make Your Own Add 2 scant teaspoons truffle shavings to 1/2 cup grapeseed or canola oil and heat gently for 1 or 2 minutes. Cool, cover, and leave at room temperature for a few days, then transfer to a ster-ile container and refrigerate. It will last for up to 1 month.

TRUFFLE OIL, WHITE – 4 or 5 drops
- 1 scant teaspoon white truffle shavings
- 5 (or more) drops porcini oil

TRUFFLE PASTE, WHITE – 1 tablespoon
- 1/2 to 1 teaspoon white truffle oil

TRUFFLE SALT (flavored finishing salt) – 3 tablespoons
Make Your Own Mix 1 scant teaspoon black truffle shavings with 3 tablespoons coarse sea salt. Tightly seal and leave at room temperature a few days for the salt to absorb the truffle flavor.

TRUFFLE SHAVINGS, BLACK, FRESH OR JARRED – 2 tablespoons
- 1 teaspoon black truffle oil

TRUFFLE, WHITE ITALIAN/PIEDMONTESE/TUBER MAGNATUM, FRESH
See also TRUFFLE, BLACK FRENCH PÉRIGORD – 1 ounce
- 1 ounce jarred white truffle peelings and pieces (less expensive)
- 1 ounce white Oregon truffle/*Tuber gibbosum/Tuber oregonense* (darker colored; smaller; less aromatic)
- 1 to 2 ounces Italian hydrated dried cèpes/*Funghi porcini secchi*

TUMBO JUICE (Peruvian tart seasoning) – 1 cup
- 1/2 cup grapefruit juice, 1/4 cup Key lime juice, and 3 tablespoons passion fruit juice
- 1 cup passion fruit juice (less tart)

TUNA/CACTUS FRUIT *See PRICKLY PEAR*

TURKISH PEPPER PASTE *See RED PEPPER PASTE, HOT; RED PEPPER PASTE, MILD*

TURMERIC ROOT, FRESH OR FROZEN (Indian seasoning) – 1-inch piece or 1 tablespoon peeled and finely chopped
- 1 or 2 teaspoons grated dried turmeric rhizome (wear plastic gloves and be careful; turmeric stains are hard to remove)

- 1 tablespoon grated carrot plus 1/2 teaspoon each powdered turmeric and grated fresh ginger
- 2 teaspoons finely chopped fresh ginger
- 1 teaspoon powdered Alleppey turmeric (orange-yellow color; for flavor) or powdered Madras turmeric (bright yellow; for color)
- 1 1/2 teaspoons generic turmeric powder (for color)
- 1/4 teaspoon finely ground annatto seeds, achiote/Bijoi powder, or mild yellow curry powder (for color only)

TURMERIC ROOT POWDER/GROUND TURMERIC – 1 teaspoon
- 1 tablespoon packed fresh grated turmeric
- Small pinch of saffron, crushed dried safflower florets, or safflower stigmas/Mexican saffron/*azafrán* (for color)
- 1 teaspoon ground annatto seeds or achiote/Bijoi powder (for color)
- 2 teaspoons ground dried marigold petals, or whole dried marigold petals steeped in a little warm water 5 minutes (use the liquid for color and discard the petals)

TURMERIC, WHITE See ZEDOARY/WHITE TURMERIC/MANGO GINGER/ AMBA HALDI

TXORIZERO PEPPER (Basque dried sweet pepper) – 1
- 1 dried New Mexico or California chili

U

UMAMI/FIFTH TASTE/SAVORY FLAVOR (flavor-enhancing foods)
⇸ Anchovies; Asian fish sauce; kombu/dried kelp; miso; mushrooms, especially morels (always cooked), porcini, portabellos, or shiitakes; Parmigiano-Reggiano or other aged cheese; red wine; smoked or cured fish; soy sauce; or tomatoes, especially vine-ripened or dried

UMAMI DUST (Japanese flavor-enhancing seasoning) – 1 ounce
⇸ 1/2 ounce crumbed dried kombu/kelp (1/2 sheet), 1/2 ounce dried shiitake caps (about 5 large), and 3 tablespoons dried bonito flakes, ground until fine

UMEBOSHI (Japanese salt-pickled dried plum) – 1 large (1 tablespoon pitted and mashed)
⇸ 1 quickly pickled salted plum/*shio-hikaeme umeboshi* (juicier, with less salt)
⇸ 1 Chinese pickled plum/*suan mei* or salted dried plum/*li hing mui/ hua mei*
⇸ 2 teaspoons jarred umeboshi puree/paste/*bainiku/neri-ume*
⇸ 1 1/2 teaspoons umeboshi plum vinegar/*ume su* (much saltier)
⇸ 2 or 3 tiny plum paste balls/*umeboshi-san*

UMEBOSHI PASTE/BAINIKU – 1 ounce
⇸ 1 ounce Japanese dried, salt-pickled plum/*umeboshi* or Chinese pickled plum/*suanmel*, ground with a mortar and pestle until smooth

UMEBOSHI VINEGAR/UME SU – 1 tablespoon
⇸ 1 1/2 teaspoons lemon juice and 1 1/2 teaspoons Japanese soy sauce or tamari
⇸ 1 (scant) tablespoon red rice vinegar or red wine vinegar plus a few drops of soy sauce

- ☞ 1 tablespoon cider vinegar plus a pinch of table salt
- ☞ 1 tablespoon sherry vinegar

URFA PEPPER FLAKES/ISOT PEPPER FLAKES/URFA BIBER (Turkish) – 1 teaspoon

- ☞ 1 teaspoon Aleppo or Maras red pepper flakes
- ☞ 3/4 teaspoon Aleppo or Urfa chili powder
- ☞ 1/2 teaspoon ancho chili powder or smoked Spanish paprika plus 1/4 teaspoon ground cayenne pepper

V

VANILLA BEAN, BOURBON/MADAGASCAR OR MEXICAN – 2- to 3-inch section
- 1/4 to 1/2 teaspoon ground whole vanilla bean
- 1 teaspoon pure vanilla extract, vanillin/vanilla powder, vanilla bean paste, vanilla bean crush, vanilla flavoring, or imitation vanilla
- 1 tablespoon vanilla sugar (reduce the sugar in the recipe by 1 tablespoon)
- 4 drops concentrated vanilla essence (add after removing from the heat)

VANILLA BEAN PASTE – 1 teaspoon
- 1 teaspoon vanilla powder
- 4 drops concentrated vanilla essence

VANILLA BEAN, TAHITIAN – 1 whole bean including scraped seeds
- 2 Bourbon-Madagascar or Mexican vanilla beans
- 1 teaspoon ground whole vanilla beans
- 1 tablespoon vanilla bean paste, pure vanilla extract, vanillin/vanilla powder, or vanilla flavoring (add toward the end of cooking, or after removing from the heat)

VANILLA EXTRACT – 1 teaspoon
- 1 teaspoon vanilla bean paste or vanilla flavoring
- 1/4 to 1/2 teaspoon ground whole vanilla beans
- 1/2 teaspoon double strength vanilla extract
- 1 (2- to 3-inch) piece Bourbon-Madagascar vanilla bean, or 1(1- to 2-inch piece) Tahitian vanilla bean, split and seeds scraped out (add early in the recipe; for puddings, custards, sauces, or ice cream)
- 4 drops concentrated vanilla essence
- 1 teaspoon imitation clear vanilla or vanillin/white vanilla powder (for no color)

☞ 1 teaspoon alcohol-free vanilla extract, such as Trader Joe's
☞ 1 tablespoon vanilla sugar (Reduce the sugar in the recipe by 1 tablespoon. Alternatively, grind a piece of vanilla bean with a little sugar, then add it to the granulated sugar before weighing or measuring.)

VANILLA EXTRACT – 8 ounces
Make Your Own Split 1 Bourbon-Madagascar, or cheaper grade B/extract, vanilla bean lengthwise. Scrape out the seeds and thinly slice the bean. Add the bean and seeds to 1 cup brandy, aged rum, or vodka in a dark-colored 8-ounce bottle; seal tightly and store in a cool, dark place for at least 3 months, shaking the bottle from time to time. (The higher the alcohol proof the better; for wheat-free extract, choose brandy or rum.)

VANILLA EXTRACT, DOUBLE-STRENGTH – 4 ounces
☞ 1 split and sectioned vanilla bean, gently inserted into a 4-ounce bottle of vanilla extract and left to steep at least 7 days

VANILLA POWDER See VANILLA BEAN PASTE

VANILLA SUGAR – 1 cup
Make Your Own Pulse 1 cup granulated or powdered sugar and 1 teaspoon vanilla powder (or half a vanilla bean cut in half) in a blender or food processor until thoroughly combined and well distributed.
Or
Split 1 vanilla bean lengthwise, then place in a jar with 1 cup granulated or powdered sugar and let sit for 1 to 2 weeks. Replenish the sugar as needed until the bean loses its flavoring capability.

VERBENA See LEMON VERBENA, FRESH

VERJUICE/VERJUS/AGRESTO/HOSRUM/KORUK/ABGHOOREH (unripe grape juice) – 2 tablespoons
☞ 1/4 to 1/3 cup hard, sour green grapes, pureed and strained to measure 2 tablespoons

- 1 tablespoon each white grape juice and cider vinegar
- 1 tablespoon each white wine and unseasoned rice vinegar
- 1 1/2 tablespoons white wine and 1/2 tablespoon distilled white vinegar or lemon juice
- 1 1/2 teaspoons dried sour grape powder and 2 tablespoons water

VERMOUTH, DRY/FRENCH (fortified white wine) – 1/4 cup for cooking
- 1/4 cup dry sherry or light, dry/Sercial Madeira
- 1/3 cup dry white wine, saké, or pure Shaoxing yellow rice wine (reduce liquid in recipe by 1 tablespoon if necessary)

VIETNAMESE BALM/GREEN PERILLA/RAU KINH GIO'I See SHISO, GREEN

VIETNAMESE CHILI SAUCE/TUONG OT TOI – 1 tablespoon
- 1 tablespoon sambal oelek, harissa, Sriracha, Sichuan chili sauce, or hot pepper sauce, such as Tabasco or Crystal
- 1 tablespoon mild Madras-type curry blend

VIETNAMESE DIPPING SAUCE/TUONG GUNG – 1/2 cup
- 1/4 cup each Vietnamese fish sauce/nuoc nam, fresh lime juice, and superfine sugar mixed together until sugar dissolves
- 2 tablespoons each unseasoned rice vinegar, water, and fresh lime juice; plus 1 teaspoon each chili-garlic paste (or Chinese chili-garlic sauce), sugar, and soy sauce stirred together until sugar dissolves

VIETNAMESE FISH SAUCE/NUOC NAM/NUOC MAM – 1 tablespoon
- 1 tablespoon premium (gluten-free) nuoc nam made with the first pressing (cot, nhi, thuong hang, phu quoc)
- 1 tablespoon Thai fish sauce/nam pla, Korean fish sauce/saengseon, Japanese fish sauce/shottsuru, or Filipino fish sauce/patis
- 1 tablespoon vegetarian fish sauce/nuoc nam chay
- 2 teaspoons anchovy essence/syrup mixed with a few drops light soy sauce
- 1/2 teaspoon Worcestershire sauce

VIETNAMESE MINT/VIETNAMESE CORIANDER/LAKSA LEAF/DAUN LAKSA, FRESH – 1 tablespoon chopped
- 1 1/2 teaspoons each chopped fresh cilantro and spearmint (or peppermint)
- 1 1/2 teaspoons each chopped fresh cilantro and lemon balm leaves (or lemon basil)
- 1 tablespoon chopped domestic garden cilantro going to seed (starting to flower)

VIETNAMESE PICKLED LEEKS/CU KIEU – 1 cup
- Cornichons or other mild cucumber pickles

VIETNAMESE SWEET-AND-SOUR DIPPING SAUCE/NUOC CHAM – scant 1/2 cup
Make Your Own Combine 1/4 cup each sugar, Vietnamese fish sauce/*nuoc nam*, and lime juice, plus 1 small minced garlic clove, and 1 minced fresh Thai or cayenne chili; stir until the sugar dissolves.
Or
Combine 1/3 cup chili-garlic sauce, 1 tablespoon Vietnamese fish sauce/*nuoc nam*, and 1 tablespoon lime juice; stir until combined (for *nuoc nam gung*, add finely chopped fresh ginger).

VIETNAMESE SWEET CHILI SAUCE/TUONG OT NGOT – scant 2/3 cup
- 2/3 cup Thai sweet chili sauce/dipping sauce for chicken/*nam jim kai*
- 3 tablespoons sambal oelek and 2 tablespoons unseasoned rice vinegar stirred into 1/3 cup mild honey

VIETNAMESE YELLOW BEAN SAUCE/TUONG OT/TUONG CU DA – 1 tablespoon
- 1 tablespoon *awase* miso (a mixture of white and red miso)
- 1 scant tablespoon Chinese yellow/brown soybean paste/*mien see* or Thai yellow bean paste/*tao jiaw* thinned with a little water
- 1 1/2 teaspoons each Japanese light and dark miso

VIETNAMESE YOGURT/SUA CHUA/DA UA – 1 cup
- 1 (3.5-ounce) can sweetened condensed milk stirred into 3/4 cup plain Greek-style yogurt until thoroughly incorporated (store, tightly covered, in the refrigerator for up to 2 weeks)

VINAIGRETTE – 1/4 cup
- 1 tablespoon olive oil and 3 tablespoons brine from jarred vegetables (olives, pickles, peppers, or other vegetables packed in brine)
- 3 tablespoons mild vinegar and 1 tablespoon oil from jarred vegetables (artichokes, sun-dried tomatoes, olives, or other vegetables packed in oil)
- 1/4 cup balsamic vinegar, chopped fresh herbs, and a pinch of xanthan gum (for nonfat dressing)

VIN COTTO (southern Italian unrefined wine syrup) – 1/3 cup See also *GRAPE MOLASSES*
- 1/3 cup Italian grape syrup/molasses/*saba/mosto cotto*
- 1/3 cup Middle Eastern pomegranate syrup/molasses/*dibis rouman/dibs rubba*
- 1/3 cup strong-flavored honey

Make Your Own Combine 1 cup fruity red wine and 5 tablespoons sugar and boil gently, stirring constantly and skimming any foam, until syrupy and reduced to 1/3 cup. It will keep in an airtight container for up to 3 months in the refrigerator.

VINEGAR (acidifying/souring agent) – 1 tablespoon
- 1/16 teaspoon ascorbic acid or 1/4 teaspoon citric acid powder (for acidulated water)
- 1 tablespoon lemon or lime juice (for salad dressings, marinades, sauces)
- 1 tablespoon sauerkraut juice (for salad dressing; omit the salt)
- 1 tablespoon lemon juice, wine, port, or sherry (for deglazing pans)
- 1 to 1 1/2 teaspoons green mango powder/*amchur*, ground sumac, or pomegranate seed powder/*anardana* (for chutneys and curries)

V

232

☞ 3/4 to 1 teaspoon tamarind paste or concentrate (for chutneys, curries, soups)

VINEGAR, MILD – 1 tablespoon
☞ 1 tablespoon unseasoned rice vinegar, white wine vinegar, or sherry vinegar
☞ 1 1/2 teaspoons each unseasoned rice vinegar and white wine vinegar
☞ 1 1/2 teaspoons each apple cider vinegar and water

VIN SANTO (Italian amber-colored dessert wine) – 1 cup
☞ 1 cup sweet Riesling, Manzanilla sherry, White Port, Madeira, or Marsala

VINO SECO (Spanish cooking wine) – 2 tablespoons
☞ 2 tablespoons red or white cooking wine
☞ 2 tablespoons dry white or red wine; adjust the salt in the recipe as needed

W

WAKAME POWDERED (Japanese condiment)
Make Your Own Cut dried wakame into small pieces and toast in a dry skillet, stirring constantly, until very crisp, about 5 minutes. Crumble or grind into a powder (use a mortar and pestle or a rolling pin sleeved in plastic). Store in an airtight container in a cool, dark place; it will last for up to 1 year.

WALNUT LIQUEUR/WALNUT-FLAVORED SPIRIT (Flaschengeist, Lantenhammer, Nocino, Nux Alpina) – 1 tablespoon for cooking
⇨ 1/4 teaspoon walnut extract and 1 tablespoon water

WALNUT OIL – 1/2 cup
⇨ 1/2 cup hazelnut, macadamia nut, or extra-virgin olive oil
Make Your Own Toast 1/2 cup shelled walnuts. Process with 1/2 cup neutral-tasting vegetable oil in a blender or food processor until smooth. Strain and refrigerate for 2 or 3 days to develop the flavor; use immediately or store, tightly covered, in the refrigerator for up to 3 months.

WASABI, FRESH (Japanese horseradish) – 2-ounce root (1 tablespoon freshly grated)
⇨ 1 or more tablespoons wasabi paste/neri wasabi
⇨ 1 tablespoon wasabi powder/kona wasabi stirred into 2 teaspoons cold water and left covered for 5 to 10 minutes to develop the flavor

WASABI, POWDERED – 1 teaspoon
⇨ 1 teaspoon horseradish or mustard powder

WASABI, PREPARED – 1 teaspoon
⇨ 1 teaspoon wasabi powder mixed with 1 scant teaspoon cold water, then left, covered, 10 to 15 minutes to develop the flavor

- 1 teaspoon fresh horseradish (or strained bottled horseradish) plus a touch of green food coloring
- 1 teaspoon mustard powder, 1/2 teaspoon vinegar, 1/4 teaspoon oil, and 1/8 teaspoon salt mixed together until smooth, then left, covered, for 10 to 15 minutes to develop the flavor

WATERCRESS, CULTIVATED – 1 ounce (1 cup)
- 1 ounce hydroponic-grown cress with roots attached (milder tasting; more tender), or wild watercress (smaller leaves; less tender)
- 1 ounce upland/land cress, or garden/pepper cress (smaller leaves; slightly more pungent)
- 1 ounce young nasturtium leaves and stems, radish sprouts, baby arugula/rocket, or young dandelion greens
- 1 ounce young garland chrysanthemum (for cooking)
- 1 ounce Japanese mugwort/*yomogi*, or tender wild mugwort/*Artemisia vulgaris*

WHEAT MALT SYRUP (non-diastatic liquid malt) – 1 tablespoon
- 1 tablespoon barley malt syrup
- 1 1/2 teaspoons granulated sugar, or 1 tablespoon light brown sugar

WHEAT STARCH SYRUP (thick, sticky sweetener) – 1 cup
- 1 cup mild, light-colored honey, or light-colored (not "lite") corn syrup
- 1 cup golden syrup (adds color)
-

WHISKEY SAUCE – 1 1/2 cups
- 1/4 cup whiskey, thoroughly stirred into a 14-ounce can warmed sweetened condensed milk (low-fat or regular)

WHITE SAUCE/BÉCHAMEL, MEDIUM – 1 cup for cooking
- 2/3 cup canned cream-style soup, such as celery or mushroom, and 1/3 cup milk, whisked together and heated
- 3 cups canned or homemade coconut milk slowly simmered, uncovered, until reduced to 1 cup (vegan)

☞ 1/3 cup plain macadamia nuts soaked in water to cover for 8 to 12 hours, then drained and processed in a blender with 1 cup water until smooth (vegan; strain through a fine-mesh sieve, then blend again if necessary)

WHITE WINE VINEGAR – 1 tablespoon
☞ 1 tablespoon champagne vinegar or unseasoned rice wine vinegar

WILD LIME LEAF See KAFFIR LIME LEAF

WINE – 1 cup for marinades
☞ 1/2 cup vinegar, 1/2 cup water, and 2 tablespoons sugar, heated to dissolve the sugar, then cooled
☞ 3/4 cup chicken stock plus 1/4 cup vinegar
☞ 1 tablespoon red wine powder (for barbecue spice rubs)

WINE – 1 cup for sweet dishes
☞ 1 cup grape juice made from varietal wine grapes, such as Merlot or Cabernet
☞ 3/4 cup unsweetened apple juice or cran-apple juice and 1 tablespoon lemon juice or mild vinegar
☞ 1 cup nonalcoholic fruity wine
☞ 3/4 cup water and 3 tablespoons lemon juice

WINE, SPARKLING –1 cup for cooking
☞ 1 cup sparkling white grape juice or sparkling apple cider

WINE, SWEETENED RICE See MIRIN

WINE, WHITE – 1 cup for cooking
☞ 3/4 cup dry white vermouth (opened vermouth will last for months in the refrigerator)
☞ 1 cup white low-alcohol wine (9% or so), or de-alcoholized wine (0.3 to 0.5%)
☞ 1 cup pear or apple cider (or unsweetened apple juice plus a few drops of cider vinegar)

- ⊩ 1 cup chicken or vegetable broth (or the juice from canned mushrooms), plus 1 teaspoon white wine vinegar or lemon juice, stirred in just before serving (reduce the salt in the recipe accordingly)
- ⊩ 1 cup ginger ale, white grape juice, or white cranberry juice drink

WINE, YELLOW RICE See SHAOXING

WING SAUCE (condiment for Buffalo chicken wings) – 1/2 cup
Make Your Own Bring 1/4 cup butter, 1/4 cup hot pepper sauce, such as Frank's RedHot, and 1 tablespoon distilled white vinegar to a simmer, then remove from the heat to cool.

WOOD EAR FUNGUS See CLOUD EAR/BLACK TREE FUNGUS

WORCESTERSHIRE SAUCE – 1 tablespoon
- ⊩ 1 tablespoon gluten-free Worcestershire sauce, such French's non-gluten; or anchovy-free vegetarian sauce flavored with molasses, soy sauce, and vinegar
- ⊩ 1/2 tablespoon steak sauce or HP sauce plus 1/2 tablespoon water and a drop or two of lemon juice or vinegar
- ⊩ 1 scant tablespoon soy sauce, 3 or 4 drops hot pepper sauce, 1/8 teaspoon lemon juice, and a few grains of sugar
- ⊩ 1 tablespoon mushroom ketchup, 3 drops hot pepper sauce, and 1/8 teaspoon superfine sugar
- ⊩ 1 tablespoon Worcestershire sauce powder (used dry in cooking or spice rubs)
- ⊩ 1 tablespoon Bragg Liquid Aminos or Coconut Aminos

X

XO SAUCE (Chinese spicy, dried-seafood-based condiment) – 1 tablespoon
> ⇨ 1 tablespoon oyster sauce plus a touch of chili oil (or sesame or peanut oil plus cayenne or other hot chili powder)

XTABENTUN (Yucatan anise-flavored spirit) – 2 tablespoons
> ⇨ 2 tablespoons Absente, anisette, Galliano, Herbsaint, ouzo, Pernod, or other anise-flavored liqueur

XYLITOL (Low-calorie natural sweetener) – 1 tablespoon
> ⇨ 1 tablespoon sucralose, such as Splenda
> ⇨ 1 tablespoon Sucanat, granulated sugar, or raw/unrefined sugar (more calories)
> ⇨ 1 to 4 drops liquid stevia (or to desired sweetness)

Y

YACÓN SYRUP (South American thick brown sweetener) – 1 cup
- 1 cup date syrup, palm honey/syrup, blackstrap molasses; amber agave syrup/nectar, coconut nectar, or Swedish dark syrup/*mörk sirap*

YAKISOBA SAUCE (Japanese stir-fry flavoring sauce) – 1 tablespoon
- 1 tablespoon Japanese brown sauce or tonkatsu sauce

YAKITORI SAUCE (Japanese grilling sauce and glaze) – 1 cup *See also*
TERIYAKI SAUCE
- 1 cup heavy teriyaki sauce (or 1 1/2 cups thin teriyaki sauce, boiled
until reduced to 1 cup)

YELLOW BEAN SAUCE *See CHINESE YELLOW BEAN SAUCE;*
VIETNAMESE YELLOW BEAN SAUCE

YELLOW SOY BEANS, SALTED FERMENTED (Chinese cooking
condiment) – 1 tablespoon
- 1 1/2 tablespoons Chinese yellow bean sauce/brown bean paste/
mien see, Thai yellow bean sauce/*tao jiew,* or Vietnamese yellow
bean sauce/*tuong ot*
- 1 or 2 tablespoons Japanese all-purpose light miso (such as *genmai*
or *shinshu*)

YERBA BUENA/WILD MINT *See MINT, FRESH*

YOGURT GARLIC SAUCE *See GARLIC YOGURT SAUCE*

YOMOGI (Japanese green leafy herb) – 1 tablespoon chopped
- 1 tablespoon chopped tender wild mugwort/*Artemisia vulgaris*
- 1 tablespoon chopped arugula or watercress leaves (different flavor)
- 1 teaspoon Yomogi powder/Japanese mugwort powder

YUZU/MISHO YUZU (Japanese small tart citrus fruit) – 1

- 1 or 2 *sudachi*
- One-half Meyer lemon (less bitter)

YUZU JUICE, UNSALTED (Japanese flavoring extract) – 1 tablespoon fresh, frozen, or bottled

- 1 tablespoon unsalted *sudachi* juice (slightly more acidic)
- 3/4 teaspoon salted yuzu juice plus 2 1/4 teaspoons fresh lemon juice
- 1 teaspoon each grapefruit, lemon, and lime juice
- 2 1/2 teaspoons fresh lime juice plus 1/2 teaspoon fresh orange juice

YUZU ZEST – 1 teaspoon

- 1/3 teaspoon dried yuzu peel, softened in 2 teaspoons warm water for 15 minutes, then finely chopped
- 3/4 to 1 teaspoon yuzu powder
- 1 to 2 teaspoons lemon zest or fully ripened Key lime zest

Z

ZA'ATAR/ZAHTAR/ZATAR SPICE (Middle Eastern spice blend) – 1 tablespoon
- 2 teaspoons lightly toasted sesame seeds, 2 teaspoons dried thyme, 1 teaspoon dried sumac berries (or 2 teaspoons lemon zest), and a pinch of salt, coarsely ground with a mortar and pestle or in a spice/coffee grinder

ZEDOARY/WHITE TURMERIC/MANGO GINGER/AMBA HALDI (Indian and Southeast Asian seasoning) – 1 dried slice
- 1 slice dried galangal/*galanga* (add directly to a soup or stew without soaking)
- 1/4 to 1/2 teaspoon ground *zedoary* powder
- 1/8 to 1/4 teaspoon powdered *kencur*, Laos powder, or galangal paste
- Tiny pinch ground ginger
- 1 small piece fresh or thawed frozen galangal

ZERESHK *See BARBERRIES*

ZINFANDEL VINEGAR – 1 tablespoon
- 1 tablespoon Cabernet Sauvignon vinegar, or other mellow red wine vinegar
- 1 tablespoon red wine

Thank you for purchasing this book, dear reader.

I hope you found it helpful. Jean B. MacLeod

BIBLIOGRAPHY

Arasaki, Seibin, and Teruko Arasaki. *Vegetables from the Sea*. Tokyo: Japan Publications, 1983.

Alford, Jeffrey, and Naomi Duguid. *Beyond the Great Wall: Recipes and Travels in the Other China*. New York: Artisan, 2008.

———. *Mangoes and Curry Leaves*. New York: Artisan, 2005.

Baljekar, Mridula. *Curry Lover's Cookbook*. London: Southwater, 2009.

Barham, Peter. *The Science of Cooking*. New York: Springer-Verlag, 2001.

Bartlett, Jonathan. *The Cook's Dictionary and Culinary Reference: A Comprehensive Definitive Guide to Cooking and Food*. Chicago: Contemporary Books, 1996.

Başan, Ghillie. *The Turkish Kitchen*. London: Southwater, 2010.

Bladholm, Linda. *The Asian Grocery Store Demystified*. Los Angeles: Renaissance Books, 1999.

Boxer, Arabella, Jocastas Innes, Charlotte Parry-Crooke, and Lewis Esson. *The Encyclopedia of Herbs, Spices, and Flavorings*. New York: Crescent Books, 1984.

Bremness, Lesley. *Herbs*. New York: Dorling Kindersley. 1994.

Cost, Bruce. *Bruce Cost's Asian Ingredients: Buying and Cooking the Staple Foods of China, Japan and Southeast Asia*. New York: William Morrow, 1988.

Creasy, Rosalind. *The Edible Herb Garden*. Boston: Periplus Editions. 1999.

D'Aprix, David. *The Fearless International Foodie*. New York: Living Language, 2001.

Davidson, Alan. *The Oxford Companion to Food*. Oxford: Oxford University Press, 1999.

DeWitt, Dave, and Nancy Gerlach. *The Spicy Food Lover's Bible*. New York: Stewart, Tabori & Chang, 2005.

——— . *The Whole Chili Pepper Book*. Boston: Little, Brown, 1990.

Elias, Thomas S., and Peter A. Dykeman. *Edible Wild Plants*. New York: Sterling Publishing, 2009.

Fortin, François, ed. dir. *The Visual Food Encyclopedia*. New York: MacMillan, 1996.

Gardiner, Anne, and Sue Wilson. *The Inquisitive Cook*. With the Exploratorium. New York: Henry Holt, 1998.

Gorsky, Faith. *An Edible Mosaic: Middle Eastern Fare with Extraordinary Flair*. Rutland, VT: Tuttle Publishing, 2012.

Grigson, Sophie. *Gourmet Ingredients*. New York: Van Nostrand Reinhold, 1991.

Gunst, Kathy. *Condiments: The Art of Buying, Making and Using Mustards, Oils, Vinegars, Chutneys, Relishes, Sauces, Savory Jellies and More*. New York: G. P. Putnam's Sons, 1984.

Hemphill, Ian. *The Spice and Herb Bible*. 2nd. ed. Toronto: Robert Rose, 2006.

Herbst, Sharon Tyler, and Ron Herbst. *The New Food Lover's Companion*. 4th ed. Hauppauge, NY: Barron's Educational Series, 2007.

Hill, Tony. *Contemporary Encyclopedia of Herbs and Spices: Seasonings for the Global Kitchen*. Hoboken, NJ: John Wiley & Sons, 2004.

Hom, Ken. *Ken Hom's Chinese Kitchen: With a Consumer's Guide to Essential Ingredients*. New York: Hyperion, 1994.

Hosking, Richard. *A Dictionary of Japanese Food Ingredients & Culture*. Rutland, VT: Charles E. Tuttle, 1996.

Hsiung, Deh-Ta. *The Chinese Kitchen*. 1st U.S. ed. New York: St. Martin's Press, 1999.

Jaffrey, Madhur. *At Home with Madhur Jaffrey: Simple, Delectable Dishes from India, Pakistan, Bangladesh, and Sri Lanka*. New York: Alfred A. Knopf, 2010.

——— . *Madhur Jaffrey's A Taste of the Far East*. New York: Carol Southern Books, 1993.

Jordan, Michele Anna. *Salt and Pepper*. New York: Broadway Books, 1999.

Karoff, Barbara. *South American Cooking: Food and Feasts from the New World*. Berkeley, CA: Aris Books, 1989.

244

Katz, Sandor Ellix. *The Art of Fermentation: An In-Depth Exploration of Essential Concepts and Processes from around the World*. White River Junction, VT: Chelsea Green Publishing, 2012.

Khalife, Maria. *The Middle Eastern Cookbook*. Northampton, MA: Interlink Books, 2007.

Kipfer, Barbara Ann. *The Culinarian: A Kitchen Desk Reference*. Hoboken, NJ: John Wiley & Sons, 2011.

Lee, Cecilia Hae-Jin. *Eating Korean*. Hoboken, NJ: John Wiley & Sons, 2005.

Mackey, Leslie, and Sallie Morris. *Illustrated Cook's Book of Ingredients: 2,500 of the World's Best with Classic Recipes*. 1st. U.S. ed. New York: DK Publishing, 2010.

Marks, Gil. *Encyclopedia of Jewish Food*. Hoboken, NJ: John Wiley & Sons, 2010.

Miller, Mark. *The Great Chili Book*. With John Harrisson. New York: Ten Speed Press, 1991.

Mitchell, Paulette. *The Complete Soy Cookbook*. New York: Macmillan, 1998.

Morgan, Lane. *The Ethnic Market Food Guide*. New York: Berkley Books, 1997.

Mouritsen, Ole G. *Seaweeds: Edible, Available & Sustainable*. Chicago: University of Chicago Press, 2013.

National Geographic. *Edible: An Illustrated Guide to the World's Food Plants*. Lane Cove, Australia: Global Book Publishing, 2008.

Nilsen, Angela, and Jeni Wright. *21st Century Cook: The Bible of Ingredients, Terms, Tools & Techniques*. London: Cassell Illustrated, 2006.

Norman, Jill. *Herbs & Spices: The Cook's Reference*. New York: DK Publishing, 2002.

Ortiz, Elisabeth Lambert, ed. *The Encyclopedia of Herbs, Spices & Flavorings*. New York: Dorling Kindersley, 1992.

Paino, Joe, and Lisa Messinger. *The Tofu Book: The New American Cuisine; A Complete Culinary Guide to Using Tofu*. New York: Avery, 1991.

Presilla, Maricel E. *Gran Cocina Latina: The Food of Latin America*. New York: W. W. Norton, 2012.

Rinzler, Carol Ann. *The New Complete Book of Herbs, Spices, and Condiments*. New York: Checkmark Books, 2001.

Roden, Claudia. *The New Book of Middle Eastern Food*. New York: Alfred A. Knopf, 2007.

Rolland, Jacques L, and Carol Sherman. *The Food Encyclopedia*. Toronto: Robert Rose, 2006.

Selva Rajah, Carol. *Heavenly Fragrance: Cooking with Aromatic Asian Herbs, Fruits, Spices, and Seasonings*. Singapore: Periplus, 2007.

Shurtleff, William, and Akiko Aoyagi. *The Book of Miso*. 2nd ed. Berkeley, Ten Speed Press, 2001.

Sinclair, Charles G. *International Dictionary of Food & Cooking*. Chicago: Fitzroy Dearborn Publishers, 1998.

Skelly, Carole J. *Dictionary of Herbs, Spice, Seasonings, and Natural Flavorings*. New York: Garland Publishing, 1994.

Solomon, Charmaine. *Encyclopedia of Asian Food*. With Nina Solomon. Sydney, Australia: New Holland Publishers, 2010.

Sortun, Ana, with Nicole Chaison. *Spice: Flavors of the Eastern Mediterranean*. New York: Regan Books, 2006.

Spieler, Marlena. *Peppers Peppers Peppers*. Buffalo, NY: Firefly Books, 1999.

United States Department of the Army. *The Illustrated Guide to Edible Wild Plants*. Guilford, CT: The Lyons Press, 2003.

Van Aken, Norman. *New World Kitchen: Latin American and Caribbean Cuisine*. With Janet Van Aken. New York: HarperCollins, 2003.

Virgin Islands Cooperative Extension Service Bulletin No. 1: Native Recipes. St. Croix, U.S. Virgin Islands, 1978.

Welanetz, Diana von, and Paul von Welanetz. *The Von Welanetz Guide to Ethnic Ingredients*. Los Angeles: J. P. Tarcher, 1982.

Zane, Eva. *Middle Eastern Cookery*. San Francisco: 101 Productions, 1974.

Zanger, Mark H. *The American Ethnic Cookbook for Students*. Phoenix: Oryx Press, 2001.

Zibat, Eve. *The Ethnic Food Lover's Companion*. Birmingham, AL: Menasha Ridge Press, 2001.

Zilkia, Janet. *Latin Food Culture*. Westport, CT: Greenwood Press, 2008.

Other Books by Jean B. MacLeod

If I'd Only Listened to My Mom, I'd Know How to Do This: Hundreds of Household Remedies

The Waste-Wise Kitchen Companion: Hundreds of Practical Tips for Repairing, Reusing, and Repurposing Food

The Waste-Wise Gardener: Tips and Techniques to Save Time, Money, and Energy While Creating the Garden of Your Dreams

The Kitchen Paraphernalia Handbook: Hundreds of Substitutions for Common (and Not-So-Common) Utensils, Gadgets, Tools, and Techniques

Baking Substitutions: The A-Z of Common, Unique, and Hard-to-Find Ingredients

CPSIA information can be obtained
at www.ICGtesting.com
Printed in the USA
LVHW031701061218
599502LV00020B/1070/P